SOLZHENITSYN

A Documentary Record

Solzhenitsyn

A Documentary Record

Enlarged Edition with the
Nobel Lecture in Literature

Edited and with an Introduction by
Leopold Labedz

Indiana University Press
Bloomington

To the memory of Manya Harari

Note to the Midland Book Edition

Since the first edition of this book was published, Solzhenitsyn's name has constantly been in public view. There were new episodes in his continuing struggle for civic and artistic integrity and there was also the publication of the first volume of his literary epic on war and revolution, *August 1914*. He has been subjected to new pressures and chicaneries, but his growing world fame has so far protected him from more drastic measures. It was not an easy situation: as he made clear in an interview with Western journalists, it was nerve-racking and precarious. He had to exert himself to the utmost to continue his literary work and his struggle. It was not only civic courage which was required to face political adversity, it also necessitated an iron self-discipline and a methodical devotion to work. Sheer guts would not have been enough to enable him to continue his artistic endeavors in such strained circumstances. The authorities were making life difficult for him in all sorts of ways. His application for a Moscow residence permit had been rejected; he had been refused a divorce from his first wife, and was thus precluded from marrying his long-time companion, Mrs. Natalya Svetlova, the mother of his two children. As his Swiss lawyer, Dr. Fritz Heeb, said (*The Times*, 18 January 1973), with reference to the article in *The New York Times* (8 January 1973) by an official of the Soviet *Novosti* agency, Semyon Vladimirov, who painted a picture of Solzhenitsyn living a life of 'luxury and leisure', he was subject to a continuous 'campaign of defamation'. Whether the conditions under which Solzhenitsyn is forced to write are conducive to artistic achievement is a question on which many reviewers of *August 1914* could have spared a thought. This is not to suggest that Solzhenitsyn's literary writings are to be evaluated on other than artistic grounds – he would be the first to oppose it. It is only to draw attention to the fact that writers do require concentration and that the obstacles which Solzhenitsyn has had to overcome in his literary work are, even technically speaking, almost unprecedented. However, it is also possible that such adverse conditions may have contributed to the increase of creative tension in Solzhenitsyn's 'encounter with destiny'.

L. L.

Contents

MANUSCRIPTS ABROAD

EXPULSION

NOBEL PRIZE

THE STRUGGLE CONTINUES: *August* 1914

Introduction

On purely literary grounds there is nothing extraordinary about the award of the 1970 Nobel Prize for Literature to Alexander Solzhenitsyn. He is widely recognized in his own country as its greatest living writer, although his works are banned there, and he is highly praised by critics and readers all over the world. His books, *One Day in the Life of Ivan Denisovich*, *The First Circle*, and *Cancer Ward*, have become best-sellers in all the countries where they were published. On the face of it there should be nothing surprising in the fact that honour has been given where honour was due. In conferring the world's highest literary award on the Russian author, the Swedish Academy was not taking a political decision. If anything, *not* to have awarded the prize to Solzhenitsyn would have been a political decision arising from other than literary considerations. This can be clearly seen from the account given to the Italian correspondent, Pietro Sormani, by a member of the Swedish Academy, the communist writer, Arthur Lundquist:*

The decision was difficult and not unanimous. The eighteen Academicians, who during the summer had examined the works of the candidates, were divided to the last between Solzhenitsyn and the Australian writer, Patrick White, the latter being a compromise choice favoured by many who wanted to avoid precisely those 'political machinations' of which they were accused by the Soviets. They even

Corriere della Sera, 25 October 1970. Arthur Lundquist is a Lenin Prize winner and a friend of Sholokhov. He is one of the committee of six which presents to the Swedish Academy the candidatures for the Nobel Prize for Literature. When Sholokhov received the award in 1965, Lundquist's praise for the Academy's decision was quoted with approval in the Soviet press which expressed great pleasure at the award and referred warmly to Dr Karl Ragnar Gierow (the same Swedish Academy spokesman who was later to notify Solzhenitsyn of his award). Gone was the abusive condemnation (made at the time of the Pasternak affair) of the Swedish Academy as 'a tool of the put out feelers in Moscow through Ambassador Jarring in an attempt to discover what the reactions of the Kremlin would be to the possible choice of Solzhenitsyn... In the end, however, the decision to award the prize to Solzhenitsyn prevailed. 'We were of course aware of the political consequences of this kind of choice,' Lundquist went on; but he vigorously rejected the charges which Moscow directed against the Swedish Academy. It was not true, as the Soviet press had asserted, that the Academy had yielded to outside pressures or that it had lent itself to the manoeuvres of 'White' émigrés in France and Germany.

As the Pasternak affair had already demonstrated, the definition of what is political is quite different in the Soviet Union from what it is elsewhere. In the Soviet Union, a refusal to submit to political dictates of the Party on aesthetic or ethical grounds is in itself termed 'political'. In the West the definition is less comprehensive; fortunately it does not yet completely cover the ethical and aesthetic.

Yet, given that this important point has been grasped, the fact remains that the decision of the Swedish Academy is one of the most remarkable it has ever taken, and it was based not only on literary criteria. The Academy was clearly aware of this when it stressed in its citation not just Solzhenitsyn's purely literary achievement, but 'the ethical force with which he has pursued the indispensable traditions of Russian literature'.

Solzhenitsyn's writings, well known in the West, provide ample evidence for this citation. But its full significance can be gauged only against the background of his life, of his fate as an individual and a writer (a fate shared by millions of Soviet citizens and hundreds of Soviet writers), and of his own ethical fortitude in adversity, a fortitude amounting to heroism. In

---

imperialists'. In the grand climax Sholokhov received a telegram of congratulation on the award, signed jointly by the Central Committee of the Communist Party of the Soviet Union and the Soviet Government (*Pravda*, 28 October 1965). On 21 October 1970 Dr Karl Ragnar Gierow informed the press conference in Stockholm that he had sent a letter to the chief editor of *Literaturnaya Gazeta*, Alexander Chakovsky. He said that the decision was taken to make the letter known to the world when *Literaturnaya Gazeta* had not had the courtesy to publish his letter or to correct in any way at all the misapprehensions and errors of fact about the administration of the Nobel prizes which it had published a week earlier.

presenting a documentary record of the Solzhenitsyn case the present volume may help the reader to understand this background.

Alexander Isayevich Solzhenitsyn was born on 11 December 1918 in Kislovodsk, a spa in the Caucasus well liked by Lermontov. His father died in an accident before his birth. When the boy was six years old, his mother moved to Rostov-on-Don to earn a meagre living as a typist. Life was even harder for a young widow with a small son than for the population in general during the twenties and thirties, the years which included the post-Revolution and post-collectivization famines.

Alexander was extremely good at school and later, while studying mathematics and physics at Rostov University, he won a Stalin scholarship for postgraduate studies. The gods are ironical: the future author of *One Day* and of *The First Circle* used it to follow his literary bent (of which he was conscious before he was ten), and enrolled at the Moscow Institute of Philosophy, Literature and History for a correspondence course which he completed in 1941. In the previous year he married a fellow-student, Natalya Reshetovskaya, and took a job as a teacher of mathematics in a Rostov secondary school. When he sent his first attempts to the journal *Znamya* they were rejected – another ironical incident, for the man who rejected them was none other than Konstantin Fedin, who nearly thirty years later was to prevent the publication of *Cancer Ward* in *Novy Mir*.

After the outbreak of the Soviet–German war Solzhenitsyn joined the army (on 18 October 1941) and served as an artillery officer all the way from Kursk to Königsberg (now Kaliningrad). He was twice decorated and in 1945 was promoted to a captaincy. What followed was the first step on his road to Calvary: he was arrested for criticizing Stalin in his letters to a friend. In July 1945, while in the notorious Lubyanka prison in Moscow, he was sentenced by the special board of the NKVD, the secret police, to eight years hard labour in a prison camp. The verdict was pronounced in his absence, a standard procedure during the years of Stalin's rule of terror.

He served his sentence partly in a special prison in Moscow, where he was sent because of his training as a physicist, and partly in the Karlag concentration camp in Dzezkazgan in the province of Karaganda where a vast network of such camps had been built. The earlier experience provided the canvas for *The First Circle*, the later for *One Day* and for the play *The Tenderfoot and the Tramp*.

On his release from the camp in 1953, Solzhenitsyn was again sentenced, this time to 'perpetual exile'. He was to serve it near Dzambul in southern Kazakhstan. During his stay there he was striken by a cancer of the stomach and was sent to Tashkent for a course of radiology. The treatment was successful. It was this experience which sets the scene of his third novel, *Cancer Ward*.

Solzhenitsyn was released from exile in 1956 and 'rehabilitated' a year later. He had spent eleven years in prisons, in camps and in exile, among millions of other prisoners, facing the questions of life and death in what was a microcosm of Soviet life at the time: Stalin's *univers concentrationnaire*. Now he settled in Ryazan, a hundred miles south-east of Moscow, and took a post as mathematics teacher in the local school. He was rejoined by his wife, who, while he was in exile in Kazakhstan, had given him up for dead and married again. He was soon to achieve world-wide fame and his genius was to be universally acclaimed, but his *via dolorosa* was not at an end. He had a debt to pay to the ghosts of his fellow-prisoners. He began to write *One Day in the Life of Ivan Denisovich*.

The period after the Twentieth Congress of the Soviet Communist Party was one of considerable political and intellectual ferment in the Soviet Union. Having denounced Stalin in his 'secret speech', Khrushchev constantly oscillated between thaw and freeze, between the policy of relaxation and the policy of repression. The sorcerer's apprentice of Soviet politics assumed the mantle of a moderate reformer who condemned Stalin's methods of rule, but who was determined to preserve as the basis of his power the machine built by his predecessor. While scolding the more liberal intelligentsia (among whom the writers were naturally the most articulate), Khrushchev was also facing the sullen resentment of the *apparatchiki* who felt their position being undermined by his demolition of the Stalin myth and his other 'hare-brained schemes'.

It was at the climax of Khrushchev's until then successful struggle with his more die-hard opponents in the Party, and because it could be used against them, that Solzhenitsyn made his explosive literary debut with the publication of *One Day* in November 1962.* It was not long, however, before the die-hards' counter-offensive began, and Solzhenitsyn drew the first fire from his critics. They still hailed his talent and had to go carefully in their attack because he was launched by Tvardovsky with Khrushchev's personal *nihil obstat*, but that only meant that the attack had to be veiled. The formula used was that he had failed 'to rise to a philosophical perception'† of the Stalin era (*i.e.* that the Party was building socialism despite Stalin's 'mistakes'). While Solzhenitsyn provided the simple truth about it, his critics demanded a more dialectical approach: 'Without a vision of historical truth, there can be no full truth, no matter what the talent.'‡

The counter-offensive fizzled out in the spring of 1963 when an interview with Tvardovsky (containing warm praise of Solzhenitsyn) appeared in *Pravda* on 12 May. But towards the end of the year the battle flared up again. So long as Khrushchev stayed in power, Tvardovsky was able to publish several short stories by Solzhenitsyn in *Novy Mir*. After Khrushchev's fall in 1964, only one more tale by Solzhenitsyn appeared in print. The struggle between his friends and enemies became more intense in 1965, with the former on the defensive and steadily losing ground.

At the meeting of the prose section of the Moscow writers'

*The introduction (by Max Hayward and the present writer) to its first American edition, published in January 1963 in New York, began with the words: '[This book] is beyond doubt the most startling work ever to have been published in the Soviet Union. Apart from being a literary masterpiece, it is a revolutionary document that will affect the climate of life inside the Soviet Union.'

†Lydia Fomenko, 'Great Expectations', *Literaturnaya Rossiya*, 11 January 1963.

‡Vadim Kozhevnikov in *Literaturnaya Gazeta*, 2 March 1963.

organization he was still supported by the majority of those present, who passed a resolution calling for the publication of *Cancer Ward*. But by then the battle for the publication of *The First Circle* in *Novy Mir* had already been lost, and at the end of 1967 Konstantin Fedin torpedoed the appearance of *Cancer Ward*, already set up in print for *Novy Mir*. By that time hundreds of 'Samizdat' ('publish-it-yourself') editions of Solzhenitsyn's novels were circulating in typewritten form in the Soviet Union, and even without the help of the KGB – which was, as it were, forthcoming – they were bound to reach the West and find publication there in spite of Solzhenitsyn's protests and pleas to the Writers' Union to have them published in Russia first. During 1966 and 1967 Solzhenitsyn was subjected to increased pressure: he became the target for a growing slander campaign and his manuscripts and archives were seized by the KGB.

During all this time he fought a vigorous defensive battle and found many supporters and admirers. His open letter to the Fourth Writers' Congress is the most eloquent plea for the freedom of literature that has ever appeared in the Soviet Union. His hard experience and his knowledge of the law were important assets in his conduct of the battle, but he increasingly was facing opponents who were not just hard-liners, but were ready to use the weapon of political provocation and so to swell the KGB file on him, a file which could be used against him at the appropriate time by his enemies. By obscure channels, his manuscripts began to reach the West. It became clear that a 'case' against Solzhenitsyn was being prepared and that he might eventually face trial, as Sinyavsky and Daniel had done. The two meetings of the Writers' Union which were held to discuss his 'case' before his expulsion already treated him like a pariah and put him in the dock. He was duly expelled from the Union, an action which he contemptuously castigated in another magnificent open letter.

His detractors accused him of being a 'tool of the imperialists' and a 'slanderer of the Soviet Union' (*Literaturnaya Gazeta*, 26 November 1969). He was called a 'liar' by the Russian Federation section of the Writers' Union which invited him to leave the country and live in the West. Sholokhov called him a 'pest' (*Literaturnaya Gazeta*, 3 December 1969).

During all this time the 'Samizdat' publications conducted a vigorous defence of Solzhenitsyn, but the Soviet 'democratic opposition' was itself coming increasingly under fire, its members being arrested and sent to mental prisons, corrective labour camps or to exile in the remoter parts of the country.

In 1970, when the Soviet authorities were preparing the final act in the Solzhenitsyn drama, the Swedish Academy announced its award of the Nobel Prize for Literature to Solzhenitsyn. Bitterly stung, the Soviet propaganda machine quickly announced the 'literary and political bankruptcy' of Solzhenitsyn and condemned the Nobel Prize Committee for its nefarious decision. It was no longer ready to concede to Solzhenitsyn even a literary talent.* Now he had become a 'run-of-the-mill writer' (*Soviet Weekly*, 17 October 1970). With his friend and protector Tvardovsky on his death-bed, Solzhenitsyn was facing the greatest honour and another great ordeal in his life.

During the Pasternak affair, and again when the Nobel Prize was awarded to Solzhenitsyn, the Soviet press denounced the Swedish Academy as 'conservative and reactionary', pointing out that in 1901 the first Nobel Prize for Literature had gone to the now forgotten French poet, Sully Prudhomme, and not to the great Leo Tolstoy (*Literaturnaya Gazeta*, 21 October 1970). The Academy has indeed made many errors of judgement during the seventy years in which the Prize has been given, but this particular argument was not used in the Soviet press when it was Sholokhov who received the award.

If there are certain historical continuities in the treatment of even the greatest Russian writers by the authorities, they only underline how much worse that treatment is now. Tolstoy was denounced by the Holy Synod, an episode which forms the basis of his novel *Resurrection* (it is also recalled in *Cancer Ward*). But the Holy Synod would hardly have dared to press Tolstoy to

*Earlier even his opponents granted him at least that. Fedin said at the meeting of the Secretariat of the Writers' Union (on 22 September 1967): 'None of us denies his talent.' And Alexi Surkov said that Solzhenitsyn was dangerous 'because he has got talent'.

renounce the Nobel Prize, if he had received the award, or to attack the Swedish Academy for making it. True, when Tolstoy died without returning to the Church, the Holy Synod forbade the local priest to say a mass for his soul and instructed the local police to exact obedience from the population to its decree forbidding the chanting of religious songs for Tolstoy and laying wreaths on his grave. Later, authorized by the governor of Ryazan, the police relented and permitted the placing of wreaths. Today the Ryazan authorities are less liberal, as the expulsion of Solzhenitsyn from the Ryazan writers' organization testifies.

Of the four Nobel Prizes awarded to Russian writers three are not acknowledged by the Soviet authorities. Pasternak was forced to renounce it, Solzhenitsyn is now being denounced for receiving it, and although Ivan Bunin, who got it in 1933 as an émigré, has been posthumously rehabilitated, an article in *Pravda* (22 October 1970) commemorating the one hundredth anniversary of his birth did not mention that he was a Nobel Prizewinner. Would any other country in the world feel 'ennobled' if it had to disclaim the highest honour for their finest writers? What would – say – the French think if they had to repudiate André Gide, François Mauriac and Albert Camus, three Nobel Prize laureates?

But perhaps in the historical perspective all this is not so important, provided of course that what one has in mind is the literary prizes and not the persecution of the writers. As we all know, literary prizes, including the Nobel Prize, do not in the long run make any difference to the stature of the writer; what matters is the quality of the writing, and here time is the most ruthless judge. It is by such criteria that Solzhenitsyn will be judged by posterity, and although literary predictions are notoriously risky, one can venture the opinion that the combination of his literary gifts and his nobility of spirit will make him immortal. In the Soviet context his historical as well as literary significance cannot be exaggerated. He is the first great Russian writer to emerge after the Revolution whose humanity can be compared to that of Tolstoy, his awareness of suffering to that of Dostoyevsky, his lack of sentimentality to that of Chekhov.

His style may seem old-fashioned in the light of literary developments elsewhere, but not in the context of the historical development of the Russian language and literature, or indeed in the general course of European culture. And who can tell what effect it will have on his readability a hundred years hence? In any case there is no doubt that Solzhenitsyn is the best example of those writers whom the late Konstantin Paustovsky described as the only ones whose works will endure (*Novy Mir*, No. 11, 1967):

They see the truth and they write the truth. Therefore their books survive. They live and they will go on living and there is no need to worry about the fate of their books. In that lies the strength of true works of art; having served their own time, they retain their irresistibility and their power of conviction even when that time moves into the past. And not only as a document, but also as a passionate human response to what is happening in the world.

Konstantin Paustovsky was, as I know from a personal conversation, an admirer of Solzhenitsyn.

Like other major novelists, Solzhenitsyn makes his own experience the centre of his literary work and the point of departure for its symbolic significance. The concentration camp and the cancer ward are for him places in which to reflect not just on the problems presented by extreme situations, but on the wider questions of Soviet reality and of our epoch of good and evil, in short of *la condition humaine*. Like other great novelists he is uncompromising in his attitude to truth and he restores to Russian literature the moral universalism which had been lost during the Stalin era. His writing is philosophical in the traditional sense; with its complexity and sense of tragedy, it is the antithesis of the shallow optimism and vulgar sociologism which, under the sign of 'socialist realism', has for so many years dominated Soviet prose writing.

One of the characters in *The First Circle* reflects that 'for a country to have a great writer is like having another government'. Solzhenitsyn is such a writer. He ended his beautiful story, *Matryona's Home*, with these moving lines:

We all lived beside her and did not understand that she was that just person without whom, according to the proverb, the village could not endure.

Nor the city.

Nor all our land.

Solzhenitsyn is himself such a person.

In regard both to the man and the writer, the Nobel award to Solzhenitsyn and the words of its citation are singularly appropriate.

LEOPOLD LABEDZ

LITERARY DEBUT

Solzhenitsyn returned from the 'house of the dead' just before Khrushchev's 'secret speech' condemning Stalin. His literary debut, the publication in the liberal Novy Mir *of* One Day in the Life of Ivan Denisovich, *was personally authorized by Khrushchev and betokened the highpoint of de-Stalinization. The novel was a literary as well as political bombshell; it received an enthusiastic reception on the part of liberal writers, a cautious one from the fence-sitters, and it infuriated the literary die-hards. This division was also reflected in the public: the novel angered obscurantist elements among the general readers but pleased all those who had suffered under Stalin. Its entire edition disappeared from the shops in hours. It immediately provided a litmus paper to test moral and political attitudes not only towards the Soviet past, but also towards its future. The literary talent of Solzhenitsyn was recognized at once: he became a classic overnight. He was also recognized as a liberating force which could release Russian literature from the shackles of socialist realism, a way of writing imposed by the Party since the early thirties which paralysed individual sense of reality and imagination. 'After Solzhenitsyn we cannot write as before', said one Soviet writer. Many felt the same and the support given by the Party leadership enhanced their hopes.*

Solzhenitsyn's rehabilitation

Supreme Court of the USSR Decision no. 4n-083/56

The Military Collegium of the Supreme Court of the USSR, presided over by Judicial Councillor Borisoglebsky and comprising Judicial Colonels Dolotsev and Konev, has examined at its session of 6 February 1956 **the Protest of the Chief**

Military Prosecutor against the decree of the Special Board of the NKVD of the USSR, dated 7 July 1945, on the basis of which, under articles 58(10), part two and 58(11) of the Criminal Code of the RSFSR, a sentence of eight years imprisonment in corrective labour camps was passed on SOLZHENITSYN, Alexander Isayevich, born 1918, a native of Kislovodsk and with a higher education. Before his arrest he had held the post of battery commander, had participated in the war against the fascist German armies and was awarded the Order of the Fatherland War, class two, and the Order of the Red Star.

Having heard the report of Comrade Konev and the statement of the Deputy Chief Military Prosecutor, Judicial Colonel Terekhov, who advocated that the protest be accepted, the Collegium **established** the following:

The charge against Solzhenitsyn was that from 1940 until the day of his arrest he had conducted anti-Soviet propaganda among his friends and undertaken steps to establish an anti-Soviet organization.

In his protest the Chief Military Prosecutor proposed the annulment of the Special Board's decree with regard to Solzhenitsyn and the cancellation of the case owing to the absence of proof of a crime.

The reasons given were as follows:

It is clear from the evidence in this case that Solzhenitsyn, in his diary and letters to a friend, N. D. Vitkevich, although speaking of the correctness of Marxism-Leninism, the progressiveness of the socialist revolution in our country and the inevitability of its victory throughout the world, also spoke out against the personality of Stalin and wrote of the artistic and ideological shortcomings of the works of many Soviet authors and the air of unreality that pervades many of them. He also wrote that our works of art fail to give readers of the bourgeois world a sufficiently comprehensive and versatile explanation of the inevitability of the victory of the Soviet army and people, and that our literary works are no match for the adroitly fashioned slanders of the bourgeois world against our country.

These statements by Solzhenitsyn do not constitute proof of a crime.

In the process of verifying Solzhenitsyn's petition the following people were questioned: Reshetovskaya, Simonyan and Simonyants – to whom Solzhenitsyn is said to have made anti-Soviet allegations. These people characterized Solzhenitsyn as a Soviet patriot and denied that he had conducted anti-Soviet conversations.

From Solzhenitsyn's military record and a report by Captain Melnikov, who served with him, it is clear that from 1942 until the time of his arrest Solzhenitsyn served on several fronts of the Great Fatherland War, fought courageously for his homeland, more than once displayed personal heroism and inspired the devotion of the section he commanded. Solzhenitsyn's section was the best in the unit for discipline and battle effectiveness.

Basing himself on the above-mentioned evidence, the Chief Military Prosecutor considers the conviction of Solzhenitsyn to have been incorrect and in this connection applies for the case against him to be closed on the basis of article 4, point 5 of the Criminal Procedure Code of the RSFSR.

Having examined the case material and the material investigation and concurring with the arguments expounded in the official protest, while also taking into account the fact that Solzhenitsyn's actions do not constitute a crime and his case should be closed for lack of proof, the Military Collegium of the USSR **resolves** that the decree of the Special Board of the NKVD of the USSR dated 7 July 1945, concerning Solzhenitsyn, Alexander Isayevich, shall be revoked and his case, for lack of proof, be closed on the basis of article 4, point 5 of the Criminal Procedure Code of the RSFSR.

The original bears the relevant signatures. Original verified, Senior Officer of the Military Collegium, Major Degtyaryov.

A biographical note on Solzhenitsyn

'A New Name in our Literature' by P. Kosolapov,
TASS Correspondent

In 1941 he joined the Soviet army. In 1942, after graduating
from the artillery school, he was appointed commanding officer
of a battery. In this position he stayed continually and uninter-
ruptedly in the front line until February 1945. He was awarded
two decorations. In February 1945, already on the territory of
East Prussia, Captain Solzhenitsyn was arrested on groundless
political accusations and was sentenced to eight years imprisonment. After serving it fully he was sent into exile, from which he
returned in 1956. In 1957 he was fully rehabilitated since he had
committed no offence.

(Sovetskaya Rossiya, 28 November 1962)

Solzhenitsyn's Autobiographical Note

I was born at Kislovodsk on 11 December 1918. My father had
studied philological subjects at Moscow University, but did not
complete his studies, as he enlisted as a volunteer when war
broke out in 1914. He became an artillery officer on the German
front, fought throughout the war and died in the summer of
1918, six months before I was born. I was brought up by my
mother, who worked as a shorthand-typist, in the town of Rostov
on the Don, where I spent the whole of my childhood and youth,
leaving the grammar school there in 1936. Even as a child,
without any prompting from others, I wanted to be a writer and
indeed I turned out a good deal of the usual juvenilia. In the
1930s I tried to get my writings published but I could not find
anyone willing to accept my manuscripts. I wanted to acquire a
literary education but in Rostov such an education that would
suit my wishes was not to be obtained. To move to Moscow was
not possible, partly because my mother was alone and in poor

health and partly because of our modest circumstances. I therefore began to study at the department of mathematics at Rostov University, where it proved that I had a considerable aptitude for mathematics. But although I found it easy to learn this subject I did not feel that I wished to devote my whole life to it. Nevertheless it was to play a beneficial role in my destiny later on, and on at least two occasions it rescued me from death. For I would probably not have survived the eight years in camps if I had not, as a mathematician, been transferred to a socalled *sharashka*, where I spent four years; and later, during my exile, I was allowed to teach mathematics and physics, which helped to ease my existence and made it possible for me to write. If I had had a literary education it is quite likely that I should not have survived these ordeals but would instead have been subjected to even greater pressures. Later on, it is true, I began to get some literary education as well; this was from 1939 to 1941, during which time, along with university studies in physics and mathematics, I also studied by correspondence at the Institute of History, Philosophy and Literature in Moscow.

In 1941, a few days before the outbreak of the war, I graduated from the department of physics and mathematics at Rostov University. At the beginning of the war, owing to weak health, I was detailed to serve as a driver of horsedrawn vehicles during the winter of 1941–2. Later, because of my mathematical knowledge, I was transferred to an artillery school, from which after a crash course I passed out in November 1942. Immediately after this I was put in command of an artillery position-finding company and in this capacity served without a break right in the front line until I was arrested in February 1945. This happened in East Prussia, a region which is linked with my destiny in a remarkable way. As early as 1937, as a first-year student, I chose to write a descriptive essay on 'The Samsonov Disaster' of 1914 in East Prussia and studied material on this; and in 1945 I myself went to this area (at the time of writing, autumn 1970, the book *August 1914* has just been completed).

I was arrested on the grounds of what the censorship had found during the years 1944–5 in my correspondence with a school friend, mainly because of certain disrespectful remarks about Stalin, although we referred to him in disguised terms. As a further basis for the 'charge' there were used the drafts of stories and reflections which had been found in my map case. These, however, were not sufficient for a 'prosecution' and in July 1945 I was 'sentenced' in my absence, in accordance with a procedure then frequently applied, after a resolution by the OSO (the Special Committee of the NKVD), to eight years in a detention camp (at that time this was considered a mild sentence).

I served the first part of my sentence in several correctional work camps of mixed types (this kind of camp is described in the play *The Tenderfoot and the Tramp*). In 1946, as a mathematician, I was transferred to the group of scientific research institutes of the MVD-MGB*. I spent the middle period of my sentence in such 'SPECIAL PRISONS' (*The First Circle*). In 1950 I was sent to the newly established Special Camps which were intended only for political prisoners. In such a camp in the town of Ekibastuz in Kazakhstan (*One Day in the Life of Ivan Denisovich*) I worked as a miner, a bricklayer and a foundryman. There I contracted a tumour which was operated on, but the condition was not cured (its character was not established until later on).

One month after I had served the full term of my eight-year sentence there came, without any new judgement and even without a 'resolution from the OSO', an administrative decision to the effect that I was not to be released but EXILED FOR LIFE to Kok-Terek (southern Kazakhstan). This measure was not directed specially against me but was a very usual procedure at that time. I served this exile from March 1953 (on 5 March, when Stalin's death was made public, I was allowed for the first time to go without an escort) until June 1956. Here my cancer had developed rapidly and at the end of 1953 I was very near death. I was unable to eat, I could not sleep and was severely affected by the poisons from the tumour. However, I was able to go to a cancer clinic at Tashkent, where during 1954 I was cured (*The Cancer Ward, Right Hand*). During all the years of exile I taught mathematics and physics in a primary school and during my hard and lonely existence I wrote prose in secret (in

*Ministry of Internal Affairs, Ministry of State Security.

the camp I could only write down poetry from memory). I managed, however, to keep what I had written and to take it with me to the European part of the country, where in the same way I continued, as far as the outer world was concerned, to occupy myself with teaching and, in secret, to devote myself to writing, at first in the Vladimir district (*Matryona's Home*) and afterwards in Ryazan.

During all the years until 1961 not only was I CONVINCED that I should never see a single line of mine in print in my lifetime but also I scarcely dared allow any of my close acquaintances to read anything I had written because I feared that this would become known. Finally, at the age of 42, this secret authorship began to wear me down. The most difficult thing of all to bear was that I could not get my works judged by people with literary training. In 1961, after the 22nd Congress of the USSR Communist Party and Tvardovsky's speech at this, I decided to emerge and to offer *One Day in the Life of Ivan Denisovich*.

Such an emergence seemed then to me, and not without reason, to be very risky because it might lead to the loss of my manuscripts and to my own destruction. But on that occasion things turned out successfully and after protracted efforts A. T. Tvardovsky was able to print my novel one year later. The printing of my work was, however, stopped almost immediately and the authorities stopped both my plays and (in 1964) the novel *The First Circle*, which in 1965 was seized together with my papers from the past years. During these months it seemed to me that I had committed an unpardonable mistake by revealing my work prematurely and that because of this I should not be able to carry it to a conclusion.

It is almost always impossible to evaluate at the time events which you have already experienced and to understand their meaning with the guidance of their effects. All the more unpredictable and surprising to us will be the course of future events.

Visiting Solzhenitsyn in Ryazan

by Victor Bukhanov

The street leading to the Oka River is blocked at one end by the churches of the Ryazan Kremlin. In this street stands the school where Alexander Solzhenitsyn taught physics until the end of last year.

In the space of a month the name of the Ryazan teacher became known in Moscow and Vladivostok, in Paris and the Antarctic. His novel One Day, *about a day in the life of a prisoner, Ivan Shukhov, aroused general interest. Victor Bukhanov, an APN correspondent, visited Alexander Solzhenitsyn and below we publish his story.*

A TEACHER OF PHYSICS

Solzhenitsyn's interests have always run in two directions and his gifts as a teacher are as indisputable as his literary talent.

Apart from having a thorough grasp of his subject, he taught in the fresh and fascinating manner of the schoolteacher whose heart was in his subject. He studied the technical magazines, and gave comprehensive talks on various subjects including space flight; amazing his colleagues with the range of the material, he constantly went 'beyond the bounds' of the bare school programme.

'He makes the lesson so interesting. He's a good speaker. I never liked physics much before, but now . . .'

'I don't know about his writing, but he's a wonderful teacher.' These are typical of the comments made by his pupils.

'This is the end of the term,' Solzhenitsyn told me, when I went to see him at the end of December. 'This is when the children's work is reviewed and they are given a chance to improve their marks. I would rather you didn't come to our lesson as it might make the children more nervous and affect their answers.'

A glass door separated me from the classroom. Through it I could see Solzhenitsyn calling out his pupils, writing on the blackboard and talking with lively gestures. As I could not hear what was being said, the scene reminded me of an old silent film.

Both his pupils and fellow-teachers, I learned, were loath to think of their physics-teacher giving up his teaching to devote himself entirely to writing. And when the day of his last lesson on December 28 arrived, all of them were sorry to see him go.

It had not occurred to Solzhenitsyn's colleagues that he had any special literary talent.

'We didn't suspect it,' they told me. 'He was just a teacher to us, better at his job than many of us, but that's all.'

Vladimir Beltsov, head of the school's curriculum department, said he had had an idea that the physics teacher was absorbed in some new interest but he thought Solzhenitsyn was writing a physics textbook or a book of problems. 'He has sufficient knowledge to do this,' Beltsov commented.

NOT A MINUTE WASTED

Here is another comment about Solzhenitsyn: 'His whole life follows a pattern known only to himself.'

It is difficult to imagine just how much energy and purposefulness Solzhenitsyn has.

When Solzhenitsyn began teaching school five years ago, he asked the principal to limit his lessons to fifteen hours a week. A year later, without explaining his reasons, he asked for the number of hours to be reduced to twelve, and ultimately he was giving only nine lessons a week. That was why his salary amounted to only 50 roubles a month.

Solzhenitsyn planned his day very carefully. He would arrive at school no more than a minute or two before the lesson began. And he never stayed after lessons were over or dropped into the staff room without good reason. He also avoided prolonged meetings. At the same time he never neglected his duties. He always kept his word, he was never late and he expected others to be as punctilious as he was. His timekeeping became a by-word.

Every summer Solzhenitsyn and his wife, sometimes with two or three friends, go on a holiday tour, preferring bicycle and boat to other forms of transport.

The writer and his wife have toured the Ryazan region on their bicycles with improvised baggage carriers on the back wheel. Solzhenitsyn has also been to the Baltic Republics, and last summer he took a trip beyond Lake Baikal.

Photography is one of the couple's hobbies, and I found the walls of their dining-room hung with photographic studies.

Recently Alexander Solzhenitsyn went hunting with a few other schoolteachers. He was armed, however, with a camera only. And while the others shot, he took photographs. He does not like to carry a gun. His father met his death while hunting, shooting himself by accident in the chest.

HIS WIFE

Natalia Reshetovskaya, the writer's wife, is a chemist with a M.Sc. degree. She teaches at the local agricultural institute. By all accounts she is a good pianist, and I noticed that half of the small Solzhenitsyn dining-room was occupied by a grand piano.

Solzhenitsyn married Natalia Reshetovskaya before the war. About a year before V-Day and Solzhenitsyn's arrest (on a false charge) Natalia went out to the battlefront to see him. When Solzhenitsyn's sentence ended and he was banished to the Djambul region, she joined him there.

Natalia Reshetovskaya was just as indisposed to talk about her husband as he was about himself. However, she let me have two photographs of her husband.

'Would Solzhenitsyn have become a writer had he not been through his prison camp experience?' I asked.

'It's hard to say. At any rate he had tried to get a literary education with a definite purpose.'

The Solzhenitsyns have no children.

WORK, WORK

Solzhenitsyn does his best to avoid publicity. He is strongly averse to discussing his work or manner of writing.

'There is only one way the writer can communicate with his reader – through his books.' Solzhenitsyn repeated this to me over and over again in different words.

The writer gives no interviews to either Soviet or foreign journalists. He is not well disposed towards newspapermen and does not hide the fact, and is annoyed with the reading public for wanting to learn and swallow the news at a single gulp.

It is therefore no easy job for a journalist to try to talk to Solzhenitsyn. His polite but firm refusals to answer questions are discouraging. He refuses to discuss either the number of pages he writes in a week or his plans for the future.

'You'll learn about all that after my funeral,' he told me without a suggestion of humour in his voice.

We know a little about him, however. One of these things is that *One Day*, his short novel, was completed four years ago, and that there has been a proposal to film it. It is also known that some time ago he read a play of his to the company of the *Sovremennik* and that it will probably be staged at this theatre. Alexander Solzhenitsyn has written and may still be writing poetry. Two of his stories have appeared. Rumour has it that he plans to return to the theme of his first work. Of his further plans we may judge from one phrase he let drop: 'I have accomplished hardly anything yet.'

There is reason to believe that Solzhenitsyn is never happier than when he is hard at work on his writing – 'quietly and peacefully at my work', as he puts it himself.

He is inclined to upbraid mildly the increasing number of admirers who come knocking on his door and disturbing him.

While I sat in the writer's dining-room my gaze strayed now and then to the books on his shelves. Among them I noticed Dumas and four volumes by Melnikov-Pechersky, which set me wondering whether it was not from the latter that Solzhenitsyn was taking lessons in style. On the piano was a pile of music and on the wall above faded pictures of Tchaikovsky and

Chopin. There were flowers and a general atmosphere of cosiness.

'Writers in the last century,' Solzhenitsyn said, 'lived and wrote, without being dragged into sensation. They were merely read, and they were fine writers.

'Too bad that reviews of my first book appeared even before it has been printed, and now overtures are being made to me before my second has come out. Such a fuss requires that I live up to readers' expectations. And what if I fail to produce anything worth while?'

(*Literaturnaya Rossiya*, 25 January 1963)

One Day With Solzhenitsyn – An Interview

by Pavel Licko* (extracts)

Our readers have already had an opportunity to read some of Solzhenitsyn's works (*Matryona's Home, An Incident at Krechetovka Station, For the Good of the Cause*, etc.), and in particular

---

*Pavel Licko, a Bratislava journalist. During the last war he worked for Soviet military intelligence. In 1948 he was editor-in-chief of Bratislava's *Economic Gazette*, and between 1949 and 1951 director of the press department of the Central Committee of the Communist Party of Slovakia. In 1953 he was director of the 'Socialist World' Publishing House. From 1962 to 1967 he was on the editorial board of the weekly *Kulturny Zivot*, and since 1968 a director of the Tatrapress Agency. He was arrested in September 1970 on charges of 'damaging the interests of the Czechoslovak Republic abroad.' *Time* magazine (28 December 1970) described his role as follows:

'Licko later visited London, where he boasted of his supposed intimacy with Solzhenitsyn; he also signed an affidavit saying that the author had entrusted him with a manuscript of *Cancer Ward* and had asked him to place it for publication in England. In addition, Licko tried to persuade Western newsmen to print an assortment of fantastic stories and patent lies that made Solzhenitsyn out to be a traitor to his country.

'When fragmentary reports reached Solzhenitsyn in Russia of his purported "authorization" of *Cancer Ward*, he sent letters to two European newspapers denying that he had authorized any Western firm to publish it. Told by friends that Licko had claimed to represent him in the sale of the novel, the author stated categorically that he had never even given the man a manuscript, let alone instructions about its publication.'

One Day in the Life of Ivan Denisovich, which was more than the spontaneous outcry of the artist's tormented soul, the label it was given when it achieved worldwide fame. Solzhenitsyn is, in fact, a writer by vocation, as I realized when I visited this fifty-year-old man, who used to teach mathematics and physics somewhere in the Soviet Union, in his Ryazan home. His whole life was a conscious preparation for creative writing. Not only self-discipline but his own experiences helped him to become a writer.

Solzhenitsyn was born in Kislovodsk in 1918 and his childhood and school years were spent in Rostov-on-Don, in Southern Russia. He studied mathematics and physics at the University of Moscow, and history, philosophy, and literature at an excellent institute in Moscow. A few days before the outbreak of the Second World War he graduated with two degrees.

I was not sure what to do next. I was good at mathematics and it was suggested that I should do postgraduate research. I never intended to devote the rest of my life to mathematics. Literature was the greatest attraction but I realized that mathematics would at least provide me with my bread and butter.

His first writings, sent to Lavrenev and Fedin, were not accepted. Some have been preserved but others are still in Lubyanka files.

Solzhenitsyn almost became an actor. According to Zavadski, a stage director who founded a drama school when deported to Rostov, Solzhenitsyn had talent but had to give up the idea of acting when it was discovered that he suffered from chronic laryngitis.

After the outbreak of war Solzhenitsyn was still convinced that his future lay in literature. . . In the army they did not know what to do with him. Although a mathematician and foot soldier, Solzhenitsyn was attached to a unit using horse-drawn transport. Together with some old and ill Cossacks, he was expected to look after almost ninety horses although he had no idea how they should be handled. He dreamed of the artillery. The military situation at the beginning of 1942 was so critical, however, that nobody had time to show any interest in Solzhenitsyn and his requests for transfer to an artillery unit went unheeded. But at last, with the help of an officer in his unit who had been at the front, the transfer came through... He finished a training course for junior officers and was afterwards sent on a fortnight's journey to the Gorki region.

All I saw and experienced there is reflected in An Incident at Krechetovka Station.

He managed to get to the front as a result of a mathematical question he asked the commander of the officers' school. The question was designed to ridicule the commander, but the latter was so impressed that he appointed Solzhenitsyn chief of a sound-ranging battery. He was promoted to the rank of captain and took part in the battles of Leningrad and Kursk, and then marched from Orel through White Russia and Poland to Berlin.

In January 1945, during the battle for Königsberg, he was summoned by the commander of the division, Major-General Travkin (later to become his close friend), who ordered Solzhenitsyn to hand over his revolver. The general was obviously ill at ease and Solzhenitsyn was unable to understand the reason behind the order. He handed over his revolver and was then stripped of his badge of rank and decorations by two officers. His only memory of that moment is of the noise made by the artillery moving away from the nearby front line. Before Solzhenitsyn was taken away, General Travkin managed to shake his hand.

That handshake was one of the most heroic acts I had seen during the whole of the war. I was arrested because of my naïve and childish ideas. I knew that it was forbidden to write of military matters in letters from the front, but I thought it was permitted to think and reflect on events. For a long time I had been sending a friend letters clearly criticizing Stalin though without mentioning his name. I thought he had betrayed Leninism and was responsible for the defeats of the first phase of the war, that he was a weak theoretician and that his language was primitive. In my youthful recklessness I put all these thoughts down on paper.

I was held in the Lubyanka prison in Moscow. After interroga-

tion, and without trial, I was sentenced by special decision to eight years imprisonment. I never thought this unjust. After all, I had expressed opinions which at that time were inadmissible.

I would never have survived the camp had it not been for mathematics. I was unfit for manual work and could not make moral compromises. I was employed on building sites near Moscow and in Moscow itself. On Leninsky Prospekt there is a large building with small towers and a shop called Spartak on the ground floor. I worked there. In a questionnaire we had to fill in, I wrote that I was a mathematician and physicist. I was then taken to a prison research institute where the standard was so high that any scientist would have been proud to work there. As a prisoner mathematician I spent four of the eight years in good conditions.

For the last three years of my sentence I was in a mining region in Kazakhstan. It was there I conceived the idea of writing One Day in the Life of Ivan Denisovich. *Since it was a special camp we all had numbers stamped on the forehead, chest, knees, and back. My number was* Shch. 232.

(A day later I went with Solzhenitsyn to the elegant Lira café for young people in Moscow. We left our coats in the cloakroom and the attendant gave us tickets. Solzhenitsyn glanced at his cloakroom ticket and smiled: 'It seems that I shall never get rid of this number.' It was 232.)

It took me two years in the camp to learn the trade of stonecutting and metal-casting. I was released in February 1953, a month after the end of my sentence. On 5 March 1953 I walked the streets of a town, a free but exiled man. An old deaf woman woke me up one morning and forced me to go out and listen to a communiqué broadcast by the local radio station. Stalin's death was announced. It was my first day of freedom.

Later on I was summoned to appear before the local committee of the security police, where I was asked to sign a document confirming my perpetual exile. It was formulated exactly in this way – perpetual exile, not exile for life. I refused to sign.

In 1956 I was living in exile on the edge of a desert to the southwest of Balkhash, in the village of Kok-Teren (Green Poplar). I was pleased to be in exile because as a free man it would have been more difficult to find employment. I was in the fortunate position of being the only mathematician in the village and was easily able to find a teaching post. Matryona's Home *had its origin there. The events in that story took place in 1956, and not 1953 as was stated in the first edition.*

While still in the camp Solzhenitsyn had an operation. The doctors correctly diagnosed a tumour, but he was not allowed to know the truth. His sufferings in 1953 were so severe that he was barely able to move, but there was nobody in the village able to give him treatment.

I was dying. But later I managed to reach Tashkent and after long treatment I recovered. The tumour does not bother me now.

Throughout his imprisonment Alexander Solzhenitsyn immersed himself in the Russian language and of course wrote poems, prose, and plays. *The Tenderfoot and the Tramp* was written in 1954. Later he wrote the novel *The First Circle*, but it did not meet with approval.

The Stalinist personality cult was the source of all the accusations levelled against Solzhenitsyn and was the reason for his arrest. It was only after the Twentieth Party Congress that he was allowed to return to normal life. His old dream of living in Central Russia could now be realized.

I know that the easiest thing for a writer is to write about himself. But I have always felt that to write about the fate of Russia was the most fascinating and important task to be performed. Of all the drama that Russia lived through, the fate of Ivan Denisovich was the greatest tragedy. I also wanted to expose the false image of prison camps. While still in the camp I made up my mind to describe one day of prison life. Tolstoy once said that a novel can deal with either centuries of European history or a day in one man's life . . .

In addition to works already published, Solzhenitsyn has also written a novel called *Cancer Ward*, running to many hundred pages (a fragment of this novel was published by the Bratislava *Pravda*). The second part was finished during my visit to

Ryazan. Solzhenitsyn considered *The Tenderfoot and the Tramp* to be the best of his earlier works. He used a verse from the Gospel of Saint Luke for another play: 'See to it then that the light within you is not darkness' (11:35).

I wanted to write a play that had nothing to do with politics or the larger national problems. The action takes place in an unknown country, the time is not precisely defined, and all the characters are given international names. My purpose was not to camouflage. I was interested in the moral problems of highly civilized societies, whether capitalist or socialist.

After Solzhenitsyn's rehabilitation in 1957, the first to read or rather to listen to *One Day* were members of the Supreme Military Court. He read his novel to the first judges he had ever seen. After its publication in book form, Solzhenitsyn sent several short stories to *Novy Mir*, and *The Tenderfoot and the Tramp* to the Sovremennik Theatre. It took about nine years to write *The First Circle*; it is about seven hundred pages long, and was finished two days after Stalin's death. The action of the novel is confined to one day and part of the night in December 1949. The characters are Stalin, a watchman, representatives of the intelligentsia, and government officials. Part of the action takes place in a scientific institute for prisoners.

After a brief silence Solzhenitsyn returned to the subject of his play, which is concerned with the moral problems existing in highly civilized societies.

I do not think it is a good play, although both the Vakhtangov Theatre and the Komsomol Theatre wanted to produce it some time ago.

It was written in 1960 but never published. He also wrote sixteen micro-stories, not more than fifteen to twenty lines each. Like many of his other writings, they were first composed and memorized, and only put down on paper after a lapse of several years. These short stories were popular throughout the area where Solzhenitsyn was living at the time. They were published without his knowledge by *Encounter* (March 1965). Literary critics in England identified the author by an analysis of the language. In 1959 he was looking for a new medium of expression and was working on a scenario for a film, but he 'has still not decided to show his latest works to his readers'.

By intuition, and by his singular vision of the world, a writer is able to discover far earlier than other people various aspects of social life and can often see them from an unexpected angle. This is the essence of talent. Talent, however, imposes certain duties. It is incumbent upon a writer to inform society of all that he is able to perceive and especially all that is unhealthy and a cause for anxiety. I was brought up with Russian literature and only circumstances prevented me from pursuing more extensive studies . . . Russian literature has always been sensitive to human suffering. We sometimes hear that literature should beautify the future. This is falsification, and justifies lying. Such literature is a kind of make-up . . . In literature cosmetics are very harmful.

(*Kulturny Zivot*, 31 March 1967)

Alexander Tvardovsky's Preface* to *One Day*

The subject matter of Alexander Solzhenitsyn's novel is unusual in Soviet literature. It echoes the unhealthy phenomena in our life associated with the period of the personality cult, now exposed and rejected by the Party. Although these events are so recent in point of time, they seem very remote to us. But whatever the past was like, we in the present must not be indifferent to it. Only by going into its consequences fully, courageously, and truthfully can we guarantee a complete and irrevocable break with all those things that cast a shadow over the past. This is what N. S. Khrushchev meant when he said in his memorable concluding address at the Twenty-second Congress: 'It is our duty to go carefully into all aspects of all matters connected with the abuse of power. In time we must die, for we are all mortal, but as long as we go on working we can and must clarify many things and tell the truth to the Party and the

* This statement by the Editor-in-chief of *Novy Mir* appeared as a preface to the novel in the November 1962 issue of that journal.

people ... This must be done to prevent such things from happening in the future.'

One Day in the Life of Ivan Denisovich is not a book of memoirs in the ordinary sense of the word. It does not consist merely of notes on the author's personal experiences and his memories of them, although only personal experience could have given the novel such an authentic quality. It is a work of art. And it is the way in which the raw material is handled that gives it its outstanding value as a testimony and makes it an artistic document, the possibility of which had hitherto seemed unlikely on the basis of 'concrete material'.

In Solzhenitsyn the reader will not find an exhaustive account of that historical period marked in particular by the year 1937, so bitter in all our memories. The theme of *One Day* is inevitably limited by the time and place of the action and by the boundaries of the world to which the hero was confined. One day of Ivan Denisovich Shukhov, a prisoner in a forced labour camp as described by Alexander Solzhenitsyn (this is the author's first appearance in print) unfolds as a picture of exceptional vividness and truthfulness about the nature of man. It is this above all that gives the work its unique impact. The reader could easily imagine many of the people shown here in these tragic circumstances as fighting at the front or working on postwar reconstruction. They are the same sort of people, but they have been exposed by fate to a cruel ordeal – not only physical but moral.

The author of this novel does not go out of his way to emphasize the arbitrary brutality which was a consequence of the breakdown of Soviet legality. He has taken a very ordinary day – from reveille to lights out – in the life of a prisoner. But this ordinary day cannot fail to fill the reader's heart with bitterness and pain at the fate of these people who come to life before his eyes and seem so close to him in the pages of this book. The author's greatest achievement, however, is that this bitterness and pain do not convey a feeling of utter despair. On the contrary. The effect of this novel, which is so unusual for its honesty and harrowing truth, is to unburden our minds of things thus far unspoken, but which had to be said. It thereby strengthens and ennobles us.

This stark tale shows once again that today there is no aspect of our life that cannot be dealt with and faithfully described in Soviet literature. Now it is only a question of how much talent the writer brings to it. There is another very simple lesson to be learned from this novel. If the theme of a work is truly significant, if it is faithful to the great truths of life, and if it is deeply human in its presentation of even the most painful subjects, then it cannot help but find the appropriate form of expression. The style of *One Day* is vivid and original in its unpretentiousness and down-to-earth simplicity. It is quite unselfconscious and thereby gains great inner strength and dignity.

I do not want to anticipate readers' judgements of this short work, but I myself have not the slightest doubt that it marks the appearance on the literary scene of a new, original, and mature talent.

It may well be that the author's use – however sparing and to the point – of certain words and expressions typical of the setting in which the hero lived and worked will offend a particularly fastidious taste. But all in all, *One Day* is a work for which one has such a feeling of gratitude to the author that one's greatest wish is that this gratitude be shared by other readers.

ALEXANDER TVARDOVSKY

Soviet reviews of *One Day*

'*About the past, in the name of the future*' by Konstantin Simonov

Solzhenitsyn creates one human portrait after another. Amongst the story's heroes there are people with wonderful human qualities, there are people who are simply good, there are people with failings, perhaps with delusions, there are the stronger and the weaker. But when through the power of Solzhenitsyn's artistic brush they are transformed into a portrait of a wide group of people, depicted against the leaden-grey background of one day of ordinary camp life, you, the reader, begin to feel these people, taken together, are none other than purely and simply a part of our society . . . and they remain for the most part the same people that they were before the camp – real Soviet people . . .

Solzhenitsyn never draws this conclusion directly or stresses it, because as an artist he had no need to. But without labouring the point, he makes you sense it, experience it, understand it. And it was with just such a feeling, overcome by the power of his truth and the power of his talent, that I turned the last page of the story . . .

The Party has called writers its helpers. I believe that Alexander Solzhenitsyn, in his story, has shown himself a true helper of the Party in a sacred and vital cause – the struggle against the cult of personality and its consequences.

The consoling thought – that Stalin did not know what was happening – which some of us tried earlier to instil forcibly into ourselves has become a myth that has been destroyed. And this heavy but sober feeling flares up in the soul with new force when you read Solzhenitsyn's story – although I cannot even remember now if the name of Stalin is mentioned in it. The story *One Day in the Life of Ivan Denisovich* is written with the sure hand of a mature, unique master. A powerful talent has come into our literature. I personally have no doubts on that score.

(*Izvestia*, 18 November 1962)

'In the name of truth, in the name of life' by V. Ermilov*

Into our literature there has come a writer gifted with a rare talent, and, as befits a real artist, he has told us a truth that cannot be forgotten, that must not be forgotten, a truth that is staring us in the face . . .

Ivan Denisovich himself is a zealous, demanding master of

---

*Vladimir Ermilov became famous for his insinuation in 1930 that Mayakovsky was 'playing the game of the Trotskyite opposition'. During the purges he was a secret-police informer who denounced many writers and intellectuals.

his trade and here in the camp he remains true to himself, a man with a true worker's conscience ...

Alexander Solzhenitsyn's story, which at times calls to mind Tolstoy's artistic power in its depiction of the national character ...

There can be no doubt that the fight against the consequences of Stalin's personality cult, taken up by the Party and the Soviet people since the Twentieth and Twenty-second Congresses of the CPSU, will continue to facilitate the appearance of works of art outstanding for their ever increasing artistic value, their ever deeper closeness to the people, works reflecting our contemporary life and the creative labour of our people ...

Here we have a lofty, epic tale ...

I think that the author's artistic and humanitarian standpoint is a lofty and noble one ...

On reading this tragic tale ... the reader feels also that a truth has been told, and that the possibility of telling this truth has been affirmed by the Party and the people, by the whole course of our country's life during recent years ...

(*Pravda*, 23 November 1962)

'The power of creative youth in the service of great ideals'

Speech by the Secretary of the Central Committee of the CPSU, L. F. Ilichev, at a session of the Central Committee's Ideological Commission in the presence of young writers, artists, composers, cinema and theatrical workers, 26 December 1962.

... Our Party has supported and continues to support truthful works imbued with the sharpest critical spirit, if they are written from a constructive standpoint and filled with the ideals of our society ...

As for the story *One Day in the Life of Ivan Denisovich* ... as you know, it deals with a bitter subject, but it is not written from a decadent viewpoint. Works like this inspire respect for the labouring man, and the Party supports them.

To excoriate, to cauterize everything bad, everything negative in people's souls, and to inspire in them a readiness for great exploits, to summon them to the fight, to creative labour, that's the way, keep at it!

(*Literaturnaya Gazeta*, 10 January 1963)

A reader writes

To the Editors of *Literaturnaya Gazeta*
Esteemed comrade Editor!

After reading the story *One Day in the Life of Ivan Denisovich* by Alexander Solzhenitsyn in *Novy Mir*, I was so shattered that I barely managed to get through my day's work ... Solzhenitsyn's story struck me right to the heart. I do not know A. Solzhenitsyn's address, so I beg you, comrade Editor, to thank him from me for his story which struck me to the heart.

(*Literaturnaya Gazeta*, 22 January 1963)

'The eternal youth of realism'
by Arkady Elyashevich

... In my view, talented works such as *One Day in the Life of Ivan Denisovich* by Alexander Solzhenitsyn ... possess a very distinct and altogether unusual stylistic tonality that immediately inspires the reader's trust ... I have in mind, of course, not only the unusual quality of the author's 'stamp' ... but also the uniqueness of content and form of these works as a whole ...

Yes, our literature affirms the present reality, but it looks all its shortcomings boldly in the face, does not avoid them or hide them from its readers.

(*Literaturnaya Gazeta*, 12 February 1963)

How people read *One Day*

A survey of letters
by Alexander Solzhenitsyn

These are letters that I shall keep. They will be precious not only to me. Our fellow-countrymen too seldom have the opportunity to express their views on social questions; this applies even more to former prisoners. They have already been disillusioned, deceived, too many times, but all the same, this time they believed that the age of truth was beginning, and that they could write for themselves. And it was as if a common cry went up. (And they have, of course, been deceived, for the *n*th time . . .)

Well, there were some who were careful. As one wrote: 'I am not giving my name because I am watching my health for the remaining days of my life.'

Others were even more careful – they did not write at all (after all, one can be traced from one's handwriting, it has often happened here; it's easy enough).

I think it is appropriate to leaf through these letters: from this reception given to the first scanty, muffled account of the camps we can measure what will happen when the truth is revealed in its entirety.

FORMER PRISONERS READ *One Day*

When former prisoners learned from the fanfares in all the newspapers that some story about the camps had appeared, and that the newspaper men were vying with each other to praise it, they decided unanimously: 'More lies! They've managed to lie, even about this!' That our newspapers, with their usual lack of restraint, should suddenly begin to praise the truth – this really did seem inconceivable! Others did not even wish to see the work.

But in the end they find out.

Markelov: 'Ivan Denisovich? That's me, sz–209. And I can give all the characters real names, not invented ones. Which camp? Ukhta, 29th encampment. Or Steplag, Balkhash, 8th section.'

Mumrikov: 'It's the No. 8 mine in Vorkuta.'

N. A. Ivanov from Cherepovets: 'We were in the 104th brigade with you, lived in the same hut.'

Voichenko: 'Solzhenitsyn has not even changed Tyurin's name. I knew him, and worked in the 104th brigade ... I remember equally well the senior guard, Ivan Poltor, from the western Ukraine, always on the make, he was. He was a big fellow with black eyes that bulged frighteningly. His real name was Burden-yuk ... I shall never forget the disciplinary officer, Sorodov, introduced in the story as Volkovoi. He did not walk round the compound, he strode majestically in a short leather coat, in smart new felt boots (made by a prisoner) – quite a picture! ... I also knew Shukhov under another name. There was one like him in every brigade.'

F. V. Shavirin: 'You have taken a picture of quite a day. ... Reading your story and comparing it with the camp, it is impossible to distinguish one from another. They are alike as two peas – the arrangement of the compound, the punishment block, and the attitude to the prisoners.'

B. D. Golitsin: 'In the story I was first of all looking for things that rank false, or were made up by the author – and I did not find one.'

S. M. Rudkovsky: 'One can see that you yourself were in a camp.'

Posya also recognizes himself in Shukhov: 'I wore the number A–691 for ten years because I was imprisoned by the Germans for two days, and I did not even seen any Germans.'

And another correspondent recognizes himself in Captain Buynovsky. 'The captain suffered because of a gift – I suffered because of a letter from the USA. I was dismissed from service in the navy; there was discrimination against me everywhere, even in my personal life.'

How They Read One Day

Rudkovsky: 'Read it through with difficulty – I was there myself.'

Belsky: 'I could not sit still. I kept leaping up, walking about and imagined all those scenes as taking place in the camp I myself was in.'

Zarin: 'When I read it, I literally felt the blast of cold as one leaves the hut for inspection.'

Voichenko: 'Reading it my hands trembled.'

Kravchenko (Yakutiya): 'Now I read and weep, but when I was imprisoned in Ukhta, for ten years I shed not a tear.'

P. V. Sharapov (Barnaul): 'Although I wept when I read it, I felt myself a citizen with full rights among other people. Up to then I felt their chilly glances and they reminded me of Pechora and Norilsk.'

E. Ya. Zaitseva: 'I got it only for New Year's night!'

Svetlana Lesovik: 'I am only a nurse, and there were professors and university teachers in the queue for the book. But because I know someone in the library, and because I was there myself, I was given it for the New Year without waiting in the queue . . . It seemed as if you were writing about the camp I was in.'

Mark Ivanovich Kononenko: 'In Kharkov I have seen all kinds of queues – for the film "Tarzan", butter, women's drawers, chicken giblets and horse-meat sausage. But I cannot remember a queue as long as the one for your book in the libraries . . . I waited six months on the list and to no avail. By chance I got hold of it for forty-eight hours.'

Olga Chavchavadze: 'After reading it, the only thing left to do is to knock a nail into the wall, tie a knot and hang oneself.' (She was not in prison herself – her husband perished.) And a young female student, both of whose grandfathers perished *there* – 'I flicked through it.'

Kaidanov from Debaltsevo: 'I got the magazine version (*roman-gazeta*) for four roubles instead of twelve kopecks . . .

My own life is described here exactly ... A loudly dressed lady with a gold ring said, "I don't like this story, it's too depressing". I answered her, "It's better to have a bitter truth than a sweet lie".'

G. Benediktova: 'It has so much life, so much pain that one's heart might stop beating. People who have not been there exclaim in horror, even say that those who informed on others should be arrested ... Just a little sympathy for those who perished is beginning to penetrate such people, and the cold indifference is beginning to give way to warmth.'

M. I. Kalinina also gave it to various other people to read. 'A teacher at the kindergarten read it avidly, and was shaken to the core, but the head of the kindergarten, a middle-aged Party member, said, "Hm, just a lot of swearing". Young workers at evening classes seized the chance to read it; a Komsomol secretary said, "I don't like that kind of book". My neighbour read it, started drinking and drank for a week.'

V. I. Zhukov was sentenced back in 1941 for 'terrorist acts against Stalin', and in the years after that lost his family, possessions and apartment; he did not even read *One Day* itself, but a review in *Ogonyok*, and at last made up his mind to write and ask for rehabilitation! (Through ignorance he did not realize that he could have had it long ago.) He wrote to the Prosecutor-General's office and soon received it.

Opinions

G. F. Polev: 'Can the time be coming when people are beginning to find out?'

Anna Matveyevna Lukyanova (Yaroslavl): 'It is a joy to realize that Shukhov's dreams – "We will live through everything, may God grant an end to it" – have come true.'

Shavirin: 'We hope that this story is a forerunner of others. Let it be painful and bitter, as long as it is the truth!'

I. Dobryak: 'This story has opened the eyes of many people to whom we were a mystery.'

Lilenkov: 'Truth has triumphed, but too late. The Far East and Siberia were created by unjustly condemned men who perished on the construction sites.'

P. N. Ptitsyn: 'Our people, guilty of nothing, reduced to the situation of the lowest of cattle, threw themselves heart and soul into this work ... And when they had finished the task (bridge, tunnel, road, palace, aerodrome) they lay dying on sackcloth, pouring out their starved, bloody insides. Eternal praise and remembrance to those unknown toilers who laid down their bones in the wild, frozen outer regions of our homeland ... Real criminals are not capable of genuine toil. Truly it is the Ivan Denisovichs who achieved something genuine ... What a drama: an enemy of the people is friend to the people. They seek to destroy a man, and he does a good deed.'

Sushikhin, military engineer: 'Some critics mock Ivan Denisovich for doing menial jobs to earn extra money. I, however, who have two higher degrees, but had no parcels or money, had to repair fountain pens, compose applications. I should like to see any of those critics in the position of a prisoner!'

N. I. Ryabinin: 'People, brought to total physical and moral exhaustion, perished in their hundreds of thousands. Those, however, who exercised this tyranny, in the majority of cases did so in full consciousness of what they were doing. And they are still walking around, although they should long ago have been dispatched to the other world.'

P. R. Martynyuk: 'When reading this story one is forced to consider the question – how could it come about, that the people were in power and that the people permitted such oppression? ... I worked on the White Sea and Volga-Moscow canals, and by a miracle stayed alive. What is described in the story is a tiny part of what I personally saw and lived through.'

L. Terenteva-Mironova (Yalutorovsk) did not suffer imprisonment – she is the wife of one who died. She has a double-barrelled name because she changed it to escape persecution. 'I see, I hear this crowd of hungry, freezing creatures, half people, half animals, and amongst them is my husband ... Continue to write, write the truth, even though they won't print it now! Our floods of tears were not shed in vain – the truth will rise to the surface in this river of tears . . . My husband wrote to me from Taishet that one of his companions in misfortune would come to me some day and tell me about him, and give me a ring that he made for me there, in his place of torment. But nobody came to me, and now will never come . . .'

V. P. Tarnovsky: 'And he broke up his food ration,
                And with it returned to me all Russia.'

N. A. Vilenchuk: 'We believed in the Party and *we were not wrong* (I spent seventeen years in the camps). We still need to have our heated arguments.'

M. Kononenko: 'You have described a comparatively bearable camp, not a punishment camp. From your story there is no answer to the question: why did so many never return?'

V. M. Eremenko: 'I am amazed that Volkovoi allowed you to publish this story. Tell me, there is something worrying me, were you never in the punishment block?'

F. Shults: 'I am astonished that they have not put both you and Tvardovsky away.'

We are astonished too . . .

PRESENT-DAY PRISONERS READ *One Day* (prisoners of the 1950s and 1960s)

We talk about all this as past history, but for them it is actuality. We have served our sentences (for good?), but they are still inside. For them this story is not the whole truth, if there will be no sequel, something *about them* and the fact that things are just the same today. They want this to be said, and for something to change! If words do not lead to deeds, then what good are they? A dog barking at night in a village?

All the fuss in the newspapers about this story, calculated to impress people outside the camps and abroad, has been to the effect that 'it happened, but will never happen again!' As always, they are lying about what matters most. Part of the truth has come out, but we are not allowed to go any further. And this has particularly provoked present-day prisoners.

Their letters are also a common cry. They want to know: 'What about us?!'

P. A. Lepekhin: 'Citizen Solzhenitsyn! Help to revise the rules and administrative regulations in the penal settlements! On the basis of my letter I beg you to print in the newspaper *Izvestia* a criticism of the accursed past system.'

I. G. Pisarev: 'One thing I do not understand – did you want to say that *that* no longer exists or that what there was before still remains?'

A. D. Korzukhin: 'The day you have described is not yet a thing of the past.'

Yu. K-i: 'Nothing has changed since the days of Ivan Denisovich except the external forms. A prisoner will read your book, and he will be hurt and embittered that everything has remained unchanged.'

Bratchikov: 'Yesterday I read your story which is still valid at the present day. In court one often hears: "You are keeping quiet, but in your heart you are still the same criminal you were ten years ago." I think these words apply most of all to the people who pronounce them. People talk and write a great deal about the cult of Stalin, but what has changed if the laws about twenty-five-year imprisonment, promulgated under him, are still in force?'

V. D. Ch-n and others: 'Why are people like the disciplinary officer Volkovoi still unpunished, for people like this even at the present time are working as "educators" in corrective penal institutions, with the one difference that they have exchanged the wolf's skin for a sheep's?'

V. I. Knyaginin: 'Probably there is no one who could rite about the present time.'

A joint letter from Ust-Nera: 'For us now it is considerably worse (than in the story). We are not beaten, but the guards like to say that we should be exterminated. Where do lads of eighteen to twenty years of age get such hatred? Evidently someone is stirring them up . . . In December 1962 (when the story appeared) out of 300 men in our camp there were 190 suffering from malnutrition.'

V. E. Milchikhin: 'Black obscurity has covered us and no one sees us . . . You at least were allowed to receive parcels, and to earn extra bread. We, on the other hand, receive 700 grammes and no parcels . . . Nowadays you writers are discovering the injustices of the days of Beria. But why does not one of you touch on the life of non-political prisoners? Why is not a single writer interested in the life of prisoners now? Why does no one deign to come to a camp and see who is inside? Of course, you can send me politely to hell, but once you have decided to reveal the truth, you should take it through to the end . . . For example, why are we, murderers, inside? (Murder in the camp.) People who had hanged and executed Soviet citizens were released under article 58, while we have to stay in prison.'

There are many different things here – truth, and envy, and nonsense. One's own pain is so close to the heart that it seems quite unnecessary to write about the past (as if books about it came out every day). There is no need to release anyone under article 58, as long as I am released! Ivan Alekseyev really took me aback: 'Minds like yours are not interested in real help. Your position is that of the rear-guard.'

The letters of today's prisoners tell about the most recent situation in the camps; and take it upon themselves to answer some general questions.

Lepekhin: 'Prisoners' complaints to the higher judicial organs are consistently rejected. After all, if one goes into a case and releases someone, then one is liable to be dismissed oneself.' (There is definitely some truth here. Not of course justice, but self-preservation is the most important goal of the present legal system.)

Yu. K-i: 'If representatives of industry visit the camps, they are taken round the best huts, shown Potemkin villages. Beforehand they are frightened with tales about the degenerates they will see . . . They blacken us as best they can in order to justify their own existence and to show that they have a difficult task too. From the meanest guard right up to the camp boss, all have a vital interest in maintaining the existence of the camps. The supervisors make a great fuss about every trifle; the security officers add all the dirt they can to our files; the head of the administration, compiling his quarterly report on infringements of the rules, always embroiders. We, who are serving twenty-five years are the bread and butter for those who are supposed to teach us virtue, corrupt though they are themselves. Did not the colonizers make out that Indians and Negroes were not fully human in this way? . . . It takes nothing at all to arouse public opinion against us. It is enough to write an article in the paper called "Man in a Cage" or to describe how a degenerate criminal violated a five-month-old baby girl, and tomorrow the people will organize meetings to demand that we be burnt in furnaces.'

'PRACTICAL WORKERS' AND THE WELL-INTENTIONED READ One Day

What are 'practical workers'? It turns out that this is how camp guards style themselves. The description is priceless; we had not heard it before.

Let us hear the other side, as is only proper. More precisely, let us receive our directives.

Not all of these correspondents identify themselves; maybe there are some who never wore blue flashes, and whose only bunch of keys belongs to his apartment, but they are all of one mind, all of the same ilk. They are the people whose pictures are never in the papers, but who wield the power. (One of them – S. I. Golovin – says he is a former prisoner. We must believe him.)

They are not victimized for reading this book, they have time to read it, to take notes, break it down point by point.

About Shukhov

Ivan Denisovich is a boot-licker. As a prisoner of the Germans he would be able to earn his bread though he might have been killed by fellow prisoners (*Oleinik*, Aktyubinsk).

I do not want heroes like that – all stomach and no brain (*Pastukhova, T. S.*, Bogorodsk).

The principal character of the story, Shukhov, is shown negatively, like all the others, who, as the story shows, disorganized life in the camp (*Grigorev, A. I.*, Monino, Nelidovsk raion, practical worker).

If he is not allowed to return to his family, then he has nothing at all to do with his freedom. Is this picture of the Soviet man of the fifties true? You feel neither sympathy nor respect for Shukhov, nor do you feel any particular anger at the injustice done to him. (*Yu. Matveyev*, Moscow. He very likely lives with his family.)

When he had washed the floor he threw the sopping cloth behind the stove and poured the dirty water on to the path used by the authorities. This shows how he respects communists and looks after socialist property . . . All he hopes for is the sick-bay. After all he is in a corrective labour camp, even if he is innocent, so he ought to set an example to the others, like a good Soviet citizen, and show how to fire the others with enthusiasm and not go to pieces! (*Zakharova, A. F.*, worked for the MVD since 1950, Lesogorsk, Irkutsk oblast).

Shukhov was rightly condemned. At the interrogation *no one could force him*, after all it was not 1937. He had his reasons: he was afraid of going back to the front. (*V. I. Silin*, Sverdlovsk, practical worker).

Vladimir Dmitrievich Uspensky from Moscow attacks Shukhov in the greatest detail of all. (He is either an investigator or a camp administrator.) Disregarding the text of the story as obviously false testimony, he makes his case against Shukhov absolutely in the spirit of *those days*:

Shukhov is not ill, since he could work today. But he is afraid for his health, and so rushes off to the medical orderly!

The only place he did a decent job of work was on his own log cabin; everywhere else he is a sloppy worker.

He never shares anything with anyone; he is a fully qualified, resourceful and merciless jackal. He is a total egoist, living only for his belly. He brings a knife into the camp in order to sell it, and a man is killed with it.

He was the first to put up his hands and hastened to give himself into captivity, he is a real traitor to his country.

In a word, ten years is too little for Shukhov. He should have received four times that!

About the Other Characters

Millions of Soviet people labour at felling timber and sing the praises of this form of toil (!), but the heroes of this story regard it with fear (*A. F. Zakharova*).

You show a captain of the second grade humiliated and deprived of his feeling of self-respect. Why is he alone in his indignation, and why is the director of the factory reconciled to this? (*Oleinik*).

The Tyurins never worked in the camp ... (*P. A. Pankov*, Kramatorsk).

Why is Tyurin inside? The sons of kulaks were not imprisoned(??). And there were *very few* Estonians and Latvians in the camps; generally they were deserters from the Red Army (*Uspensky*).

Since when has *Novy Mir* taken upon itself the mission of defending bourgeois nationalists from whose bullets thousands of activists perished? (*Belousov*, Uzhgorod).

About Camp Regulations

Why give someone who does not work a lot to eat? His strength will remain unspent ... Prisoners were dressed *according to the season*, and were fed no worse than the free labour force ... The criminal world is still treated too gently (*Sergei Ivan. Golovin*, Tselinograd, served ten years).

How dare you slander camp regulations in this way? In the camps there is less abuse than in any other Soviet institution?! (Patriotically said.) I maintain that things have grown *more severe* in the camps now (*Karakhanov*, foreman).

Nothing has changed even now, for example, in the searching, or to use the language of the author, in the frisking of prisoners on being led out and on re-entering the camp. And repeated roll-calls if the numbers do not tally ... And nowadays also the guards always walk with sub-machine guns at the ready, and at a fixed distance go men with dogs. As regards the food regulations it must not be forgotten that *they are not at a resort.* For this reason they must redeem their guilt by honest toil (senior official *Bazunov*, Oimyakon, fifty-five years old, veteran of the camp service).*

How is it possible to discontinue body searches when prisoners try to take out of the camp letters of a slanderous nature attacking the Soviet Communist party and the Soviet government? ...

(About the whip.) We all know perfectly well that corporal punishment was abolished in our country with the coming of Soviet power ...

Solzhenitsyn describes the working of the camp as if there were no control by the Party. Earlier, as now, Party organizations existed and directed all activities as conscience required (*Zakharova*).

Once you have camps, arbitrary individual acts are possible (*P. A. Pankov*).

---

*Bazunov's lengthy letter was sent to a *closed* journal of inspection and security with the noble title 'Towards a New Life'. In the general excitement the journal had been foolish enough to print a sour but positive review of my story, and in answer was showered with indignant letters from its readers. The spell was still so great that the editors sent me Bazunov's letter for me to reply. This I willingly did, but times had changed and my answer never appeared.

[Footnote comments throughout this section are Solzhenitsyn's own.]

About Informers

According to Solzhenitsyn, if one of the prisoners who is more conscious of his duties tells something to the authorities, then it is 'self-preservation at someone else's expense'. Some patriot, I must say! The Soviet people should say only thank you to this prisoner who has come to a proper understanding (*Zakharova*).

How informers are murdered is described as if it were a good thing. Everyone knows what an informer is. In the Soviet Union *these* people are respected, because they are progressive, politically aware people, who help to bring into the open the enemies of Soviet power and to unmask traitors. In the camps they are those prisoners who have recognized their guilt. If there were no informers, there would be escapes. And what is a prisoner *doing at liberty*? (*Silin*).

About the Guards

But the main thing which astonishes – I make bold to express myself thus – in this story, is the fact that the author so defames our soldiers and guards. A soldier is a soldier, he is true to his oath, carries out all the commands of his superiors ... What a serious and responsible task falls to the soldier who takes the prisoners out to work ... This story insults soldiers, sergeants and officers of the Ministry for the Preservation of Public Order [MOOP, now MVD]. The people are the creators of history, but how are the people represented in the figures of soldiers, sergeants and officers? They are represented as 'parrots' [camp slang for sentries], blockheads, idiots in greasy field shirts and torn greatcoats (*Bazunov*).

To my mind there is no shame in protecting the peaceful toil of Soviet people. But according to Solzhenitsyn there is nothing more shameful. The people have glorified our heroic Soviet troops, but Solzhenitsyn makes them into 'parrots' ... And what would happen if the camp guards stopped doing their work! How the people would suffer!? (*Zakharova*).

About the 'Practical Workers' Themselves. About Camp Administration and Surveillance

Solzhenitsyn has spoken out against workers who are carrying out a difficult but worthy task. The entire day of the story is filled with the negative behaviour of the prisoners without any indication of the role of the administration; if it is mentioned at all, it is only negatively. But the keeping of prisoners in camps *is not a result of the cult of personality*, but is due to the carrying out of sentences ...* The security officers are called 'godfather' – a term used only by a few bad characters among the prisoners ... The negative attitude of the prisoners to the authorities ... does not correspond to the tasks laid down at the present time (*Grigorev, A. I.*).

The security forces did not know why people were put inside† (*Karakhanov*).

Of what are the staff and the officers guilty? Are they guilty of being called by the Party and the government to bear the heaviest burden of our time – work with the criminal world? ... We, the officials, living in remote places, are deprived of all elementary human conditions in comparison with city dwellers. Occasionally we do not have enough to eat(!) ... We are working with the rejects of society, we carry the most difficult burden for the good of the whole of the people. So why are our names besmirched? ...

(About the authorities in the story.) They were only carrying out their orders, instructions and regulations. They did nothing of their own accord, did not take advantage of the freedom from restraint afforded by the period of the cult of personality. *The same people are working now who worked then* (!). Maybe about ten per cent are new.

Solzhenitsyn calls the security officers a 'godfather'. Who gave him the right to pour scorn on a post laid down in the statutes of the MVD? ... And what are we to think about 'blockhead guards'? They hold responsible positions ...

---

*'We only carried out orders', 'We did not know'.
†Very significant testimony. Present-day convicts say the same.

In Ozerlag, to my knowledge, there was no thieving.* But he calls everyone a thief (*Zakharova*).

And why be displeased that the convicts are building houses, for free people to live in? (*Bazunov*).

About the Story as a Whole

If your story is a work of art, then it should be like a rallying cry.

Instead of depicting the destruction of the most loyal people in 1937, the author chose 1941, when by and large it was self-seekers who were sent to the camps.† In 1937 there were no Shukhovs,‡ and they went to their deaths grimly and in silence, wondering for whose benefit it was§ . . . They did not lick food bowls there (*Oleinik*).

I feel no pity or sympathy for these convicts. Surely the communists who got into trouble were not like that? (*Anon.*)‖

Not one of those who were unjustly punished ever blamed comrade Stalin for his misfortunes – the thought did not even occur to them. This is the watershed dividing those who suffered innocently and the real criminals. The latter, as a rule, abused both Soviet power and Stalin (*Vinokur*, engineer). He has practically no victims of 1937, *in other words* innocent people (*Medne*, Elgava).

They are not the people of 1937, but are all part of the post-war crowd. I feel no pity for them.¶ These miserable people with foul deeds in their hearts *were sentenced too mildly*. I am not sorry for the dubious personalities from the time of the Patriotic War (apart from POWs) (*Ignatovich*, Kimovsk, worked as a foreman on public transport in Karaganda).

*Perhaps this is why there was such a careful search for letters at the exit?
†Indeed: simple people, prisoners of war.
‡How many were there even then!
§What intellectual profundity! By the way, they did not really go in silence, but with constant confessions and pleas for mercy.
‖He too conceals his identity, just in case: the devil only knows which way the wind may blow next?
¶Of course they were only the simple people with no Party affiliations.

How much unbelievable effort the Chekists put into restoring lost folk to society! Why did he not show how our people worked for twenty-four hours at a stretch, not because of the threat of the stick, but because they knew the value of wolfram and molybdenum in wartime! In what a frenzy about one thousand people worked seventy-two hours together up to the knees and waist in cold water. Who was able to inspire such a feat of patriotism? The Chekists!* (*S. I. Golovin*).

The convicts' work, which is the basis of their re-education, is similarly not shown in a positive light in the story. The prisoners in the story break the rules (!) not only in their daily routine, but also while on the job . . . The story teaches a careless attitude to socialist property – 'They broke off wires to make spoons, concealing them in the corner' . . . In our opinion, Shukhov's 'days' inside the camp should not have been taken up with this kind of thing. If such negative acts on the part of the convicts did actually take place, there were constant attempts to put a stop to them, but about this the story says nothing. There were so many positive features, and still are! Surely such inadmissible acts on the part of the prisoners would not have been tolerated. The story would have had a beneficial influence if it had responded to the tasks set before corrective labour establishments† (*Grigorev*).

We have never before had to put up with such rubbish. This is not only my opinion; there are many like us, *their name is legion*.‡

The author is making use of his unsuccessful work to attach himself to the great task which has already been performed by our Party, namely, the task of clarifying the harm done and the consequences of the cult of personality. (*Bazunov*. He adds: 'This is not only my opinion, but that of all military personnel who have read the story.')

*The reader will see that this profound comment also defines the general purpose of literature.

†Yet another profound comment defining the general purposes of literature.

‡It is true that they are legion. Only in their haste they forgot to check the Bible. The legion is of *devils*.

I am absolutely disgusted, like all the officials of MOOP. All are burning with wrath and indignation. It is quite astonishing how much bile there is in this work ... (*Zakharova*).

And more briefly: 'The story told by Solzhenitsyn should be removed immediately from all libraries and reading rooms!'

This in fact was done, only more gradually.

And finally: 'This book should not have been published; the material should have been handed over to the MVD' (*Anon.*; child of October).

This is almost what happened; the dead child is not far off ...

What about the Author Himself?

You, who are not in a fit state to stand firmly on your feet (?), trample honest Soviet people into the dirt ... You have tackled a good subject in a spirit that is not quite pure ... Why (in the story) does no one protest at the practice of bribery? It is repulsive to Soviet man. Or did you *yourself* get your freedom with the aid of a bribe? (*Oleinik*).

You are a wet blanket, comrade Solzhenitsyn; we cannot sense in you any faith in the new life (*Kamzolova*).

Spite has clouded the gaze of this man Solzhenitsyn, and so he cannot take a sober view of his surroundings. He thinks that only his petty personality, soured by spineless malice, is typical in literature ... This man is not capable of understanding the great things in life (*N. D. Marchenko*, st. Udelnaya).

He deliberately incites the people against the organs of the MVD ... And why is he allowed to mock the people who work in MOOP? *It is a disgrace!* (*Zakharova*).

Hear that! A disgrace! It was alright to torment people in camps for forty years, but to publish a story about it is a disgrace!

Finally, and more broadly: *the philosophical approach.*

You wish to infect Soviet man with these sores from the past (*Oleinik*).

History never has any use for the past (!!) – least of all the history of socialist culture (*A. Kuzmin*).

We paid too dearly for Soviet power to allow its activities to be debased (*Golovin*).

I would not have published this. For what reason and for whom is it? One tries to conceal one's own shortcomings instead of advertising them. We need neither sympathy nor charity (*Medne*).

Criticizing the cult of personality is necessary and inevitable, and we are all doing it at the moment. It is not, however, necessary to drag in people who are not involved ... This authority of M O O P has been finally undermined before the people and cannot now be restored ... (*Zakharova*).

Why do we have to make a big fuss over what was done during the personality cult? The unmasking of illegal acts is like an epidemic, writers and poets are trying to kick a dead lion ... Perhaps Stalin and his toadies invented the class enemy as well? ...* What is the point of nosing about in the dirty linen of a past which has vanished for ever into the waters of Lethe? ...

> Do you hear that, Russia,
> On our consciences
> There is not a single spot! (*Anon.*)

Once again that wretched *Anon*! One would so much like to know whether he shot people himself, or only sent them to their death, or whether he is just an ordinary orthodox citizen.

And here at last is a more comprehensive historical view, the first scientific explanation of all our misfortunes:

After the original (?) slogan, 'the son is not responsible for his father', the shattered remains of the privileged classes strove to insinuate themselves into every part of the Soviet system, never abandoning thoughts of revenge for the privileges they had lost. They were particularly active in 1937(!).† They collaborated in the police forces of the enemy

*Who else?

†i.e. the day after the 'original' slogan they had all already seized the N K V D and established their authority over the Party.

in 1941; from their very first day in the army, they shouted, 'Everyone for himself!', and led others after them into captivity (*Pankov*).

Now we know at last it was the class enemy that decimated the Party, and let Hitler get as far as Stalingrad, only then handing over to our brilliant generals and the wise Generalissimus.

This is what is frightening – this is the way they write history . . .

(*Survey*, No. 74/75, Winter/Spring 1970)

NEW TROUBLES

Khrushchev's visit to the Manège exhibition of modern Soviet art on 1 December 1962 and his angry denunciation of artists who painted 'with a donkey's tail' served as a signal for a general counter-attack against liberal artists and writers. Khrushchev led the chorus of condemnation in his notorious speech of 8 March 1963, but was curiously defensive in some respects. He defended Solzhenitsyn, Tvardovsky and Yevtushenko who were then the object of attack by the neo-Stalinists, sensing – rightly as he was soon to discover – that the latter were challenging his own authority. But the struggle went on and Solzhenitsyn became a central figure in it. The attitude towards him encompassed in a symbolic form all the basic questions affecting Soviet political evolution: cultural, social and economic. Not surprisingly, Solzhenitsyn became both a protagonist and a target in these preliminary skirmishes which presaged the fall of Khrushchev and the limited re-Stalinization afterwards. The liberal writers tried to secure the Lenin Prize for Solzhenitsyn but a pitched battle behind the scenes ended in their defeat. Little did Solzhenitsyn know that after a period of tribulation he was destined to receive another, much more prestigious, literary prize abroad.

Khrushchev on Solzhenitsyn

In their creative work in recent years, writers and artists have been paying great attention to that chapter in the life of Soviet society which is bound up with the Stalin personality cult. All this is quite logical and there is every reason for it. Works in which Soviet reality during those years is truthfully reflected from party positions have appeared. One could give as illustrations, among other works, Alexander Tvardovsky's *Distant*

Horizons, Alexander Solzhenitsyn's *One Day in the Life of Ivan Denisovich*, some of Yevgeny Yevtushenko's poems, and Grigory Chukhrai's picture *Clear Skies*.

The party gives its backing to artistic creations which are really truthful, whatever negative aspects of life they may deal with, so long as they help the people in their effort to build a new society, and so long as they strengthen and weld together the people's forces.

(*Literaturnaya Gazeta*, 12 March 1963)

Meeting of Moscow writers

... 'It is the task of Soviet writers to educate youth by positive examples, lead it to a bright future, to communism', said V. Tevekelyan. From this point of view the position of the editors of the journal *Novy Mir* is not clear. We know not only the story *One Day in the Life of Ivan Denisovich* by Alexander Solzhenitsyn, published in this journal, but also his story *Matryona's Home*. When you read this story you get the impression that the peasant's psychology has remained the same as it was sixty years ago. But this is not true! We need works which are historically truthful, and tell of the enormous revolutionary changes that have taken place in the Soviet village.

(*Literaturnaya Gazeta*, 19 March 1963)

Attacks on Solzhenitsyn

1. by Sergei Pavlov, First Secretary of the Young Communist League

Under the pretext of the struggle against the consequences of the cult of the individual and dogmatism, certain writers, film makers and artists have begun somehow to 'be embarrassed' to speak of lofty ideas, of communism. Juggling with the lofty concept of 'truth to life' and distorting this idea, they populate their works with people who stand aside from great public interests and are immersed in a narrow little world of philistine problems. And it is these philistines whom some writers portray with greatest sympathy! ...

So our educators have to fight the baneful influence of some books intended for young people. Bourgeois propaganda, on the other hand, eagerly arms itself with such works, translates and advertises them extensively. At the Eighth World Festival of Youth and Students, representatives of American, French, Italian, and other delegations told us that the young people of their countries often ask: Why do we meet good Soviet people in real life, but some Soviet books write about utterly different kinds? Indeed, one need merely read I. Ehrenburg's memoirs, A. Yashin's *Vologda Marriage*, V. Nekrasov's travel essays, V. Aksyonov's *Halfway to the Moon*, A. Solzhenitsyn's *Matryona's Home*, V. Voinovich's *I Want to Be Honest* (and all from the magazine *Novy Mir*) – these works breathe such pessimism, mustiness, hopelessness that I fear they could mislead an uninformed person who did not know our life. Incidentally, *Novy Mir* prints such works with utterly inexplicable consistency.

(Komsomolskaya Pravda, 22 March 1963)

2. by Mikhail Sokolov

It is impossible to agree with those who claim that we had a period of disorder, of ideological hesitation. There was no disorder whatsoever, no sort of hesitation either among literary people or among others in cultural activities. We went where the Party called us. There were private mistakes. But these mistakes were made by living people. And it is time to inquire about these people, it is time to bring order into our writers' organization.

Why, for example, is it precisely in the pages of *Novy Mir* that there appears now one, now another, then a third work, upon reading which one can only shrug one's shoulders – Ehrenburg's memoirs, Nekrasov's notes, Solzhenitsyn's stories, and others?

(Literaturnaya Gazeta, 2 April 1963)

Tvardovsky on Solzhenitsyn

A. Solzhenitsyn's *One Day in the Life of Ivan Denisovich*, which first appeared in *Novy Mir* – a story by a Ryazan teacher whom no one had heard of until recently – is in my opinion a particularly important and significant phenomenon. This is not only because it is based on specific materials and shows the anti-popular character of the phenomena associated with the consequences of the cult of the individual, but also because its whole aesthetic structure confirms the unchanging meaning of the tradition of truth in art and decisively counters false innovationism of the formalist, modernist sort.

In my opinion, *One Day* is one of those literary phenomena after whose appearance it is impossible to talk about any literary problem or literary fact without measuring it against this phenomenon.

I will never forget how N. S. Khrushchev responded to this tale by Solzhenitsyn – to its hero, who retains the dignity and beauty of the man of labour under inhuman conditions, to the truthfulness of the account, to the author's Party approach to bitter and stern reality. At the first meeting Nikita Sergeyevich mentioned Solzhenitsyn in the course of his speech and introduced him to all of those present in the Palace of Meetings on the Lenin Hills.

If it were necessary to demonstrate the breadth of the views of our Party's Central Committee concerning literature and art, the sole fact that it approved this story by A. Solzhenitsyn would be more than sufficient. Incidentally, this once again irrefutably proves the complete baselessness of the hostile talk of the 'restrictions' and 'regimentation' that according to certain people characterize Soviet literature.

(*Pravda*, 12 May 1963)

The battle over Solzhenitsyn reopens

1. The Opening Move

WHAT IS 'RIGHT'?

The writing career of the author of *One Day in the Life of Ivan Denisovich* evolved in so dramatic and unusual a manner, and his talent is so individual and so interesting, that nothing which now flows from his pen can fail to excite the liveliest interest. *An Incident at Krechetovka Station* and *Matryona's Home*, whatever your opinion of them, showed that we are in the presence of a gifted writer who has not the slightest intention of confining himself within the limits of the prison-camp theme. Now we have a new story. And, it would appear, a 'new' Solzhenitsyn – writing about present-day Party officials, the youth, and so forth . . .

The phrase 'for the good of the cause', which Solzhenitsyn has made the title of his story, has an obviously sarcastic undertone – the words are discredited by the demagogue Khabalygin. Yet these words are not only mouthed by demagogues; they have a real, and most important, meaning. But this is completely ignored by the author. So what happens? Real, living bonds and relationships are destroyed, and we are presented with an artificially constructed, imaginary world, where honest, decent, but weak-willed champions of justice are found to be helpless, not so much in the face of the Knorozovs and Khabalygins as in the face of some indifferent, unfeeling force, which can be sensed behind the faceless, nameless representatives of unnamed institutions ('a comrade from the Department of . . .' and 'the head of the Electronics Section from . . .').

It would be wrong to suppose that these serious defects in the very conception of Solzhenitsyn's story do not affect its literary qualities. Truth to life is an intellectual and aesthetic category, and the slightest deviation from it is fraught with failure in the 'purely' artistic sphere. Here and there in the story *For the Good of the Cause*, in the occasional vivid touches or observations or in a particular word, we can detect the hand of Solzhenitsyn, but the plasticity and organic qualities of the language which won us over in the best pages of his other prose are lacking on this occasion.

And so, it's a failure ... But is there a single artist, and especially an artist who is still trying to find his way, who is immune to failure?

Of course not.

And maybe it would not be worth talking about this failure of Solzhenitsyn's if the shortcomings of this story did not have much in common with what the critics noted in, for example, *Matryona's Home*. I refer to his attempts to resolve the most complex intellectual and moral problems, to pass judgements on people and their actions, without reference to actual, living relationships; he operates in abstract categories which are not invested with a concrete social content. In *Matryona's Home* it was the 'righteous woman' without whom neither the village nor the town nor 'our whole land' was supposed to be worth anything. In this story it is the 'little' people who have racked their brains in fruitless efforts to answer a scholastic question, posed without reference to space or time: What *is* 'right'?

It might seem that *For the Good of the Cause* is the most topical of Solzhenitsyn's stories. But if you think it over and ignore such completely extraneous features as the sail-boats and palm-trees on the shirts, the short crew-cuts, and the 'supermodern' views of the young people on literature – if all this is thrown out – then the writer's view of life and his attitude towards it will be seen to have remained just as unmodern, and in many respects as archaic, as they were in *Matryona's Home*. We have not found the 'new', truly modern Solzhenitsyn here.

And yet we are undoubtedly in the presence of a writer of great and honest quality who is uniquely sensitive to any manifestation of evil or untruth or injustice. This is a great force, but only when it is combined with a knowledge and deep understanding of the laws governing the movement of the real world and an ability to see clearly the direction of that movement.

I think and I believe that our encounter with the 'new' Solzhenitsyn is still to come.

YURI BARABASH*

(*Literaturnaya Gazeta*, 31 August 1963)

2. Counter-move

IS THE CRITIC RIGHT?

It so happened that I read Yuri Barabash's review of Solzhenitsyn's *For the Good of the Cause* before reading the story itself. As a result, I approached the story with an unconscious prejudice, having been put on my guard by the serious criticism contained in what seemed a convincing review – all the more so since it was written in a tone of quiet good-will that inspired confidence. However, Solzhenitsyn made me change my mind, convinced me of the rightness of his case, and, moreover, made me take up my pen and enter into a debate, despite my lack of experience as a critic . . .

The democratization of our life has been marked in recent years by efforts to do everything possible to widen participation in the administration, in supervisory work, and likewise in Party and Soviet work. There are people who are upset by this democratization. Why? How do they act, what are their tactics, their methods, what is their philosophy? This is the object of Solzhenitsyn's interest.

Seriously and courageously he poses a moral and social problem: What does 'for the good of the cause' mean? He raises this problem to the level of the high moral demands of a communist society. He fights passionately for faith in the people who are furthering that cause and who alone have the right to judge what is useful to the cause and what is not. He exposes those who, while using the interests of the state as a cover, look after their own little affairs at the expense of the state. He demands justice, and how can one call his approach 'scholastic' when he is trying to defend justice and further it? Only a story filled with

*A well-known conservative critic.

the joy and the pain that come from real knowledge of life can excite and move us in this way.

It would be ridiculous for me to claim that all my judgements are unassailable. Like any other work of art, this story examines life in all its complexity and contradictions. And various interpretations and objections may arise. But they must at least deal with what is actually in the story.

DANIL GRANIN*
(*Literaturnaya Gazeta*, 15 October 1963)

3. The Attack Develops

BEHIND THE TIMES

... Yes, all sorts of things happen in real life. I myself know of a school that was 'moved out' of premises belonging to it. But in that case it was quite obvious that the motives for the decision really were unjust. It happened near Leningrad and it became known immediately – as it was bound to, for today that sort of thing gets out right away. Such actions invariably run into firm opposition on the part of the general public. All the forces of our democratic system at once come into play, and people start banging on every door in their efforts to see justice done. Can that atmosphere of passivity and helplessness described by Solzhenitsyn exist today in any community? I don't think so. At least not in any of the educational communities with whose life I am acquainted. That is why it is difficult to sense in Solzhenitsyn's story any feeling for the life of today. It seems rather to evoke echoes of life the day before yesterday ... It is not inertia or passivity that is characteristic of Soviet man; nor are these features typical of our public life. Genuine justice, fought for and won by the Party and our whole people – and not 'abstract' justice – runs through our life today and is triumphant!

A writer who takes it upon himself to deal with an important contemporary theme cannot fail to take all this into account.

R. N. SELIVERSTOV

*A liberal Leningrad novelist.

THE EDITORS SPEAK

(Seliverstov's article was accompanied by the following statement from the editors of Literaturnaya Gazeta.*)*

In publishing Yuri Barabash's article 'What Is "Right"?' the editors felt – and still feel – that the critic's comments on Solzhenitsyn's story were well founded ...

Solzhenitsyn's story obviously would not in itself have provided material for a continuing discussion had not some general questions of principle – primarily the question of the class approach versus the 'universal', extra-social approach to the concepts of humanism and justice – arisen in the course of the debate. These problems have attracted the attention of the critics and of our readers ...

A keen ideological battle is going on in the modern world. And we must not for a single moment lower our ideological and ethical standards in our assessment of literary works. It is because we respect a writer's talent that we cannot make allowance for his artistic mistakes.

Soviet art knows no limitations in the choice of subject matter. All aspects of life are open to it, including the negative ones. But a socialist-realist artist handles themes from the standpoint of the communist view of the world.

THE EDITORS
(Literaturnaya Gazeta, 19 October 1963)

4. The Counter-attack

AN AUTHOR'S SUCCESS

We, former Party propagandists, have always believed that it is very important to support everything that is truthful and just, as the Party teaches us.

And this is particularly important at the present time, when our whole people is building communism – the most just society on earth.

Alexander Solzhenitsyn is absolutely right when he stresses

this side of the question in his story *For the Good of the Cause*, where it is a matter of such vital importance for this large and fine group of nine hundred young men and women standing on the threshold of life. This is not an abstract presentation of the question, as Yuri Barabash mistakenly supposes, but a very important problem of bringing up young people in the spirit of the Party's teachings. Such things ought not to be forgotten, especially by a literary critic.

Barabash's ironic remarks on the title of the story, *For the Good of the Cause*, are irrelevant. The author of the story is right. In reality, petty bureaucrats (and there are still plenty of them, and quite unreformed ones, in our country) frequently conceal their bureaucratic desires and actions by imaginary 'considerations of state' and by appeals to 'the good of the cause'. Here Solzhenitsyn exposes just such a situation . . .

We, old communists, consider that articles such as that of Barabash lead large numbers of readers astray – especially our young people.

So it turns out in fact that Solzhenitsyn's supposed 'failure', which Barabash writes about, is nothing of the sort. On the contrary, *For the Good of the Cause* is another success both for the author and for us, the readers.

Y. YAMPOLSKAYA, member of the CPSU since 1917
I. OKUNYEVA, member of the CPSU since 1919
M. GOLDBERG, member of the CPSU since 1920
(*Novy Mir*, October 1963)

AN OPEN LETTER TO YURI BARABASH

Dear comrade Barabash,

You were the first to comment in *Literaturnaya Gazeta* on Solzhenitsyn's story *For the Good of the Cause*, and on the whole you are right in demanding that an artist should deal with highly controversial moral problems in a concrete, historical manner and should not allow them to be diluted, so to speak, in high-minded abstractions. This demand would evoke sympathy and support if certain of your arguments did not themselves

suffer from abstractness and if they were not extremely controversial . . .

You are right when you call Solzhenitsyn a writer of great and
honest quality. And there can be no argument that every talented
writer should be subjected to serious criticism. But you will
agree that a great talent deserves above all a positive interpretation . . . I am sure that *for the good of the cause* and for the sake
of justice (that is, for the sake of the national interest), we must
offer every kind of support to a talented writer when he appears
in our midst and explain the strength of his talent and his works,
and not lead readers astray through categorical and basically
inaccurate and unjust criticism. That is why I have written this
letter and I hope that you will understand me and agree with
me.

L. REZNIKOV
Lecturer at the University of Petrozavodsk
(*Novy Mir*, October 1963)

5. Final Rebuttal

The editors of *Novy Mir* have had their say in this controversy
[about Solzhenitsyn's work] by publishing three letters from
readers.

There appears to us to be no particular need to reiterate what
has been said by the editors of *Literaturnaya Gazeta* about the
commendable vigour of the story's attack on bureaucracy and
officialdom, as well as the work's serious failings. They were
dealt with in detail in Barabash's article and Seliverstov's letter.

We would simply like to point out that the editors of *Literaturnaya Gazeta*, having provided an opportunity for *different*
opinions about Solzhenitsyn's story to be voiced in its pages,
find it only natural that at the end they should express their
editorial opinion as well. The editors of *Novy Mir* apparently
consider this type of discussion too democratic. The letters *they*
have published contain only unqualified praise of the story and
are unanimous in their attacks on the author of the critical
article in *Literaturnaya Gazeta*.

It stands to reason that the opportunities which a magazine

has for praising works which it publishes are truly unlimited. But it is scarcely necessary to point out that this is done at great cost – at the expense of objectivity and a sense of proportion.

We have no reason whatsoever to doubt the sincerity of the authors of the contributions published in *Novy Mir*. What is strange, however, is that, in making their selection of letters, the editors found it impossible to mention, let alone publish, any readers' letters containing criticisms of the story. It is difficult to believe (and this is borne out by *Literaturnaya Gazeta*'s own mail) that the editors of *Novy Mir* received only letters singing the story's praises ...

In this connection we would like to say the following: Any editorial board is responsible not only to its readers; it also bears a moral responsibility towards the writer whose work it publishes. It is the sacred duty of editors to help a writer, to draw attention to his weak points, and help him to overcome them. In summing up the discussion about *Novy Mir*'s statement on Solzhenitsyn's story, it is worth pointing out that true respect for a writer excludes any form of indulgence towards his weaknesses and errors as an artist ...

(*Literaturnaya Gazeta*, 12 December 1963)

6. Final Rejoinder

... Thus the editors of the magazine [*Novy Mir*] are in effect being accused of misrepresenting the views of its readers. This compels us to give an account of the mail which the magazine has received about Solzhenitsyn's story.

The editors of *Novy Mir* received a total of fifty-eight letters dealing with *For the Good of the Cause*. Many of them amount in effect to long articles of between ten and twenty typed pages of detailed argument. The authors of fifty-five letters, three of which we published, thoroughly approve of Solzhenitsyn's story and take issue with his critics ...

It should be pointed out that twelve of these letters were carbon copies of originals sent to *Literaturnaya Gazeta*. This is the case with two of the letters which we printed. In view of this, *Literaturnaya Gazeta*'s chosen method of conducting a debate is hardly likely to strike anybody as 'too democratic'. Of course, any editorial board is free to disagree with the majority of its readers about the value of a work and may express a contrary opinion. But in that case, it probably ought to be done openly and the readers should have the mistakenness of their views explained to them, rather than have their views misrepresented in this manner.

And now for that part of *Novy Mir*'s mail containing 'critical comments' on Solzhenitsyn's story, which *Literaturnaya Gazeta* demanded that we publish. Two letters contain comments on the language used in the story . . .

Only one of the fifty-eight letters (from N. L. Marchenko, railroad station Udelnaya, Moscow region) expresses disapproval of Solzhenitsyn's story. However, there is not a word in this letter about the actual content of the story, its subject or its characters. It was apparently only an excuse for the writer to condemn Solzhenitsyn's work as a whole. N. L. Marchenko considers the publication of any of Solzhenitsyn's works as harmful. We find that we cannot quote from this letter, because it is written in an inadmissibly offensive manner. But we are ready at any moment to show it to the editors of *Literaturnaya Gazeta*.

We recognize the justice of *Literaturnaya Gazeta*'s demand that readers' mail should be treated objectively and some idea should be given of the range of opinion expressed by readers, if only by indicating the *number* of letters supporting either side in a controversy. *Novy Mir* proposes to follow this practice in future in its 'Readers' Forum'. It is much to be desired that *Literaturnaya Gazeta* do likewise.

EDITORIAL BOARD OF *Novy Mir*
(*Literaturnaya Gazeta*, 26 December 1963)

The Lenin Prize for Solzhenitsyn?

The Proposal*

In the USSR Council of Ministers, Committee for the Lenin Prizes in the field of Literature and Arts.

The Committee for the Lenin Prizes in the field of Literature and Arts reports that the following candidates have been proposed for 1964 Lenin Prizes:

In the field of literature:

17. *Solzhenitsyn, A. I.* – Short novel *One Day in the Life of Ivan Denisovich.*

Proposed by the editorial board of *Novy Mir* magazine and by Central State Archives of Literature and Art.

(*Literaturnaya Gazeta,* 28 December 1963)

'High Requirements'

After quotations from letters which allegedly were received by editors from readers whose addresses are not given, a Pravda *article states:*

They all come to the same conclusion: A. Solzhenitsyn's short novel deserves a positive assessment but it cannot be placed among such outstanding works which are worthy of the Lenin Prize.

(*Pravda,* 11 April 1964)

Tvardovsky looks back

... How difficult it is in our literary life to get rid of the sad legacy of the past years, when all kinds of falsification and distortion of truth were flourishing, creating among the people a

*It was significant that the candidature of Solzhenitsyn for the Lenin Prize advocated by the liberal writers appeared in *Pravda*'s list only in the seventeenth place. The prizes are awarded by a jury consisting mostly of reliable, 'conservative' members.

distrust of our printed word. It was too serious an experience to gloss over and thereby to leave open the possibility of its repetition ... A notorious period in the life of our country ... was destroying the habit of expressing one's personal feelings or reflections on paper in one form or another; it was paralysing the genuine human memory about the events through which one lived, about the significance and the real role in them of individuals with unmentionable names. Not only we, but the generations to come will have cause to regret it. There was also something else: deliberate forgeries of 'personal testimonies', distortions of historical facts in bogus memoirs, the adaptation of the 'memory apparatus' to the needs of the day by their authors ... The situation has changed decisively since the Twentieth Congress. I doubt whether there was ever a time when so many people turned to the pen with such an irrepressible desire to describe their lives, to reveal so many things which were hidden, to explain the past for the sake of the present and the future ... [Solzhenitsyn's] novel, published two years ago, simply had to be created. Somehow it seems as if it was already there, such as it actually is, and was just waiting to appear ... The reader badly needs the full truth about life; he is sickened by evasiveness and hypocrisy ...

(*Novy Mir*, January 1965 [40th Anniversary Issue])

Mihajlo Mihajlov*: 'Moscow Summer 1964'
An Interview with V. I. Lakshin†

He had won wide popularity thanks to his long and important essay 'Ivan Denisovich, his Friends and Foes', published in the January 1964 issue of *Novy Mir*, in which he took up a brilliant defence of Solzhenitsyn. Practically the entire Soviet press descended upon Lakshin for the publication of his essay. Fortunately, apart from verbal roars, there was nothing else to which the critic had been subjected. 'Today', he told me, 'nobody can do anything through administrative means to us who work on *Novy Mir*, because the attack on one of us would be an attack on all the editors of the paper.' This would, of course, also mean an attack on Tvardovsky, the editor-in-chief. Tvardovsky is now one of the most outstanding personalities, not only in the Writers' Union, and is in a favourable position to play an extremely important part in the process of the liberalization of culture in the Soviet Union.

After the publication of Lakshin's essay on Solzhenitsyn and the uproar that followed it, the young critic was receiving up to 150 letters a day in which readers praised him for his courage and expressed their solidarity with him. When I asked him why

*Mihajlo Mihajlov, a Yugoslav literary critic. Born in Paicevo (near Belgrade) of Russian parents who emigrated to Yugoslavia after the Russian Civil War, Mihajlov was educated at the Universities of Belgrade and Zagreb and became a university lecturer in Slavic languages and literature at the Zadar branch of Zagreb University. He is a specialist on Dostoyevsky. His writings on the Soviet scene in the Yugoslav journals irritated the Soviet Embassy in Belgrade. After Tito's intervention, Mihajlov was arrested in Zadar on 4 March 1965, tried on 29–30 April 1965 and sentenced to nine months' imprisonment. This sentence was suspended on appeal by the Croatian Supreme Court in Zagreb on 23 June 1965. He was, however, arrested again when he tried to launch a new magazine and sentenced on 22 September 1965 in Zadar to one year; before he had served half of the term he was on trial again for sending critical articles abroad. He was sentenced this time to four and a half years in prison at Belgrade on 19 April 1967. He was released from prison in February 1970.

†Deputy editor of *Novy Mir* at the time.

the letters were not published, he said that the editorial board did not want to confine the polemics to Solzhenitsyn alone. 'Whenever they attack us,' he said, 'we publish something even more outspoken and thus the debate is constantly shifting from one subject to another.'

I found it very interesting to hear from him that the following saying is widely circulating in the Soviet Union: 'Tell me what you think of *One Day*, and I will tell you who you are'.

(*Delo*, Belgrade, January 1965)

THE STRUGGLE INTENSIFIES

In 1965 the liberal writers tried to counter the pressure of the hard-liners but without success: the situation was steadily deteriorating under the new post-Khrushchev leadership. Tvardovsky was still steadfastly defending liberal positions in Novy Mir, *but his accolade to Solzhenitsyn, printed there on the occasion of the fortieth anniversary of the journal, did not stop the intensified campaign against Solzhenitsyn. After a long-drawn-out battle, his novel* The First Circle *was finally prevented from appearing; it was seized by the secret police, together with other unpublished manuscripts, after a search at the home of a friend to whom he had entrusted them. When in the following year he was unable to find a publisher for the first part of his new novel,* Cancer Ward, *a writers' meeting was convened in Moscow to debate his 'case'. At the meeting, in November 1966, Solzhenitsyn's detractors were subdued by the outspoken support of the majority of his fellow-writers who, far from condemning his novel, passed a resolution actively supporting his efforts to have it published. This brief euphoria was soon dispelled. The campaign of slander against Solzhenitsyn was intensified. He was not only banned from publishing: even his name could no longer be mentioned in the Soviet press except to be vilified. The dissonant voices in Soviet literature, abandoning hope of expressing their views in official publications, appeared more and more frequently in the underground literature of 'Samizdat'.* After three years of harassment, Solzhenitsyn appealed in an open letter to the delegates of the Fourth Soviet Writers' Congress. This*

*'Samizdat', literally 'Self Publishing House', consists of underground writings which are reproduced, mainly in typewritten form, and circulated among the reading public. Each typescript is copied often and is thus given additional circulation. Since 30 April 1968 a regular 'Samizdat' underground periodical called *Chronicle of Current Events* has been appearing every two months. It gives details about both repressions by the authorities and the resistance activities of the 'democratic opposition'.

powerful document found strong support among his fellow-writers, a fact which was not mentioned, needless to say, in the official press. Solzhenitsyn now engaged in a protracted contest with the Soviet Establishment. A meeting with the secretaries of the Writers' Union in September 1967 sharply contrasted with the meeting held a year earlier. Now Solzhenitsyn found himself in the dock, subjected to scurrilous attacks from the literary bureaucrats who dominated the session. Soon afterwards he was falsely castigated by the editor-in-chief of Pravda, M. V. Zimyanin. *Again he found many supporters, and such respected literary figures as Tvardovsky and Kaverin continued vigorously to defend his cause. But despite their mediation, this battle too was lost:* Cancer Ward, *which was scheduled to appear in* Novy Mir, *was suppressed through the intervention of the First Secretary of the Writers' Union, Konstantin Fedin. Solzhenitsyn and his allies went on protesting and their voices, now amplified by 'Samizdat', were increasingly echoed abroad.*

Solzhenitsyn's manuscripts seized

The manuscript of Solzhenitsyn's new novel* (actually his *first* novel) was returned to him by the editor of a magazine, with a note to the effect that the novel could not, alas, be published. The writer put the four big parcels containing copies of the manuscript into his case and prepared for the journey back to his home in Ryazan, some 115 miles from Moscow. But before setting off, he decided to do some shopping for his family. Weighed down by his heavy load and very tired – after many

*The novel in question was *The First Circle* and it was rejected by *Novy Mir*. Contrary to this report, which repeats a very widespread rumour circulating in the Soviet Union at that time, the manuscript of the novel was *not* returned to Solzhenitsyn by the KGB, nor were his personal archives confiscated together with the novel (see Solzhenitsyn's open letter, p. 106). *Neuer Zürcher Zeitung* (10 November 1965) reported that the Soviet Writers' Union 'in answer to its inquiry [about the seizure of Solzhenitsyn's manuscripts and archives] received the explanation that this was a "security measure", intended to prevent Solzhenitsyn's manuscripts from reaching capitalist countries, as a result of inadequate protection, where they could be published in an arbitrary manner by profit-hungry publishers'.

years in a prison camp his health is not good – Solzhenitsyn dropped in on one of his Moscow friends, with whom he left the case containing the manuscript, intending to pick it up the next time he was in Moscow.

That night, agents of the KGB called on Solzhenitsyn's friend and confiscated the novel. When he heard about this, Solzhenitsyn rushed immediately back to Moscow and demanded an interview at the KGB. They agreed, and, so the story goes, he told them that his friend was innocent and had no idea what was in the case. Solzhenitsyn added that if his novel constituted a criminal offence, they had better arrest him, since he was used to that sort of thing. And if it was not, they should return the manuscript to him at once, since it was *his*. The KGB were evidently very polite to him, explaining that they had taken the novel to prevent it from being passed around illegally. If he promised not to give it to anybody to read, he could have the novel back.

The KGB did in fact return it to him, and, as far as I know, Solzhenitsyn has kept his word and shown it to no one. In any case, up to my departure from the Soviet Union, none of my friends, people who never miss a single piece of writing, had laid hands on the novel. This is a great loss, because others – people working on magazines who have read the novel in the course of their work – have let it be known that it is a really shattering achievement.

LEONID VLADIMIROV, *The Russians*
(Praeger, New York, 1968) pp. 176–8

Moscow writers on *Cancer Ward*

Transcription of a discussion of the first part of the novel Cancer Ward *at a meeting of the prose section of the Moscow writers' organization,* * *17 November 1966.*

G. BEREZKO: I am very glad that so many people have turned up

* The Soviet Writers' Union is divided both territorially and functionally, having organizations in the Republics and even in major towns of the Soviet Union. It also has special sections of prose-writers, poets, etc. which form separate committees.

today to our meeting, which is not usually so well attended.
We have discussed manuscripts before. My comrades and I
consider this one of the most important sides of our work.
This sort of discussion of a manuscript, so essential for our
literature, takes place mainly when there is some difference
of opinion between the author and the publisher. Our intervention is sometimes helpful.

A writer is by the very nature of his work condemned to
solitude. In the course of his work a natural desire arises to
consult with his comrades by trade – or by art – according to
the way you look at it.

We have been approached with a request by the writer A.
Solzhenitsyn – I would like you to come up here on to the
platform [*Solzhenitsyn takes his place at the table*]. I am very
pleased that our first encounter with a work of considerable
talent is taking place in such a businesslike manner. This is a
working discussion of an unfinished novel. I hope it will be
fruitful. [*Turning to Solzhenitsyn*] You don't wish to say
anything?

SOLZHENITSYN: No.

A. BORSHCHAGOVSKY: I will begin by making a confession as a
reader. In preparation for today's discussion I got hold of a
copy of the manuscript with the idea of skipping through it
quickly – I had read the manuscript quite recently – but it
didn't happen that way. I read the whole of *Cancer Ward*
through again, from beginning to end, without putting it
down and without missing anything out. I am not, of course,
saying this to boast of my prowess. I believe that when I get
my hands on the book when it is published – and I am sure
that it *will* be published – I shall again read the whole of it
through again.

The book is written on the basis of the most difficult
material; it cuts into life at a most difficult point; and it does
not get across to the reader at once. It may be said that it is
difficult to discuss an unfinished book. And that is not just a
formal objection. There are things in the book which you
cannot understand, no matter how much thought you give to
them. You cannot answer the simplest questions which a

reader may put about the fate of various characters in the book, and such questions cannot be passed over. The second book will provide the complete answer to all these questions. But even now what there is in the first part is so significant, so capable of assessment, so joyful to my way of thinking, and so necessary, that we are scarcely likely in the near future to come across another work which is so needed.

Solzhenitsyn has chosen to take the most essential cross-section of life and in this he is helped by the outstandng nature of his gifts – it would be easier to say these words if you were not here, Alexander Isayevich. *Cancer Ward* is a work of the same depth as *The Death of Ivan Ilyich*; or, if you take its satirical elements, of the same level as *Gospoda Golovlevy*.*

Our literature is rising to a new level, but it is doing so by moving along the outskirts, along the ditches, in new works by Belov and Mozhayev, and there is taking place an infinitely important inquiry into the nature of man, of man as he is and not as he might be constructed.

All of this we find in *Cancer Ward*. Remember how we kept on struggling everlastingly with the problem of the 'positive hero', which really turned into a sort of curse?

What sort of a person is Yefrem? He had not led a particularly praiseworthy sort of life. But however late it was, even though only three days before his life came to an end, he at least began to reflect on those things about which a man ought to start thinking sooner. And it is precisely the job of writers to move people in the direction of such thoughts. As with Solzhenitsyn's other main characters, I can see Yefrem. I can feel the weight of his footsteps round the ward. He teaches me an important moral lesson: if *he* is able to start thinking about the meaning of life when it might seem there was nothing left for him to do but howl like a beast and hate everybody who remained alive – that means he was a decent man.

The ward in which the action takes place appears in a

*The author of *The Death of Ivan Ilyich* is Leo Tolstoy; the author of *Gospoda Golovlevy* is Saltykov-Shchedrin.

variety of ways. When it is shown through the eyes of Rusanov we see it filled with cattle, non-Russians, the smell of pus, sheer horror. But all the other characters eye each other in a much more approving light. The reader is presented with an idea of the sort of people created and educated by our society. They do not make fine speeches about friendship between the peoples. But they have in them true friendship and a peace arising from a deep consideration for others, the sort of consideration which is found in a person from the people, not a tactfulness instilled into him because it is 'the done thing' but a true tactfulness. The ward is full of people who have been condemned to death, not by a malicious author but by life.

The copy of the manuscript which I read had already been read by quite a few writers. It was covered with somebody's scribbles of a purely censorious character. If one allows oneself to be detached from the multifarious streams of life, then sentences dragged out of their context may shock you. Particularly some of the things said by Kostoglotov. He is irritable, he can't be otherwise and he has a right to be like that – but I see in him many of the excellent qualities of my contemporaries. Like everybody else I have my own private list of favourite literary characters – and they will now have to move aside and make room for Kostoglotov.

The date at which the action in the novel takes place is indicated precisely – February 1955, the eve of that purifying storm at the marvellous Twentieth Party Congress, to which the whole communist world is faithful and will remain faithful.

The character of Rusanov does not appear to me to be a complete success in the book. The outright hatred he shows as a citizen is so great – and it is completely understandable – that it has deprived Solzhenitsyn, the artist, of the use of the nuances and the Tolstoyan methods by means of which Rusanov could have been made true to life and not just a journalistic figure, a caricature.

I did not like anything in the book which dealt with literary life. It is not, of course, that, as a literary man myself, I want to defend literature; it is simply that in *Cancer Ward* the talk is journalistic, likely to set your teeth on edge ... The books mentioned are very casually chosen. The character of Dyoma, the young boy, so full of life, is magnificently drawn, but I do not really believe that he came across an article about sincerity or that he initiated a discussion about that article. That's just too contrived.

Why is the figure of Rusanov so necessary? Hasn't everything already been said about such people as he in Party documents? Only very simple-minded people could believe that. Alexander Isayevich keeps returning to him with good reason. Literature must still keep on dealing with such people, whether it's now or in fifteen years' time. Because it is essential to educate people to hate people like Rusanov. Very striking in this connection is the chapter of the dream – the punishment which is dealt out to Rusanov in his sleep. It is essential to inculcate hatred into people for the purpose of combating the living survivals of Rusanov's ways. In this lies the great social value of the book.

Cancer Ward is an outstanding work which will, of course, reach the printing press and will contribute much that is new to our understanding of life. It also brings us closer to those boundaries without which our society cannot advance further.

v. KAVERIN: When you have worked for many years in the field of literature you begin to see it, not from the point of view of a month or even of a year, but of ten, fifteen or even twenty-five years. We have entered into a new period without noticing it. It happened imperceptibly. I recall an incident when I was walking with Yuri Tynyanov. A lorry went by and I drew into the side. 'Is it worth it?' said Tynyanov. 'Dust is like time: even without noticing it, you have to live by it.'

The whole of Solzhenitsyn's work is characteristic of our time. The new writing has arrived, and the old, reptile-like, crawling literature, which recognized only a stright line, is finished. Who now remembers the books that were published in millions of copies, books full of lies and praise of Stalin, open or camouflaged?

That scarecrow Lysenko who brought so much shame on our country is also finished. I was for many years connected with the world of science and I know what that means. The writers who are being published and are popular with the readers are those who stood their ground and who resisted falsehood – Platonov, Zoshchenko, Babel, Bulgakov, Zabolotsky. Literature is recovering its brilliance and originality. This writing will enjoy success throughout the world if no obstacles are put in its way.

Not a month goes by but new names appear and new works, evoking surprise, joy or envy. I will name a few of them – Kazakov, Konetsky, Syomin, Mozhayev. Among them I put Solzhenitsyn in the first place. In what consists the strength of his talent? It is not only in his ability to make vivid what he has experienced – although in this he also achieves unusual heights. I have already spoken about the amazing harmony of *One Day in the Life of Ivan Denisovich*. He has two other precious qualities – an inner freedom and a powerful striving for the truth. What is inner freedom? You see, we, the writers of the older generation, for many years concealed ourselves from ourselves, got mixed up in our own contradictions – that was the natural consequence of twenty years of Stalin's rule. Solzhenitsyn and the best people in the new writing are free of all that. They have rid themselves of every imposed aim, except the desire to tell the truth . . .

Solzhenitsyn is a very considerable writer. It depends on him whether he is to become a great writer. Everybody knows that there exists in our country a typewritten literature which is passed from hand to hand. Among this literature there are excellent works; for example, a first-class story by Solzhenitsyn called 'The Right Hand'.

Why are we now discussing a manuscript and not a book? Why has Bek's novel *A New Appointment* still not appeared? The best and most experienced men of letters spoke in favour of Bek's book being published. On the other side of the scales was the opinion of some woman. And the woman's opinion outweighed the others. Both in industry and in science attention is already being paid to the opinions of the specialists, but not in literature.*

What is the idea behind the still unfinished book *Cancer Ward*? It is to place people of various professions, of various levels of education and of various degrees of moral sensitivity face to face with death. It is a tremendous task – greater than that set in *The Death of Ivan Ilyich*. I have great hopes that this problem will be resolved by the author. He carries out an intelligent psychological cross-section, and people become aware of depths hitherto unknown to themselves. That cannot fail to move the reader. We shall all find ourselves one day face to face with death. The characters are not only drawn: they seem to be striving towards self-knowledge. Yefrem is very profoundly conceived. Kostoglotov is animated not only by the will to live but by a lack of fear of death. That is a great thought, and a profoundly constructive one. An absence of fear of death was the guarantee of our victory in the war. Absence of fear of death became the guarantee of the preservation of science and art under the terror and in the camps.

The author performs a vivisection on Rusanov, in the precise pathologic and anatomic sense of the word, and a frightful emptiness is revealed. I agree with Alexander Mikhailovich [Borshchagovsky] – maybe Rusanov is too single-minded. The author exposes his fear with a scalpel. Rusanov is a powerful incarnation of the dead idol of Stalinism. Vadim is interesting, and so are the Kadmin couple – although this is rather long-drawn-out. (BEREZKO: 'But in my opinion there is too little about them, about these wonderful people.') And it is not by chance that at the end we sense the footsteps of history. Like the rest of us, Kostoglotov is moved not by malice or by hate, but by hope.

It is difficult to judge an unfinished work, but even now it can be said that this is a book of tremendous honesty, such as

*This novel by Alexander Bek, originally called *Nichto* ('Nothing') and then *Novoe Naznacheniye* ('A New Appointment'), is a critical work about Soviet bureaucracy. It was to appear in *Novy Mir* No. 8, 1966, but it was stopped. In a modified form it was prepared for publication in the May 1968 issue of *Novy Mir* but once again did not pass the censor. *Novy Mir* (No. 8, 1970) announced the publication of 'a new Bek novel'.

always inspired Russian literature. There is no story in the usual sense of the word; nothing happens, and yet how it grips the reader! Why has this manuscript not yet been printed? Are there morally deformed people to be found who will defend the Rusanov terror? Is it really not clear that here is freedom, goodness and hope – all the things on which our revolution was founded, the concepts which were distorted by people like Rusanov?

The new writing constitutes a bridge between the fifties and the sixties. All efforts to silence Solzhenitsyn are doomed to failure. He cannot write differently from the way he writes.

I. VINNICHENKO: I will preface my remarks by saying that I am rather embarrassed, because I did not come prepared to speak. I simply read through the manuscript. I am not a critic or a novelist. But I read it through in one go and I was so moved by it that I consider it my duty to speak. I don't agree with Kaverin – it seems to me we are fortunate to be discussing a book in manuscript, so that we can deal with the creative process itself. Much has been said here about the power of Solzhenitsyn's talent. I don't think he should be called great – that will do no good. But he is undoubtedly an outstanding writer. I have heard the expression 'to tell lies about the truth'. He is a writer who is organically incapable of lying about the truth. I will start with his merits as an artist. Solzhenitsyn has departed somewhat from his original style. His first works were overcrowded with dialecticisms.

It is said that the manuscript contains naturalistic details, that there is a discussion of the sad state of oncology. But here too we have no reason to fear the truth. But perhaps the author ought to take into account the possibly painful reaction of the readers.

I do not agree with those who consider that the manuscript is infused with pessimism and lack of faith in science. Doubts have also been expressed because *Cancer Ward* deals with the notorious theme of the prison camps. People started writing about the camps, and then people began to ask whether they had not gone too far. Ought they to go on writing on that theme? But in this case we are dealing with a real work of art revealing a cancerous growth in our society.

It is difficult to judge by the first part alone. I would like the author to tell us today how he intends to construct the second part.

N. ASANOV: From my point of view, our sense of the ideal which we have been developing in ourselves for forty years ought to give every writer the right to publish his works without such discussions. Every one of us is capable of being his own editor. And it is only this strange lack of faith in our clan which forces us to meet here in such a large number and discuss a work which is superior to the majority of books written by us. We ought to revolt against such a situation – revolt, of course, not on a large scale but on a small scale; we must defend what is in need of defence.

I was not very pleased with the panegyrics in A. Borshchagovsky's speech. But then even he later took up the position of an editor, prompter and adviser. They have no faith in us; they all want to help us, even the censors.

[They say] Solzhenitsyn's work is very dangerous. Vinnichenko, for example, referred to the cancerous growth, suggesting that this inevitably has other implications – a cancerous growth, cancer is incurable not only in the case of human beings. Supposing in fact it refers to society? We, of course, hope that our society will be cured. But this is more dangerous than certain sentences marked with a red pencil. The point is that the book should, with our help, appear.

What is the most powerful element in the book and at the same time the most painful to read? It is the working day of doctor Dontsova. There is the feeling that cancer is about to attack her too. She is in charge of a department and she is an excellent doctor, but her life outside the hospital is wretched and frightful. And that is the truth. The situation of the intelligentsia in our country is very distressing; engineers and doctors earn little and are responsible for everything, except the administration of the state. [*Laughter in the hall*.]

A. MEDNIKOV: A. Borshchagovsky made the most thorough analysis of the work and we are, consciously or otherwise, following in his footsteps. But there is also an international theme running through *Cancer Ward*. There are many Germans in the ward. I have a personal connection with this theme. At the beginning of the war I was a private in an NKVD 'killer' battalion. Along with other tasks we were given the special job of removing all Germans from Moscow in the course of one night. It was a very unpleasant task. We shipped them all out – members of the party, women and children. I don't know, I won't go into the question of whether such a preventive measure was necessary. but I wondered at the time how those people were going to live in the future. In Solzhenitsyn's book I saw them, I saw Federau, Vera Gangart – good, wonderful people.

I have also been thinking – why is the book called *Cancer Ward*? In fact everything described in the book might have taken place in a mine or in a factory. The author chose a cancer ward for greater dramatic effect.

Solzhenitsyn is a writer whom all writers read. In the course of time the critics will determine why he has occupied such a place in literature and in public life. He is a writer on a tragic theme. Even if his life had worked out differently he would still have been a tragic writer. If Solzhenitsyn had not been born, what he has said would inevitably have been said by someone else.

L. SLAVIN: . . . As I read the book I began to find symptoms of cancer in myself, as medical students discover all illnesses in themselves. But the author's power as an artist is not there but in his diagnosis of society, which is performed very precisely. By means of the tumour we are given a cross-section of society. A duel with death is taking place. The merciless honesty of the author stands out on the background of the democratic nature of death. I was waiting with excitement to learn who would win – would the author defeat death or would it be the other way round? Would he find what overcomes death? Or would he succumb? . . .

Even now this is one of the most powerful and most necessary works of recent years, with which I can compare only Bek's *A New Appointment*.

z. KEDRINA: It seems to me that the fact that we are able to talk here about a work which is far from being run-of-the-mill ought not to be taken badly. We are working, and we ought not to be afraid of saying something which may not please the author. After all, we are not dealing with a nervous beginner whom we are afraid to shock; we are dealing with an undoubtedly talented and mature writer. We should do our work with good-will, so that this particular author may develop in the most natural way. [*During Kedrina's speech people start leaving the hall; the chairman appeals to them to listen to the end.*] It seems to me very interesting to discuss the foundation and the tradition on which this interesting author has grown. It is the tradition of Tolstoy. *Cancer Ward* is less clearly written than Solzhenitsyn's other works. This is natural, because when an author enters into an argument with a publishing house he reveals himself more completely. [*Loud laughter. People continue to leave. The chairman appeals to the audience: 'Respect the platform!' and points to Solzhenitsyn. Kedrina goes on talking.*] There is nothing special in this; that's the way things always happen with us, nothing surprising in it. It is a creative argument if, of course, the author is a good man and the editor a good man too.

It is true that *Cancer Ward* has been likened to *The Death of Ivan Ilyich*. This is very topical for us – a man on the frontier between life and death – the thing that Fedin emphasized in Tolstoy's vision of the world. Heirs of a tradition do not simply follow it; they develop it. Solzhenitsyn overcomes what in Tolstoy is connected with non-resistance to evil. But the author's position in this connection is not clearly expressed. From this follows the contradictory opinions of the work: some people like Kostoglotov, others don't; some like Rusanov, others don't. We agree with Kostoglotov in his hatred for Rusanov, and not a single person will be found to defend Rusanov. [*Shouts from the audience: 'Except for people like Rusanov themselves!'*] ...

Kostoglotov, depicted in all his thirst for life, is very well drawn. He is contrasted with Rusanov. But what is it that is not satisfactory in the opposition of these two characters?

Only Rusanov speaks of the things which are most sacred for us. Yes, he is only covering himself up with these words. But who in the novel utters such words seriously? Who reflects the things which move our society forward? Yes, a certain atmosphere is created by Dontsova and Gangart. But after all there are also social ideals and social passions. This must be reflected. Kostoglotov reflects a thirst for life in general, but he does not express social passions.

The Tolstoy theme itself is very convincing in the book. I would like Yefrem to be more vividly depicted. There are naturalistic details and there are superfluous things. I hope the author himself will see that. But he is not on the whole a naturalistic author . . .

It is a very interesting work, and I have no doubt that it will be printed. But it still requires a lot of work, not to get it through the editors, but for it to bring out more fully the author's ideas and for the author's attitude on social problems to be more precisely indicated.

Intermission

L. KABO: I would like to tell you of the immediate impression made by reading the book. It is unusually difficult to start reading it; everything in you fights against it; you don't want to be dragged into that world of suffering, death and horror. But then quite unexpectedly things begin to become clear. Face to face with death you begin to think of the most important things, of what we have been very little accustomed to by Soviet literature – about the meaning of life, not in the straightforward but in the most profound sense of the word. I did not feel the lack of a sense of the world outside the hospital. The people in the ward have had the most varied experience of life and bring their experience with them. They are all reduced to the same level only by suffering and danger, and how differently they react to that danger! . . .

Kostoglotov is the author's most tremendous success. Above all he has a most active self-assertiveness, a determination to dispose of his own affairs. That is quite natural in view of what he had lived through before entering the hospital.

I am certainly not in agreement with Asanov in his criticism of the way love is depicted. Our precious Soviet literature inculcated the rationalistic view of love, according to which if you are good you will love a good person, and if you are better you will love a better one, and so forth. But in Solzhenitsyn it is striking how we have a contradictory, earthly feeling . . .

The character of Rusanov is drawn unevenly . . . Everything he has lived through and his hatred of Rusanov seizes the author by the throat and that is understandable. I repeat — how fortunate it is that we have a work which reveals the author as being as passionate and as partial as today's readers are.

There is a magnificent passage in Rusanov's life story when, still a young worker, he is sent to purge the intelligentsia. The roots of a great deal that we suffered in 1937 and later were put down then, in the twenties, when the foundations were laid for the terror. And I want to thank the author for that.

The manuscript produces the most tremendous impression. Of course it will be turned into a book. I support what has already been said about the unsatisfactory nature of the last chapter. In that chapter Alexander Isayevich appears at less than his full stature.

B. SARNOV: In one of his articles written long ago Shklovsky pointed out that Bulgarin did not persecute Pushkin – he simply issued directives to him. A lot of water has passed under the bridge since then and a great revolution has taken place, but Kedrina and Asanov continue to give Solzhenitsyn directives.

There is a purpose behind our discussion of this manuscript. Solzhenitsyn's literary fate is unique. About ten years ago a young man said to me that great Russian literature ended with Bunin and it was only in 1956 that young writers started everything again from the beginning. That point of view is based on ignorance; to talk like that you would have to know nothing about Babel, Platonov, Bulgakov, Zoshchenko,

Akhmatova and Pasternak. Among these names Solzhenitsyn occupies a special place.

The author of a letter to the editors about *One Day in the Life of Ivan Denisovich* said that until Solzhenitsyn literature had managed to get by without the use of coarse words. And nobody thought of replying to him that until Solzhenitsyn, literature unfortunately had to get by without many things. When I had read *One Day* I had a feeling of joy and happiness – that great writing had been resumed. I would not put *Cancer Ward* alongside the story *One Day* . . .

I wish Alexander Isayevich many long years of life, but I would also like all his works to appear during his lifetime. After all, Bulgakov's *Theatrical Novel* was deprived of twenty-five years of literary existence.

YU. KARYAKIN: In his last testament Lenin expressed the passionate and tragic hope that people whom we needed would come along with the following qualities: they would not say a word contrary to the dictates of their conscience; they would not fear to speak out about any mistakes; they would not be afraid of conflict. We forget those words, although we often quote the testament. But Solzhenitsyn answers to these criteria.

In Dostoyevsky's notes we find the words: what would it have been like if Tolstoy had lied or if Goncharov had lied. What a state of immorality it would have been if they had lied. Please excuse the involuntary pun – but Solzhenitsyn will not lie ['*ne solzhyot*']. In the upper reaches both of politics and of culture the demands are the same – a thirst for uncompromising truth. The novel *Cancer Ward* corresponds with these criteria . . .

It is obvious to everyone that *Cancer Ward* must be published. I want to adduce political arguments in defence of this idea. And I mean political, and not pseudo-political. I had to gather together practically all the foreign reviews of the book *One Day*. That book was condemned unanimously in the pages of the Trotskyist, Chinese, Albanian and Korean press. The overweight majority of favourable reviews came from the leaders of the biggest communist parties, the most outstanding Marxists of the present day. By publishing that novel we acquired a tremendous number of allies, because people believed that, as Kaverin rightly said, the ideas which people like Rusanov had destroyed regained their validity . . .

Comrade Kedrina assured us here that people like Rusanov were finished and that today no one would support him. That is a delusion – I do not know whether it is deliberate or not, but at all events it is untrue. Rusanov is not a past danger, not just a danger of 1955. People like him are still alive and still dreaming of their day. Perhaps, as today's discussion suggests, their dreams are utopian.

I have just one private disagreement with the author which I find difficult to formulate. I see Solzhenitsyn as a man who cannot forgive Rusanov for what he has done. But when he received the Nobel Prize, Camus said that art of the higher kind should not play the part of the prosecutor. You can look at man in many different ways. It would be a great victory for Solzhenitsyn as an artist if, hating Rusanov and being glad that death at least provides the Rusanovs with their just reward, he were able nevertheless to find, to reveal in him something human. If that is impossible, then we are left with the hopeless concept of original sin.

E. MALTSEV: It was only yesterday that I finished re-reading this remarkable book. I don't intend to try and teach Sarnov any lessons. You can't surprise me with sharply-worded speeches: I'm a pretty lively speaker myself . . . I read the manuscript a second time and found a great deal that was new in it, many new nuances. What disturbed me most of all was the thought of man's responsibility to life and to himself. People must answer the question: what did they live for, did they live as they should have done?

As Lyubov Rafailovna [Kabo] rightly said, as you read the book you pass gradually from confusion in the face of cruelty to enlightenment. You arrive at the thought that it is very difficult in this life to be a human being to the very end. Some people have argued about the symbolism in the chapter headings. It has been suggested that the book is about a cancerous growth in our society. If our society were incurably sick, we should not be sitting here together discussing this work. I definitely reject this interpretation . . .

We met together here in the Union and discussed the novel by Bek. Serious people gathered then and no one thought for a moment that Bek's novel would not be published. I am today sure that it will be published. Complex and irreversible processes of democratization are at work in our country; dogmatic and subjective people may obstruct those processes, but they can't stop them.

I want to see Solzhenitsyn's manuscript in print. As I read it I experienced a tremendous feeling of joy and of celebration, and I am happy today to have been able to get to know the author.

P. SAZHIN: I cannot rid myself of doubts whether we have the right to offer the author advice. After all, the second half is yet to come. One thing we do have the right to do is to say that the book is a great success . . .

E. TAGER: All speakers so far have agreed on one thing: that we are dealing with a very remarkable artistic work. Therefore there is no doubt: the difficulties over the printing of Solzhenitsyn's novel are based on the fact that it includes portrayals of unpleasant aspects of life in our country. But the whole history of world literature teaches us that we must not suppress knowledge of evil. It only becomes more powerful as a result. Solzhenitsyn is on the level of the great tradition and will not be lost in it.

[General] G. BAKLANOV: What should literature reflect – life itself or somebody's conceptions of what life ought to be like? Everyone will reply to this simplest of questions: of course, life itself. Meanwhile we have been judging this work by the extent to which it reflects the artificial concepts of life . . .

In the army I became accustomed to the fact that when the senior officers asked for advice, that by no means meant that they really wanted to listen to the advice given. It seems to me that some speakers today have abused their right to offer advice to Private Solzhenitsyn. [*Laughter*]

A. BELINKOV: The outstanding merit of the works of Alexander Isayevich Solzhenitsyn consists mainly in the fact that they were actually written. A man got to the point of writing the books he wanted to write.

I know many people who would also be able to write very good books, but they have not found a way of doing so. It so happens that people possessing a great experience of life sometimes know more than it is good for a writer to know. For example, they know that it is always possible that something will happen and that their book may not be published.

I have not invented the people I mentioned just now. I am talking about people whom we all know very well. Some of them have even come here today. I am talking about those who at one time wrote well but who later decided that it would be much better for society if they started writing badly. And many of them actually succeeded in doing just that . . .

Alexander Isayevich Solzhenitsyn came to the point of writing excellent books.

Such books can be written if two qualities come together: talent and courage. This is the essential minimum without which nothing can be achieved in art. *167/85*

Alexander Solzhenitsyn's talent and courage were revealed in the fact that, after a certain interruption which occurred in the history of our art, he began to speak with the voice of great literature, which is distinguished from insignificant literature mainly by the fact that it is concerned with the categories of good and evil, of life and death, and the relationships between man and society, authority and individuality. In great literature the main characters may be the giant Prometheus or the theomachist ('God-fighter') Cain, but for the great art what is important are not the high ranks but significant artistic ideas. That is why the novel about the sufferings of Akaki Akakievich Bashmachkin revealed to people with indisputable persuasiveness the categories of good and evil, although there is not a single word in the whole book which might be found in a philosophical dictionary, and as for important persons there is only a passing reference to an 'important individual' with the rank of general, far removed from Prometheus, to say nothing of Cain.

Alexander Isayevich Solzhenitsyn did not write a tragedy about a giant, nor did he write a mystery-play about a theomachist. He wrote a novel, about '*One* Day . . .' and short stories about *one* 'home', and *one* 'incident'.

I have read comment in a respected review and heard talk in the much esteemed Union reproaching Solzhenitsyn for producing only parts from which the readers are expected independently to reproduce the whole. They did not want the writer to give them the world in parts. They demanded to have the whole world at once, and what's more such a world as never was. This is quite natural for the thinking of people who understand very well that a part can be only the product of shortcomings, whereas the whole will undoubtedly produce the whole power-station at once.

Having read the comment and entered into the conversation I realized in the end that one writer cannot satisfy the demands of a whole national literature. I recalled that even Balzac was aided in providing an accurate and exhaustive picture of his epoch by other good writers: Constant, Stendhal, Musset, Hugo, De Vigny, Mérimée. Solzhenitsyn the writer exists in one literature along with other writers, and a correct and, most important, exhaustive picture of the epoch will be created by him along with them. All writers in our valiant literature will do their best to produce a many-sided and triumphant image of the time. Thus, the writer Sofronov produces the optimistic Stryapukha, while the writer Solzhenitsyn produces the pessimistic Matryona. If we put them together we have the whole hydro-electric power-station. The writer Solzhenitsyn succeeded, as did other great artists, in revealing yet another hitherto unnoticed aspect of the period. The many-sidedness of art is so important and so repulsive to certain art historians that the first demand which arises in people with an inborn love of order is to do something with the polyhedron. For example, to make it into a triangle. For that reason they try to get rid of everything that is unnecessary. In this way manuscripts are turned into books . . .

Since the attention of the reader is concentrated in the first place on a writer's linguistic style and imagery, and since in Solzhenitsyn these seem similar to the usual great Russian prose, they easily and readily came to regard his writing as traditional. But great art is never traditional – this does not have to be proved; it is sufficient to run through the names: Aristophanes, Dante, Shakespeare, Goethe, Pushkin, Balzac, Dostoyevsky, Blok, Pasternak – they are not like anyone else. Solzhenitsyn creates a new system of Russian prose, because he introduces into the composition of his art new, unknown or forgotten ideas of good and evil, of life and death and of the relationship between man and society. The apparently traditional nature of his style is similar to the art of the Renaissance, which was close to the art of the ancient world, but only at a distance and on a casual inspection. Solzhenitsyn's writing is not only similar to the Renaissance; it is in fact the Renaissance of Russian spiritual life . . .

Solzhenitsyn belongs to those remarkable writers who are reviving in Russian literature the great categories of good and evil, of life and death.

He has told us about what is so important for all of us, what we come up against every day and therefore know ourselves. But the difference between him and other writers lies in the fact that the other writers did not write about it, while he did. He did what is possible only for a person of true talent and real courage. That is the significance and the sense of the art of Alexander Solzhenitsyn.

A. SOLZHENITSYN: The main feeling which I have experienced today is one of gratitude. I have been moved by the attention which the prose section of the Moscow writers' organization has devoted to my work and by the very favourable opinions which, among others, have been voiced here. I could not have obtained anything like that in the Ryazan writers' organization of which I am a member.

In conditions where I am writing book after book without them being printed, such a discussion is the only possibility I have of hearing a professional opinion and criticism.

I stayed at home writing year after year without for a moment thinking about whether what I was writing would be printed or whether it would please anyone. That situation is now past. It had its advantages, but it also had its disadvantages. It turns out that in that single-handed battle with a piece of paper, when I had just a few readers, I inevitably became less demanding of myself.

And so when I came out into the open I felt how I had lacked professional opinion of my works. I still lack it, since my works are not published, but today I experienced a tremendous sense of satisfaction.

As for the unfinished state of *Cancer Ward*, I decided it would be possible to discuss the first part on its own. There have been cases in the history of literature when second parts have not been written at all or they have been destroyed – all sorts of things have happened.

I have not been offended by a single speech made here. I am so flattered by everything I have heard that I know only one way of justifying the high opinions given – by the quality of the second part. But shall I be able to do it?

A few specific questions: About the title. There was a battle over this in *Novy Mir*. I lost that battle. The prison camps were, of course, a tumour. But I was not afraid to use such a title because I reckoned I would overcome it. I did not wish either to depress or to crush the reader. I hope to overcome on the main issue – the conflict of life against death.

Literature can never grasp everything in life. I will take an image from mathematics and explain it: Every work can become just a bunch of surfaces. This bunch of surfaces passes through one point. You choose this point according to your own personal bias, your life history, your superior knowledge, and so forth. The point which I chose – a cancer ward – was suggested to me by my own illness. I had to make a serious study of oncology in order to check up on the way they were treating me. But I do not feel the necessity to describe the territory of the republic beyond the limits of the cancer ward. You can't reflect everything, but that part of the whole picture which is essential can be depicted through that single point.

A great deal of what has been said about Rusanov confirms

that I have done something wrong with him. I do not dare to argue with such a large number of critics. But what to do constructively I don't know. Karyakin's idea is very important – it goes beyond the limits of my book and of my writing – that in a work of art there must be a correlation between the present time and eternity. This is a most difficult problem. Like every writer I would like to cultivate in myself a sense of harmony. I tried to depict even Rusanov sympathetically, sometimes with all my resources – well, I suppose, not with *all* of them. [*Laughter*] After all, Rusanov's entry into the ward is autobiographical – that is me crossing the threshold of the cancer ward.

There is a well-known rule – when you are depicting a good man, try to show his bad side, and when you are depicting a scoundrel, try to show his good side. The trouble is that, in doing this, you may lose the scoundrel altogether.

Baklanov is right – in Rusanov I attack the consequences, and I ought artistically to get down to the causes. The fate of my work will probably not be any easier as a result [*laughter*], but it is a fair comment and I accept it.

As for Avieta – they say it is journalistic – I agree. They say it is farce – I agree. They say I broke away from my own style – I agree. But the journalism is not mine and the farce is not mine. I adopted here an impermissible device – there is not in the section about Avieta a single word of my own – she uses words spoken in the last fifteen years by our most important writer and literary critics. From the point of view of eternity there is no need for that chapter. But after all words like that were being spoken for such a long time from platforms higher than this one and to audiences bigger than this one. Is it right to forget this? Yes, it is undisguisedly a farce, but it's not mine.

Here, in a professional gathering, it is not difficult to persuade you that Kostoglotov is not the author. I tried my best to keep as far away from him as I could, and if the distance is still not sufficient I shall put in some more work on it. There are autobiographical elements in other passages. It is said that the discussion about the article on sincerity is not very credible.

When I returned from exile I immediately came across a blue tattered book with that article in it. Yura Maslov, from whom I drew Dyoma, got talking to me about the article. And, when I started to write *Cancer Ward* and had to go through the literary history of the year, I read the article again and I consider that for that period it was very important. I invented nothing. And the tenth volume of Tolstoy in the 'Ogonyok' edition of 1928 was in my ward.

That is the way it happens: a writer cannot fight against his own memories. You know that you ought to paint your main character in white, but you can only remember him as black. And there's nothing you can do about it.

I shall end with the same as I began – with gratitude.

Novy Mir has returned my manuscript to me, and I have sent it off to two other reviews: to *Zvezda* and to *Prostor*. I have not yet received a reply. [*Loud applause*]

G. BEREZKO: We have no reason to regret the work we have done. It will be an excellent thing if such an important writer as Solzhenitsyn devotes some more thought to certain things. It is not a question of offering elementary advice. It is a question of more important things.

I liked very much and I was greatly encouraged by Solzhenitsyn's remark 'I do not intend to depress the reader or reduce him to despair'.

The novel creates an overwhelming impression; it is a work of unusual artistic force. The comrades who spoke of weaknesses in the way the character Rusanov was drawn are right in certain respects.

*

The bureau [of the organization] along with some of the more active members passed a resolution: to take steps to bring about the publication of the novel *Cancer Ward*. It was decided to send a transcript of the discussion to *Zvezda* and *Prostor*.

O. Voitinskaya considered that the prose section ought to take an active part in fighting for *Cancer Ward*. 'We ought to demand that our review *Moskva* should print this work.'

When the discussion ended and everybody stood up, Bella

Akhmadulina rushed up to the platform and, turning to Solzhenitsyn, shouted: 'Wonderful man! Let us pray to God to grant good health to Alexander Solzhenitsyn!'

Jaures Medvedev* on the fate of Solzhenitsyn's wife

N. A. Reshetovskaya, wife of A. I. Solzhenitsyn, physical chemist and biochemist, candidate of chemical sciences, was selected for the post of senior research worker in the laboratory of chemical dosimetry in our Institute. Before that she had worked in the Ryazan Agricultural Institute and the Ryazan Polytechnic Institute as a reader in chemistry. Although the overwhelming majority of the academic board of our Institute cast their votes for Reshetovskaya (18 votes for and 2 against), steps were taken in Moscow to prevent Solzhenitsyn from moving to Obninsk. What is more, at that time (September 1965) three copies of the novel *The First Circle* together with part of the writer's personal archive were confiscated from a friend's flat in Moscow.

Solzhenitsyn was not happy in Ryazan. He and his family lived in a damp, dilapidated wooden house without sanitation and the local authorities for a long time had been refusing to improve the writer's living and working conditions.

Everything was in Reshetovskaya's favour, (but) . . . after the voting, the Obninsk local authorities became worried. The possibility of Solzhenitsyn coming to the town became real and they could not prevent it because all the residential houses in the

*Jaures Medvedev (born 1924), geneticist and gerontologist, wrote a book about Lysenko, *Biological Science and the Personality Cult*, which circulated in 'Samizdat' and was eventually published in an English translation in the United States. He attacked Lysenko in the journal *Neva* in 1963. Following this his writings were censored and confiscated on the instructions of the then head of the Party's Ideological Commission, Leonid Ilyichev. From 1964 he worked in the Obninsk Institute of Medical Radiology from which he was dismissed in 1969. On 29 May 1970 he was forcibly placed in a mental asylum. An outcry from scientists and intellectuals at home and abroad led to his release on 17 June 1970. Subsequently he was appointed a Senior Research Officer at one of the institutes of physiology and biochemistry.

town belonged to the Institute. All this happened between June and July 1965. Before that the town had been very quiet. Party and other official bodies had no worries. But now they had to give Solzhenitsyn and his family a flat. And he was a man in whose life all the high authorities from time to time took an interest. The whole system of surveillance had been well organized in Ryazan and now there was a problem of organizing a whole new system. Besides, while in Ryazan the writer was almost isolated. Here in Obninsk he would come into contact with the restive scientific community. And Moscow was quite near too. I do not know what course events took, but at the end of July the academic secretary of the Institute whispered to me 'in secret' that Reshetovskaya had been excluded from the list of successful candidates being sent for confirmation to the Academy of Medical Sciences of the USSR.

> JAURES MEDVEDEV, *International Scientific Cooperation and National Boundaries* (Macmillan, 1970)
> (Extract from Russian edition; English version will appear in 1971)

Solzhenitsyn's open letter to the Fourth Soviet Writers' Congress

To the Presidium and the delegates to the Congress, to members of the Soviet Writer's Union, and to the editors of literary newspapers and magazines:

Not having access to the platform at this Congress, I ask that the Congress discuss:

1. The no longer tolerable oppression, in the form of censorship, which our literature has endured for decades, and which the Union of Writers can no longer accept.

Under the obfuscating label of GLAVLIT, this censorship – which is not provided for in the Constitution and is therefore illegal, and which is nowhere publicly labelled as such – imposes a yoke on our literature and gives people unversed in literature arbitrary control over writers. A survival of the Middle Ages, the censorship has managed, Methuselah-like, to drag out its existence almost to the twenty-first century. Of fleeting significance, it attempts to appropriate to itself the role of unfleeting time – of separating good books from bad.

Our writers are not supposed to have the right, are not endowed with the right, to express their cautionary judgements about the moral life of man and society, or to explain in their own way the social problems and historical experience that have been so deeply felt in our country. Works that might express the mature thinking of the people, that might have a timely and salutary influence on the realm of the spirit or on the development of a social conscience, are proscribed or distorted by censorship on the basis of considerations that are petty, egotistical, and – from the national point of view – shortsighted. Outstanding manuscripts by young authors, as yet entirely unknown, are nowadays rejected by editors solely on the ground that they 'will not pass'. Many members of the [Writers'] Union, and even many of the delegates at this Congress, know how they themselves have bowed to the pressures of the censorship and made concessions in the structure and concept of their books – changing chapters, pages, paragraphs, or sentences, giving them innocuous titles – just for the sake of seeing them finally in print, even if it meant distorting them irremediably. It is an understood quality of literature that gifted works suffer [most] disastrously from all these distortions, while untalented works are not affected by them. Indeed, it is the best of our literature that is published in mutilated form.

Meanwhile, the most censorious labels – 'ideologically harmful', 'depraved', and so forth – are proving short-lived and fluid, [in fact] are changing before our very eyes. Even Dostoyevsky, the pride of world literature, was at one time not published in our country (still today his works are not published in full); he was excluded from the school curriculum, made unacceptable for reading, and reviled. For how many years was Yesenin considered 'counter-revolutionary'? – he was even subjected to a prison term because of his books. Wasn't Mayakovsky called 'an anarchistic political hooligan'? For decades the immortal poetry of Akhamatova was considered anti-Soviet. The first timid printing of the dazzling Tsvetayeva ten years ago was declared a 'gross political error'. Only after a delay of twenty to thirty years were Bunin, Bulgakov, and Platonov returned to us. Inevitably, Mandelshtam, Voloshin, Gumilev and Klyuev will follow in that line – not to mention the recognition, at some time or other, of even Zamyatin and Remizov.

A decisive moment [in this process] comes with the death of a troublesome writer. Sooner or later after that, he is returned to us with an 'explanation of [his] errors'. For a long time the name of Pasternak could not be pronounced out loud; but then he died, and since then his books have appeared and his verse is even quoted at ceremonies.

Pushkin's words are really coming true: 'They are capable of loving only the dead.'

But the belated publication of books and 'authorization' [rehabilitation] of names does not make up for either the social or the artistic losses suffered by our people as a consequence of these monstrous delays and the suppression of artistic conscience. (In fact, there were writers in the 1920s – Pilnyak, Platonov, Mandelshtam – who called attention at a very early stage to the beginnings of the cult [of personality] and the peculiar traits of Stalin's character; but these writers were silenced and destroyed instead of being listened to.) Literature cannot develop in between the categories of 'permitted' and 'not permitted', 'about this you may write' and 'about this you may not'. Literature that is not the breath of contemporary society, that dares not transmit the pains and fears of that society, that does not warn in time against threatening moral and social dangers – such literature does not deserve the name of literature; it is only a façade. Such literature loses the confidence of its own people, and its published works are used as wastepaper instead of being read.

Our literature has lost the leading role it played at the end of the last century and the beginning of this one, and it has lost the brilliance of experimentation that distinguished it in the 1920s. To the entire world the literary life of our country now appears immeasurably more colourless, trivial and inferior than it actually is – [or] than it would be if it were not confined and hemmed in. The losers are both our country – in world public opinion – and world literature itself. If the world had access to all the uninhibited fruits of our literature, if it were enriched by our own spiritual experience, the whole artistic evolution of the world would move along in a different way, acquiring a new stability and attaining even a new artistic threshold.

I propose that the Congress adopt a resolution which would demand and ensure the abolition of all censorship, open or hidden, of all fictional writing, and which would release publishing houses from the obligation to obtain authorization for the publication of every printed page.

2. The duties of the Union towards its members.

These duties are not clearly formulated in the statutes of the Soviet Writers' Union (under 'Protection of copyrights' and 'Measures for the protection of other rights of writers'), and it is sad to find that for a third of a century the Union has not defended either the 'other' rights or even the copyrights of persecuted writers.

Many writers have been subjected during their lifetime to abuse and slander in the press and from rostrums without being afforded the physical possibility of replying. More than that, they have been exposed to violence and personal persecution (Bulgakov, Akhmatova, Tsvetayeva, Pasternak, Zoshchenko, Platonov, Alexander Grin, Vassily Grossman). The Writers' Union not only did not make its own publications available to these writers for purposes of reply and justification, not only did not come out in their defence, but through its leadership was always first among the persecutors. Names that adorned our poetry of the twentieth century found themselves on the list of those expelled from the Union or not even admitted to it in the first place. The leadership of the Union cravenly abandoned to their distress those for whom persecution ended in exile, labour camps, and death (Pavel Vasilev, Mandelshtam, Artem Vesely, Pilnyak, Babel, Tabidze, Zabolotsky, and others). The list must be cut off at 'and others'. We learned after the Twentieth Party Congress that there were more than 600 writers whom the

Union had obediently handed over to their fate in prisons and camps. However, the roll is even longer, and its curled-up end cannot and will not ever be read by our eyes. It contains the names of young prose-writers and poets whom we may have known only accidentally through personal encounters and whose talents were crushed in camps before being able to blossom, whose writings never got further than the offices of the state security service in the days of Yagoda, Yezhov, Beria and Abakumov.

There is no historical necessity for the newly-elected leadership of the Union to share with its predecessors the responsibility for the past.

I propose that all guarantees for the defence of Union members subjected to slander and unjust persecution be clearly formulated in Paragraph 22 of the Union statutes, so that past illegalities will not be repeated.

If the Congress does not remain indifferent to what I have said, I also ask that it consider the interdictions and persecution to which I myself have been subjected.

(1) It will soon be two years since the state security authorities took away from me my novel, *The First Circle* (comprising thirty-five author's sheets [*avtorskie listy*]),* thus preventing it from being submitted to publishers. Instead, in my own lifetime, against my will and even without my knowledge, this novel has been 'published' in an unnatural 'closed' edition for reading by an unidentified select circle. My novel has [thus] become available to literary officials but is being concealed from most writers. I have been unable to obtain open discussion of the novel within writers' associations and to prevent misuse and plagiarism.

(2) Together with this novel, my literary papers dating back fifteen to twenty years, things that were not intended for publication, were taken away from me. Now, tendentious excerpts from these papers have also been covertly 'published' and are being circulated within the same circles. The play, *Feast of the Victors*, which I wrote in verse from memory in camp, where I

---

* 'Author's sheets' are printed pages, each containing 40,000 typographical characters, used in the Soviet Union for computing the author's fee.

went by a four-digit number – and where, condemned to die by starvation, we were forgotten by society, no one outside the camps coming out against [such] repressions – this play, now left far behind, is being ascribed to me as my very latest work.

(3) For three years now, an irresponsible campaign of slander has been conducted against me, who fought all through the war as a battery commander and received military decorations. It is being said that I served time as a criminal, or surrendered to the enemy (I was never a prisoner-of-war), that I 'betrayed' my country and 'served the Germans'. That is the interpretation being put now on the eleven years I spent in camps and in exile for having criticized Stalin. This slander is being spread in secret instructions and meetings by people holding official positions. I vainly tried to stop the slander by appealing to the Board of the Writers' Union of the RSFSR and to the press. The Board did not even react, and not a single paper printed my reply to the slanderers. On the contrary, slander against me from rostrums has intensified and become more vicious within the last year, making use of distorted material from my confiscated papers, and I have no way of replying.

(4) My novel *Cancer Ward* (comprising twenty-five author's sheets), the first part of which was approved for publication by the prose department of the Moscow writers' organization, cannot be published either by chapters – rejected by five magazines, or in its entirety – rejected by *Novy Mir*, *Zvezda*, and *Prostor*.

(5) The play, *The Tenderfoot and the Tramp*, accepted in 1962 by the Sovremennik Theatre, has thus far not been approved for performance.

(6) The screen play, *The Tanks Know the Truth*; the stage play, *The Light That is in You*; a short story entitled *The Right Hand*; the series, *Tiny Stories* – [all these] cannot find either a producer or a publisher.

(7) My stories published in *Novy Mir* have never been reprinted in book form, having been rejected everywhere – by the 'Soviet Writer' Publishers, the State Literary Publishing House, and the 'Ogonyok' Library. They thus remain inaccessible to the general reading public.

(8) I have also been prevented from having any other contacts with readers [either] through public readings of my works (in November 1966, nine out of eleven scheduled meetings were cancelled at the last moment) or through readings over the radio. Even the simple act of giving a manuscript away for 'reading and copying' has now become a criminal act (ancient Russian scribes were permitted to do this five centuries ago). Thus my work has been finally smothered, gagged, and slandered.

In view of such flagrant infringements of my copyright and 'other' rights, will the Fourth Congress defend me – yes or no? It seems to me that the choice is also not without importance for the literary future of several of the delegates.

I am of course confident that I will fulfil my duty as a writer in all circumstances – from the grave even more successfully and more irrefutably than in my lifetime. No one can bar the road to truth, and to advance its cause I am prepared to accept even death. But may it be that repeated lessons will finally teach us not to stop the writer's pen during his lifetime?

At no time has this ennobled our history.

A. I. SOLZHENITSYN

16 May 1967

(*Problems of Communism*, July–August 1968)

Telegrams and letters of support for Solzhenitsyn

Letter from eighty members of the Writers' Union to the Presidium of the Fourth All-Union Soviet Writers' Congress

The letter by A. I. Solzhenitsyn confronts the Writers' Congress and each one of us with questions of vital importance. We consider it impossible to pretend that this letter does not exist and simply take refuge in silence. To keep silent would inevitably do grave damage to the authority of our literature and the dignity of our society.

Only an open discussion of the letter, secured by wide

publicity, can serve as guarantee for the healthy future of our literature, which has been called upon to be the conscience of the people.

We consider it our civic duty to inform the Congress of our opinion.

Members of USSR Writers' Union:

K. PAUSTOVSKY	G. BAKLANOV	F. ISKANDER
V. KAVERIN	V. SOLOUKHIN	V. AKSYONOV
V. TENDRYAKOV	B. BALTER	A. GLADKOV
YU. TRIFONOV	G. SEMYONOV	A. TARKOVSKY
K. VASHENKIN	V. OGNYOV	T. LITVINOVA
B. SARNOV	G. SADOVSKY	L. LEVITSKY
V. VOINOVICH	L. PINSKY	N. OTTEN
YU. SOTNIK	E. STARIKOVA	A. SHAROV
V. KORNILOV	YU. STREKHNIN	N. PANCHENKO
M. POPOVSKY	YU. MORITS	A. RYBAKOV
S. KRUTILIN	A. SOSNIN	A. EFRON
S. YERMOLINSKY	N. TARASENKOVA	M. LORIYE
A. SMIRNOV-	R. OBLONSKAYA	V. BUSHIN
CHERKEZOV	N. DOLININA	YA. VOLCHEK
N. KORZHAVIN	L. TOOM	S. BONDARIN
V. MAKSIMOV	I. FRADKIN	V. BOGOMOLOV
B. MOZHAYEV	B. OKUDZHAVA	N. IVANTER
F. SVETOV	G. SVIRSKY	N. VOLZHINA
YU. KAGARLITSKY	V. CHESHIKHINA	A. BERZER
E. GERSHTEIN	I. VARLAMOVA	D. NIKOLAYEV
K. BOGATYRYOV	YU. VRONSKY	M. ROSHCHIN
A. ANIKST	V. AMLINSKY	I. BORISOLVA
N. ADAMYAN	N. KHARKOVA	A. GALICH
A. GLADILIN	A. IVICH	M. TUROVSKAYA
N. ILINA	YU. LEVITANSKY	N. DAVYDOVA
YU. DAVYDOV	E. GOLYSHOVA	B. SLUTSKY
L. LAZAREV	V. KOROSTYLEV	V. BYKOV

May 1967

Telegram from V. Katayev to the Presidium of the Fourth All-Union Soviet Writers' Congress

Moscow
Kremlin
Presidium of Writers' Congress

Dear comrades,
   Being unable to attend the Congress owing to difficult family circumstances and the state of my health, I have to inform you that I consider an open discussion by Congress of the [well]-known letter by Solzhenitsyn, with the basic principles of which I am in full agreement, absolutely indispensable.

Delegate to Congress, member of Presidium
VALENTIN KATAYEV

Telegram from three members of the USSR Writers' Union to the Fourth All-Union Soviet Writers' Congress

Moscow
52 Vorovsky Street
Fourth Soviet Writers' Congress

We support the letter by Alexander Solzhenitsyn. We insist on a discussion of the letter by Congress.

Members of USSR Writers' Union (Order of Lenin)
VLADIMIR VOINOVICH
VLADIMIR KORNILOV
FELIKS SVETOV

Letter from D. Dar to the Presidium of the Fourth
All-Union Soviet Writers' Congress

Copy to Editorial board of *Literaturnaya Gazeta*

Dear comrades!

Having no opportunity to speak at the Congress, I beg you to add the following open letter from myself to the materials of the Congress:

When reviewing the fifty years' development of Soviet literature, each of us must realize that despite harsh repressions, slander, victimization and persecution by various petty officials of the state and Party apparatus, the finest representatives of Soviet literature, such as Akhamtova, Pasternak, Yesenin, Tsvetayeva, Zoshchenko, Bulgakov, Mandelshtam, Solzhenitsyn and many others, guided not by decrees drawn up in various departments, but solely by the voice of their own civic conscience, have won an absolute victory in the struggle with officialdom, and have earned the love and recognition of readers in the Soviet Union and throughout the world.

From this fact we must conclude that the time has come to put an end to the illusion that state or Party employees know better than artists what serves the interests of Party and people and what damages these interests. How many Benkendorfs, Ilichyovs and Polikarpovs there were in [pre-revolutionary] Russia, trying without success to choke, to enslave Russian art! And how many of them even now still dictate to us in the name of Party and government how to write books, paint pictures, or direct films, and decide which works of art must become the nation's property and which should be hidden from the people.

The present Congress must call by its true name the phenomenon of bureaucratic realism which in our country goes sheepishly and hypocritically by the name of socialist realism. Only that which is to the taste of officials and clerks in various departments (including that so bureaucratic department, the Writers' Union) gets given the life-saving label of socialist realism, and everything that does not suit [these] officials' tastes and does not fit in with their bureaucratic interpretations, is declared to be in conflict with socialist realism.

The present Congress can only have any significance if it declares for all to hear that the interests of our people and our native land are no less dear to us Soviet writers than to clerks in state and party offices, and that we are not in need of any guardian. And any *litterateur* who does not consider he has a right to independent creativity, who through his stupidity, ignorance, inexperience or cowardice feels the need to be prompted, guided and watched over, is simply not worthy of the lofty title of writer.

Member of Soviet Writers' Union

Leningrad, 19 May 1967   D. DAR

Letter from V. Konetsky to the Presidium of the Fourth All-Union Soviet Writers' Congress

I have received the letter by A. I. Solzhenitsyn on the arbitrariness of censorship in our literature, and I must state that I fully share all the anxiety and pain with which this letter is filled . . .

In this jubilee year of Soviet power, arbitrariness and tyranny in censorship have reached their zenith, and this is blasphemy.

Therefore I join fully with A. I. Solzhenitsyn in his declaration. The question of censorship must be included in the agenda of the Congress and discussed. I disagree only with Solzhenitsyn's [suggestion] that the question could be formulated in as extreme a way as he words it: 'the abolition of all censorship – open or hidden – of all fictional writing'. Probably the formulation ought to be worked out collectively . . .

I fully agree with every word of the second part of Solzhenitsyn's letter.

Concerning the third part, I must state that it was only yesterday, when I read Solzhenitsyn's letter, that I learned of his appeal to the Board of the RSFSR Writers' Union to protect him from slander, although I should have been informed of a statement of this kind by a Soviet Russian writer, since I am a member of the Board's inspection committee.

All the problems raised by A. I. Solzhenitsyn in his letter to the Fourth Soviet Writers' Congress are radical and basic problems for our literature and hence for our people and our country. The time for their solution has arrived with relentless historical necessity. No one will ever forgive the delegates to the Congress if they retreat into hiding before the complexity of these problems.

20 May 1967   Member of Inspection Committee,
                Board of RSFSR Writers' Union; Member of Board,
                      Leningrad branch, RSFSR Writers' Union
                                              V. KONETSKY

*Letter from S. Antonov to the Presidium of the Fourth
All-Union Soviet Writers' Congress*

A few days before the start of the Congress I received the letter by A. Solzhenitsyn concerning the state of affairs in literature. I learned from this letter that it had been sent also to the Presidium of the Congress.

We have already had three days of the Congress, and its Presidium has kept enigmatic silence as though this important document did not exist under the sun.

I share many of the principles Solzhenitsyn proposes for discussion, consider them extremely important for the destiny of art, and beg the Congress Presidium not to conceal A. Solzhenitsyn's letter from the delegates.

Concerning the matters [he raises], I should like to add [the following]:

1. Present-day censorship, apart from fulfilling its traditional functions (the seizure of publications damaging to security, [or] attacks on the régime, and the suppression of pornography and war propaganda), interferes uncontrolledly in absolutely every artistic aspect of a work . . .

2. Censorship is doubly arbitrary insofar as employees of GLAVLIT because of some regulation or other do not have the right to enter into any contact with authors, and we, the writers,

have to pretend that this censorship does not exist. In my booklet *I read a story*, after all the corrections and approvals, someone or other without my knowledge crossed out from the list of contemporary Soviet story-writers the name of A. Solzhenitsyn. I never found out exactly who did it. The book's editor said that Solzhenitsyn's name had evidently not been in that list.

3. Censorial arbitrariness is further encouraged by being allowed to operate anonymously and hence with impunity . . .

4. Not only literature is suffering irreparable losses through lawless censorship. Films like *The Adventures of a Dentist* (directed by Klimov), *Earthly Stars* (based on a story by O. Bergolts), *A Nasty Joke* (directed by Alov and Naumov), *The Passions of Andrei* [Andrei Rublyov] (directed by Tarkovsky) are to this day 'lying on the shelf', that is, in plain words, they have been banned by the Committee on Cinematographic Affairs, which degenerated long ago into what is in effect one of the censor's departments – films that were placed, by an overwhelming majority of votes in the certifying commission, in the highest category for their quality . . . And as for what goes on when the works of artists and sculptors are selected for exhibition – the mere mention is repugnant.

5. Because the functions of censorship have undergone unlimited expansion, and because every common clerk can uncontrolledly and irresponsibly assume these functions under the guise of 'vigilance', the fate of Soviet art is in the hands not of its creators but of bureaucrats who understand little about it, or mediocre workers in the arts who have degenerated into bureaucrats. What this leads to is shown by, amongst a host of other lamentable facts, the unjust and shameful treatment of one of our most talented writers, A. Solzhenitsyn.

I request the Presidium of the Congress to give me the opportunity of reading this letter at the Congress, or bringing this letter to the notice of the delegates.

S. ANTONOV

*Letter from G. Vladimov to Presidium of the Fourth
All-Union Soviet Writers' Congress*

Copy to A. Solzhenitsyn

Dear comrades!

I, like you, have received the letter of A. Solzhenitsyn and
wish to make known my opinion on all the points in that letter.

I would venture to remind Congress that the main purpose of
writers' congresses is not to deliver reports on our brilliant
creative victories, or to hear the greetings of foreign guests, nor
is it [to express] solidarity with the peoples of Africa and the
struggling Vietnamese; it is first and foremost [to express] our
solidarity with our own people, first and foremost to solve our
own pressing problems, [for] without such a solution Soviet
literature cannot go on living and developing. Without freedom
of creativity, complete, limitless freedom to express any opinion
on any aspect of the social and moral life of the people, [it
cannot continue] however much we may curse this legitimate
demand of every artist who has the slightest power of thought,
the slightest sense of honour.

... And I must say that such freedom does exist. It is put
into practice, not in officially recognized, censored literature,
but in the activities of so-called 'Samizdat', of which you are
probably well aware. Passing from hand to hand, from reader to
reader, in typed seventh or eighth copies, are the unpublished
works of Bulgakov, Tsvetayeva, Mandelshtam, Platonov, and
others alive today whose names I refrain from mentioning for
fully understandable reasons ...

Organize mass search raids, seize all the tapes, all the copies,
arrest their authors and those responsible for their circulation –
even so, at least one copy will escape, and having survived will
be duplicated in even greater quantities, because forbidden
fruit is sweet ... This process whereby art is being liberated
from all the fetters of 'official directives' is developing and
expanding, and to fight against it is as stupid and senseless as to
ban tobacco or spirits ...

I have read many works in 'Samizdat' and can say of nine-tenths of them with full responsibility that they not only *can* be published – they *must* be ... There is nothing anti-national in them – no artist in his right mind would ever think of it – but there is the breath of talent, brilliance, the radiance of unfettered artistic form, there is a love for man, an authentic knowledge of life, and at times echoes of pain and anger for the writer's fatherland, or bitterness and hatred towards its enemies who pose as friends and protectors.

Naturally, everything I have said above applies also to the unpublished works of Solzhenitsyn. I have had the good fortune to read almost all that he has written; he is the writer of whom my Russia is most of all in need, who is destined to glorify her in this world and to answer all our burning questions about the tragedy we have suffered. I know no other author who might have a greater right to this task and greater strength for it. I do not intend to insult Congress when I say that probably nine-tenths of the names of its delegates will not survive to cross the threshold of the century. But the name of Alexander Solzhenitsyn, the pride of Russian literature, will reach beyond them ...

A ban on publication or performance, search raids and confiscation of his archive, 'restricted' editions of works the author himself did not intend for publication and, in addition, malicious slander against a military officer who fought through the whole war ... it is painful, agonizing, shameful to read about. And this is going on in a proletarian state. This is going on in the fiftieth year of the Revolution. This is going on, lastly, in a civilized society in the second half of the twentieth century ...

So I should like to ask the plenipotentiary congress: are we a nation of scum, sneaks, and informers, or are we a great people which has presented the world with an unrivalled galaxy of geniuses? Solzhenitsyn will fulfil his task; I believe that as firmly as he himself does. But ourselves, what of us? Did we protect him from the search raids and the confiscations? Did we push, his works into print? Did we shield his face from the slimy, fetid hand of slander? Did we in our editorial offices and our boards at least answer him intelligibly when he sought an answer?

We were listening to greetings from Mr Dürrenmatt and Mrs Hollman at the time. After all, that was business too, just like solidarity with the struggling Vietnamese and the suffering Greeks. But time will pass, and we shall be asked: what did we do for ourselves, for our near ones for whom living and working were so difficult?

The letter by Solzhenitsyn has already become a document which cannot be evaded by silence – that would be unworthy of honest artists. I suggest that Congress discuss this letter at an open session, pass a new and unequivocal resolution on it, and lay this resolution before the government of the country.

Excuse the sharp language of my appeal – but after all, I am talking to colleagues.

Yours respectfully,

Moscow, 26 May 1967   G. VLADIMOV

Letter from Pavel Antokolsky to the Secretary of the Central Committee of the CPSU, P. N. Demichev

Dear Peter Nilich,

Along with other delegates to our Congress, I received the well-known letter of the writer Alexander Isayevich Solzhenitsyn, and it greatly moved me as well as some other comrades. As an old writer and a communist I feel it my duty to convey to you my feelings.

Alexander Solzhenitsyn seems to me to be a writer of rare talent, a man of growing promise for our realist literature, and heir to the great humanistic tradition of Gogol, Tolstoy, and Gorky. We should appreciate and cherish such cultural figures. The criticism of the published works of Solzhenitsyn was shocking because of its passionate hostility and lack of proof.

Confiscating his manuscripts, as described in detail in his letter, appears to be an incredible abuse, which is unworthy of our socialist society and our Soviet state. It is even more horrible because only a few years ago the same thing happened with the manuscript of the second part of the novel of the late Vasily Grossman. Is this kind of seizure of our writers' manuscripts to become a legalized custom?

This cannot and must not be! Such a brutal attitude to works of art is incompatible with our basic laws and unthinkable in any normal human community. If there is anything questionable or unclear in the works of Solzhenitsyn, if they contain any political errors, they should be subject to open discussion in our [writers'] community. There are many such possibilities for writers.

I have been working as a writer for fifty years. I have behind me many books and my whole life, and I have been through many difficult moments. There were times when I had great fears for the fate of our literature and the fate of individual comrades: Bulgakov, Pasternak, Titian Tabidze – I recall these because they were close to me.

Having lived such a life, I just cannot imagine that at the end of my days this kind of fear should arise again, and that it should happen on the eve of our great and famous anniversary.

If a Soviet writer felt compelled to address to his fellows such a letter as that of Solzhenitsyn, it means that we have all to bear responsibility before him and before our readers. If he cannot say what he wants to say to the readers in our country, then I, an old writer, have no right to face the readers either.

PAVEL ANTOKOLSKY
(*Survey*, No. 67)

Letter from A. E. Kosterin to M. A. Sholokhov

Mikhail Alexandrovich!

It took me a long time to decide whether there was any point in writing to you. My doubts on that score are fully understandable.

After your speech at the Twenty-third Congress of the Soviet Communist Party,* L. Chukovskaya sent you an intelli-

*At the Twenty-third Party Congress, Sholokhov attacked Sinyavsky and Daniel, implying that they should have been shot: 'If these scoundrels with their black consciences had been caught in the memorable twenties, when people were tried not on the basis of closely defined articles of the criminal code, but "in accordance with revolutionary justice", then, my goodness,

gent and courageous letter. The aim of this letter was, I believe, not only to expose the misanthropic nature of your speech, but also to help you realize the danger of the path you have taken, for yourself as a writer.

From the summit of your 'majesty' you did not deign to 'notice' that letter ... Therefore I am justified in thinking that you, as a literary 'star' of ultra-powerful magnitude, will not notice me or hear my voice in the glorious radiance, the peals of chiming bells surrounding your person.

... Under the influence of recent events in our literary life, I have as it were trodden the length of the path of suffering which has fallen to the lot of Soviet writers and journalists. In his courageous letter to the Writers' Congress, Solzhenitsyn pointed to an insignificantly small part of the misfortunes which have befallen and continue to befall us.

Hundreds of writers and poets, 'lost without trace' in prisons and camps!

This one fact is enough to fill even me, an old convict, with horror, all the more since amongst those who have perished there are many of my friends.

... Apart from those who have perished in the prisons and the camps, hundreds more of the 'poor in spirit' have perished for literature, by taking your path, the path of the time-server 'for gold and fame's sake'. History will discredit them and their fame, achieved by political manoeuvring.

... You have spoken out against freedom of the press, against creative freedom, and have thereby gone over to the camp of obscurantism, the camp of the stranglers of free thought, without which there can be no progress, that is, progress along the path to communism.

We can be thankful to you for one thing only. You did not follow the example of those excessively zealous Stalinists who assert that our country has 'the freest press in the world'. In his letter Alexander Solzhenitsyn proved very convincingly that

---

they would have got something quite different, these turncoats!' Sholokhov was severely rebuked for this statement by Lydia Chukovskaya in an open letter which circulated in 'Samizdat' (see *On Trial*, ed. Leopold Labedz and Max Hayward, Collins and Harvill Press 1967, p. 292).

there is not the slightest trace of any such freedom in our country, and showed what a mockery is made of authors' rights and with what scorn people engaged in creative labour are regarded. You agreed with his arguments by your silence, and now you call anathema upon the heads of the champions of creative freedom.

To the facts cited by Solzhenitsyn one could add tens and hundreds more. But Solzhenitsyn is mistaken if he thinks that we have only to abolish GLAVLIT and KGB interference in literary matters and the reign of 'freedom of the press' will begin. No, to achieve this it is essential to ensure that the printing-presses and paper are used in the interests of the working people, that is, that they are used in the way Lenin proposed.

And this is what he had to write on the subject: '. . . Freedom of the press means that any citizen may freely express any opinion' . . .

That, Mikhail Alexandrovich, is the Leninist interpretation of freedom of the press . . . And in the twenties these directives of Lenin's were put into practice. We had the 'Moscow Fellowship of Writers', without any specially appointed editors or censorship (with the exception of military censorship); we even had the right to 'authors' [private] editions' . . .

But nowadays, not only is 'every working man' (or group of workers of any size) deprived of the possibility of freely expressing his opinion in print; [this applies] even to rank-and-file Party members. Things have gone so far that it is impossible even to publish protests at the misinterpretations of history and of Marxist classics which are frequently to be found in our press.

And this in a country which, on the eve of the fiftieth anniversary [of Soviet power], has declared:

'The victory of socialism has created the social, political and spiritual prerequisites necessary for the transition towards the building of a communist society' (see *Theses of Central Committee*) . . . When he demanded freedom of the press, Solzhenitsyn also expected the Writers' Congress to assure him protection from the arbitrary treatment accorded to him personally. You read Solzhenitsyn's letter, of course. And how did you respond to this cry for help? How did you help your fellow-writer? Was it, for instance, in the same way that Russian public opinion once came to the assistance of Maxim Gorky?

No, you took another road – the logical one for yourself. You in effect answered Solzhenitsyn's letter from the Congress platform, knowing perfectly well that the author of the letter would not be offered a platform either at the Congress or in the press. You joined with those who are systematically hounding a talented writer . . .

My advice to you, Mr Sholokhov, is – read the diary of Nikitenko, a former censor during the reign of Nicholas I. This petty official of the tyrant, the gendarme of Europe, was in thought and deed more cultured and nobler than you.

This is what that censor and teacher of Russian literature wrote in December 1844:

'I am obliged to teach Russian literature – but where is it? Does literature enjoy the rights of a citizen among us? There is only one refuge – to resort to the graveyard of theory. I deceive and am deceived when I speak the words: development, trends of thought, basic concepts of art. All this means something, and even means a great deal in countries where public opinion exists, and where there is a [real] interest in intellectual and aesthetic matters, but here it is just empty words in the air. Words, words, words! To live in words and for words, one's soul craving for truth, and one's mind striving for genuine, substantial results – that is indeed a profound misfortune.'

Nikitenko, a petty official of Tsar Nicholas, did not have the courage to speak out openly and fearlessly against censorship, but at least he did not attempt to defend it in his public statements, and 'poured out his soul' in his conversations with his diary. But you walk onto the highest platforms, and, like that buffoon Shchukar, proclaim to the whole world truths worthy of Skalozub and Famusov* . . .

If you really do have courage and believe that you are defending a just cause, then do not hide behind the backs of those who to this day are depriving your opponents of any opportunity to speak. Go out into an honest literary fight. Have the letters of

*Shchukar is a character in one of Sholokhov's novels; Skalozub and Famusov are characters in Griboyedov's *Woe from Wit*.

L. Chukovskaya, A. Solzhenitsyn, and also this one of mine published, and give an open answer to them.

No, once again you will take refuge within the walls of your estate, guarded by policemen.

I add my signature to the letter from L. Chukovskaya and her assertion that by your speeches you have struck yourself off the list of honest writers and are digging your own inglorious grave.

Moscow, July 1967   A. KOSTERIN

Letter from Solzhenitsyn to the Writers' Union

12 September 1967
To the Secretariat of the Board of the Union of Writers of the
USSR – All Secretaries

Even though supported by more than a hundred writers, my letter to the Fourth Soviet Writers' Congress has been neither published nor answered. The only thing that has happened is that rumours are being spread in order to assuage public opinion. These rumours – highly uniform and evidently coming from a centralized source – aver that *Cancer Ward* and my archives and novel have been returned to me, and that a book of [my] stories is being printed. But, as you know, this is a lie.

In a conversation with me on 12 June 1967 [some of the] secretaries of the Board of the Union of Writers of the USSR – G. Markov, K. Voronkov, S. Sartakov, and L. Sobolev – declared that the Board of the Union of Writers deemed it a duty to refute publicly the base slander that has been spread about me and my military record. However, not only has this refutation failed to materialize, but the slanders continue; at instructional meetings, at activist meetings, and at seminars, a new batch of fantastic nonsense is being disseminated about me – [*e.g.*,] that I have run off to the UAR or to England (I would like to assure the slanderers that it is, rather, they who will be doing the running). Prominent persons persistently express their regret that I did not die in the camp, that I was ever liberated. (Incidentally, immediately following *One Day*, the same regret was voiced.

This book is now being secretly withdrawn from circulation in [public] libraries.)

These same secretaries of the Board promised at least to 'examine the question' of [approving] publication of my latest novel, *Cancer Ward*. But, in the space of three months – one-fourth of a year – no progress has been made in this direction either. During these three months, forty-two secretaries of the Board have been unable to make an evaluation of the novel or to make a recommendation as to whether it should be published. The novel has been in this same strange and equivocal state – no direct prohibition, no direct permission – for over a year, since the summer of 1966. While the journal *Novy Mir* would now like to publish the story, it lacks the permission to do so.

Does the Secretariat believe that my novel will silently disappear as a result of these endless delays, that I will cease to exist, and that [therefore] the Secretariat will not have to decide whether to include it in or exclude it from Soviet literature? While this is going on, the book is being read avidly everywhere. At the behest of the readers, it has already appeared in hundreds of typewritten copies. At the 12 June meeting I apprised the Secretariat that we should make haste to publish the novel if we wish to see it appear first in Russian, that under the circumstances we cannot prevent its unauthorized appearance in the West.

After the senseless delay of many months, the time has come to state that, if the latter does happen, it will clearly be the fault (or perhaps the wish?) of the Secretariat of the Board of the Union of Writers of the USSR.

I insist that my story be published without delay.

SOLZHENITSYN
(*Problems of Communism*, July–August 1968)

Secretariat meeting with Solzhenitsyn

Proceedings of a session of the Secretariat of the Union of Soviet Writers

22 September 1967

The session was attended by some thirty secretaries of the Writers' Union and by comrade Melentiev of the cultural department of the Central Committee. K. A. Fedin was chairman. The session, which discussed letters written by Solzhenitsyn, started at 1:00 and ended after 5:00 PM.

FEDIN: I have been shaken by Solzhenitsyn's second letter. His claim that things have come to a standstill seems to me to be without foundation. I feel that this has been an insult to our collective. By no means is three and a half months a long time to spend examining his manuscript. I have sensed something in the nature of a threat [in the letter]. This strikes me as offensive! Solzhenitsyn's second letter seems to urge us to take up his manuscripts in all haste and to publish them immediately. The second letter continues the line of the first, but the first letter spoke more concretely and with more fervour about the fate of the writer, while the second, I feel, was offensive. Where do we stand with regard to the complex question of publishing Solzhenitsyn's things? None of us denies that he is talented. [Yet] the tenor of the letter veers in an impermissible direction. His letter is like a slap in the face; it is as if we are reprobates and not representatives of the creative intelligentsia. In the final analysis, he himself is slowing down the examination of the question with these demands. I did not find the idea of literary comradeship in his letters. Whether we want to or not, today we must get into a discussion of Solzhenitsyn's works, but it seems to me that generally speaking we should discuss the letters.

[*Solzhenitsyn requests permission to say a few words about the subject of discussion. He reads a written statement.*]

It has become known to me that in preparation for the

discussion of *Cancer Ward*, the secretaries of the Board were instructed to read the play *Feast of the Victors*, which I myself have long since renounced; I have not even read it for ten years. I destroyed all copies of it except the one that was confiscated and that has now been reproduced. More than once, I have explained that this play was written not by Solzhenitsyn, member of the Writers' Union, but by nameless prisoner Shch. 232 in those distant years when there was no return to freedom for those arrested under the political article, at a time when no one in the community, including the writers' community, in either word or deed spoke out against repression, even when such repression was directed against entire peoples. I now bear as little responsibility for this play as many other authors bear for speeches and books they wrote in 1949 but would not write again today. This play bears the stamp of the desperation of the camps in those years when man's conscious being was determined by his social being and at a time when the conscious being was by no means uplifted by prayers for those who were being persecuted. This play bears no relationship whatsoever to my present works, and the critique of it is a deliberate departure from a business-like discussion of the novel *Cancer Ward*.

Moreover, it is beneath a writer's ethics to discuss a work that was seized in such a way from a private apartment. The critique of my novel *The First Circle* is a separate matter and should not be substituted for a critique of the story *Cancer Ward*.

KORNEICHUK: I have a question to put to Solzhenitsyn. How does he regard the licentious bourgeois propaganda that his [first] letter evoked? Why doesn't he dissociate himself from it? Why does he put up with it in silence? How is it that his letter was broadcast over the radio in the West even before the Congress started?

[*Fedin calls upon Solzhenitsyn to reply. Solzhenitsyn replies that he is not a schoolboy who has to jump up to answer every question, that he will deliver a statement like the others. Fedin says that Solzhenitsyn can wait until there are several questions and then answer them all at the same time.*]

BARUZDIN: Even though Solzhenitsyn protests against the discussion of *Feast of the Victors*, we shall have to discuss this play whether he wants to or not.

SALYNSKY: I would like Solzhenitsyn to tell us by whom, when, and under what circumstances these materials were removed. Has the author asked for their return? To whom did he address his request?

[*Fedin asks Solzhenitsyn to answer these questions. Solzhenitsyn repeats that he will answer them when making his statement.*]

FEDIN: But the Secretariat cannot begin the discussion until it has the answers to these questions.

VOICES: If Solzhenitsyn wants to refuse to talk to the Secretariat at all, let him say so.

SOLZHENITSYN: Very well, I shall answer these questions It is not true that the letter was broadcast over the radio in the West before the Congress: it was broadcast *after* the Congress closed, and then not right away. Very significant and expressive use is made here of the word 'abroad', as if it referred to some higher authority whose opinion was very much cherished. Perhaps this is understandable to those who spend much creative time travelling abroad, to those who flood our literature with sketches about life abroad. But this is alien to me. I have never been abroad, but I do know that I don't have time enough left in my life to learn about life there. I do not understand how one can be so sensitive to opinion abroad and not to one's own country, to pulsing public opinion here. For my entire life, I have had the soil of my homeland under my feet; only *its* pain do I hear, only about *it* do I write.

Why was the play *Feast of the Victors* mentioned in the letter to the Congress? This is apparent from the letter itself: in order to protest against the illegal 'publication' and dissemination of this play against the will of the author and without his consent. Now, concerning the confiscation of my novel and archives. Yes, I did write several times, beginning in 1965, to protest about this matter to the Central Committee. But, in recent times, a whole new version of the confiscation of my archives has been invented. The story is that Teush, the person who was keeping my manuscripts, had some tie with another person who is not named, that the latter was arrested while going through customs (where is not mentioned), and that something or other was found in his possession (they do not say what); it was not something of mine, but it was decided to protect me against such an acquaintance. All this is a lie. Teush's friend was investigated two years ago, but no such accusation was made against him. The items I had in safekeeping were discovered as a consequence of [police] surveillance, wiretapping, and an eavesdropping device. And here is the remarkable thing: barely does the new version [of the confiscation] appear than it crops up in various parts of the country. Lecturer Potemkin has just aired it to a large assemblage in Riga, and one of the secretaries of the Writers' Union has passed it on to writers in Moscow, adding his own invention – that I supposedly acknowledged all these things at the last meeting at the Secretariat. Yet not a single one of these things was discussed. I have no doubt that I will soon start getting letters from all parts of the country about the dissemination of this version.

VOICE: Has the editorial board of *Novy Mir* rejected or accepted the novel *Cancer Ward*?

ABDUMOMUNOV: What kind of authorization does *Novy Mir* require to print a story, and from whom does it come?

TVARDOVSKY: Generally, the decision to print or not to print a particular thing is a matter for the editorial board to decide. But in the situation that has developed around this author's name, the Secretariat of the Union must decide.

VORONKOV: Not once has Solzhenitsyn appealed directly to the Secretariat of the Writers' Union. After Solzhenitsyn's letter to the Congress, some of the comrades in the Secretariat expressed the desire to meet with him, to answer questions, to talk [with him] and offer assistance. But, after the letter appeared in the dirty bourgeois press and Solzhenitsyn did not react in any way . . .

TVARDOVSKY [*interrupting*]: Precisely like the Writers' Union!

VORONKOV: . . . this desire died. And now the second letter has come. It is written in the form of an ultimatum; it is offensive and disrespectful to our writers' community. Just now,

Solzhenitsyn referred to 'one of the secretaries' who addressed a party meeting of Moscow writers. I was that secretary. [*To Solzhenitsyn*] People were in a hurry to inform you, but they did a bad job of it. As to the confiscation of your things, the only thing I mentioned was that you had admitted at the last meeting that the confiscated items were yours and that there had been no search made of your house. Naturally, after your letter to the Congress, we ourselves asked to read all your works. But you should not be so rude to your brothers in labour and writing! And you, Alexander Trifonovich [Tvardovsky], if you consider it necessary to print this story and if the author accepts your corrections, then go ahead and print it yourself; why should the Secretariat be involved?

TVARDOVSKY: And what happened in the case of Bek? The Secretariat was also involved then and made its recommendations, but, all the same, nothing was published.

VORONKOV: What interests me most of all, now, is the civic person Solzhenitsyn: Why doesn't he answer the malicious bourgeois propaganda? And why does he treat us as he does?

MUSREPOV: I have a question, too. How can he possibly write in his letter: 'Prominent persons persistently express regret that I did not die in the camp'? What right does he have to write such a thing?

SHARIPOV: And by what channels could the letter have reached the West?

[*Fedin asks Solzhenitsyn to answer these questions.*]

SOLZHENITSYN: What other things have been said about me? A person who, right now, occupies a very high position publicly declared that he is sorry he was not one of the triumvirate that sentenced me in 1945, that he would have sentenced me to be shot then and there! Here [at the Secretariat] my second letter is interpreted as an ultimatum: either print the story, or it will be printed in the West. But it isn't *I* who presents this ultimatum to the Secretariat; life presents this ultimatum to you and me both. I write that I am disturbed by the distribution of the story in hundreds – this is an approximate figure – in hundreds of typewritten copies.

VOICE: How did this come about?

SOLZHENITSYN: My works are disseminated in one way only: people persistently ask to read them, and, having received them to read, they either use their spare time or their own funds to retype them and then give them to others to read. As long as a year ago, the entire Moscow section [of the Writers' Union] read the first part of the story, and I am surprised that comrade Voronkov said here that they didn't know where to get it and they asked the KGB. About three years ago, my 'short stories' or poetry in prose were disseminated just as rapidly; barely had I given them to people to read when they quickly reached various cities in the Union. And then the editors of *Novy Mir* received a letter from the West from which we learned that these stories had already been published there. It was in order that such a leak might not befall *Cancer Ward* that I wrote my insistent letter to the Secretariat. I am no less astonished that the Secretariat could fail to react in some way to my letter to the Congress before the West did. And how could it fail to respond to all the slander that surrounds me? Comrade Voronkov used here the remarkable expression 'brothers in writing and labour'. Well, the fact of the matter is that these brothers in writing and labour have for two and a half years calmly watched me being oppressed, persecuted, and slandered . . .

TVARDOVSKY: Not everyone has been indifferent.

SOLZHENITSYN: . . . and newspaper editors, also like brothers, contribute to the web of falsehood that is woven around me by not publishing my denials. I'm not speaking about the fact that people in the camps are not allowed to read my book. It was banned in the camps, searches for it were conducted, and people were put in punishment cells for reading it even during those months when all the newspapers were loudly acclaiming *One Day in the Life of Ivan Denisovich* and promising that 'this will not happen again'. But, in recent times, the book is secretly being withdrawn from libraries outside [the camps] as well. I have received letters from various places telling me of the prohibition against circulating the book; the order is to tell the readers that the book is in the bindery, that it is out of print, or that there is no access to the shelves [where the book is kept], and to refuse to circulate it. Here is a letter recently received from the Krasnogvardeisky region in the Crimea:

In the regional library, I was confidentially told (I am an activist in this library) of an order that your books be removed from circulation. One of the women workers in the library wanted to present me with [a copy of] *One Day* as a souvenir, since the library no longer needs it, but another woman immediately stopped her rash girlfriend: 'What are you doing, you mustn't! Once the book has been assigned to the Special Section, it is dangerous to make a present of it.'

I am not saying that the book has been removed from *all* libraries; here and there it can still be found. But people coming to visit me in Ryazan were unable to get my book in the Ryazan oblast reading room! They were given various excuses, but they did not get the book . . .

The circle of lies becomes ever wider, knowing no limits, even charging me with having been taken prisoner and having collaborated with the Germans. But that's not the end of it! This summer, in the political education schools, *e.g.*, in Bolshevo, the agitators were told that I had fled to the UAR and changed my citizenship. Naturally, all this is written down in notebooks and is disseminated a hundred times over. And this took place not more than a few miles from the capital! Here is another version. In Solikamsk (PO Box 389), Major Shestakov declared that I had fled to England on a tourist visa. This is the deputy for political affairs – who dares to disbelieve him? Another time, the same man stated: 'Solzhenitsyn has been *forbidden* to write officially'. Well, at least here he is closer to the truth.

The following is being said about me from the rostrums: 'He was set free ahead of time, for no reason'. Whether there was any reason can be seen in the court decision of the Military Collegium of the Supreme Court, Rehabilitation Section. It has been presented to the Secretariat . . .

TVARDOVSKY: It also contains the combat record of Officer Solzhenitsyn.

SOLZHENITSYN: And the expression 'ahead of time' is used

with great relish! After the eight-year sentence, I served a month in transit prisons, but, of course, it is considered shameful to mention such a petty detail. Then, without being sentenced, I was permanently exiled. I spent three years in exile with that eternal feeling of doom. It was only because of the Twentieth Congress that I was set free – and this is called 'ahead of time'! The expression is so typical of the conditions that prevailed in the 1949–53 period: If a man did not die beside a camp rubbish heap, if he was able even to crawl out of the camp, this meant that he had been set free 'ahead of time' – after all, the sentence was for eternity and anything earlier was 'ahead of time'.

Ex-minister Semichastny, who was fond of speaking on literary issues, also singled me out for attention more than once. One of his astonishing, even comical, accusations was the following: 'Solzhenitsyn is materially supporting the capitalist world; why else doesn't he claim his rights [*i.e.,* collect his royalties] from someone or other for his well-known book?' Obviously, the reference was to *One Day*, since no other book of mine had been published [at that time]. Now if you knew, if you had read somewhere that it was absolutely necessary for me to wrest the money from the capitalists, then why didn't you inform me about it? This is a farce: whoever collects fees from the West has sold out to the capitalists; whoever does not take the fees is materially supporting them. And the third alternative? To fly into the sky. While Semichastny is no longer a minister, his idea has not died; lectures of the All-Union Society for the Dissemination of Scientific Information have carried it further. By way of example, the idea was repeated on 16 July of this year by Lecturer A. A. Freifeld at the Sverdlovsk Circus. Two thousand persons sat there and marvelled: 'What a crafty bird, that Solzhenitsyn! Without leaving the Soviet Union, without a single kopek in his pocket, he contrived to support world capitalism materially'. This is indeed a story to be told at a circus.

We had a talk on 12 June, right here, at the Secretariat. It was quiet and peaceful. We seemed to make some progress. A short time passed, and suddenly rumours were rampant throughout all of Moscow. Everything that actually took place was distorted, beginning with the fabrication that Tvardovsky had been shouting and waving his fist at me. But everyone who was there knows that nothing like that took place. Why these lies, then? And, right now, we are all simultaneously hearing what is said here, but where is the guarantee that after today's meeting of the Secretariat everything will not be distorted again? If you really are 'brothers in writing and labour', then my first request is that when you talk about today's session, don't fabricate and distort things.

I am one person; my slanderers are numbered in hundreds. Naturally I am never able to defend myself, and I never know against whom I should defend myself. I wouldn't be surprised if I were declared to be an adherent of the geocentric system and to have been the first to light the pyre of Giordano Bruno.

SALYNSKY: I shall speak of *Cancer Ward*. I believe that it should be printed – it is a vivid and powerful thing. To be sure, it contains descriptions of diseases in pathological terms, and the reader involuntarily develops a phobia about cancer – a phobia that is already widespread in our century. Somehow this [aspect of the book] should be eliminated. The caustic, topical-satirical style should also be eliminated. Another negative feature is that the destinies of almost all the characters are connected with the camp or with camp life in one form or another. This may be all right in the case of Kostoglotov or Rusanov, but why does it have to be applied to Valim, to Shulubin, and even to the soldier? At the very end, we learn that he is no ordinary soldier from the army, that he is a camp guard. [Still] the basic orientation of the novel is to discuss the end of the difficult past. And now a few words about moral socialism [a concept expounded in the novel]. In my opinion, there is nothing so bad about this. It would be bad if Solzhenitsyn were preaching amoral socialism. If he were preaching national socialism or the Chinese version of national socialism – that would be bad. Each person is free to form his own ideas on socialism and its development. I personally believe that socialism is determined by economic laws. But, of course, there is room for argument. Why not print the story, then? [*He subsequently calls upon the Secretariat to issue a statement decisively refuting the slanders against Solzhenitsyn.*]

SIMONOV: I do not accept the novel *The First Circle* and I oppose its publication. As for *Cancer Ward*, I am in favour of publishing it. Not everything in the story is to my liking, but it does not have to please everyone. Perhaps the author should adopt some of the comments that have been made, but, naturally, he cannot adopt all of them. It is also our duty to refute the slander about him. Further, his book of stories should be published. The foreword to the latter book would be a good place in which to publish his biography, and, in this way, the slander would die out of its own accord. Both we and he himself can and must put an end to false accusations. I have not read *Feast of the Victors*, nor do I desire to do so, since the author doesn't wish it.

TVARDOVSKY: Solzhenitsyn's position is such that he cannot issue a statement. It is we ourselves, the Union, who must make a statement refuting the slander. At the same time, we must sternly warn Solzhenitsyn against the inadmissible, unpleasant way in which he addressed the Congress. The editorial board of *Novy Mir* sees no reason why *Cancer Ward* should not be printed, naturally with certain revisions. We only wish to receive the Secretariat's approval or at least word that the Secretariat does not object.

[*He asks Voronkov to produce the Secretariat's draft communiqué which was prepared back in June. Voronkov indicates that he is in no hurry to produce the communiqué. During this time voices are heard:* They still haven't decided. There are those who are opposed!]

FEDIN: No, that isn't so. It isn't the Secretariat that has to print or reject anything. Are we really guilty of anything? Is it possible, Alexander Trifonovich, that you feel guilty?

TVARDOVSKY [*quickly, expressively*]: I? No.

FEDIN: We shouldn't search for some trumped-up excuse to make a statement. Mere rumours don't provide sufficient grounds for doing so. It would be another matter if Solzhenitsyn himself were to find a way to resolve the situation. What is needed is a public statement by Solzhenitsyn himself. [*To Solzhenitsyn*] But think it over, Alexander Isayevich – in the interest of *what* will we be publishing your protests? You must protest above all against the dirty use of your name by our enemies in the West. Naturally, in the process, you will also have the opportunity to give voice to some of the complaints you've uttered here today. If this proves to be a fortunate and tactful document, we will print it and help you. It is precisely from this point that your acquittal must proceed, and not from your works or from this bartering as to how many months we are entitled to examine your manuscript – three months? four months? Is that really so terrible? It is far more terrible that your works are used there, in the West, for the basest of purposes.

[*Approval is expressed by members of the Secretariat.*]

KORNEICHUK: We didn't invite you here to throw stones at you. We summoned you in order to help you out of this trying and ambiguous situation. You were asked questions, but you declined to answer. By our works, we are protecting our government, our Party, our people. You have sarcastically referred here to trips abroad as if they were pleasant strolls. We travel abroad to wage the struggle. We return home from abroad worn out and exhausted, but with the feeling of having done our duty. Don't think that I was offended by the comment concerning travel sketches. I don't write them. I travel on the business of the World Peace Council. We know that you suffered a great deal, but you are not the only one. There were many other comrades in the camps besides you. Some were old communists. From the camps, they went to the front. Our past consists not of acts of lawlessness alone; there were also acts of heroism – but you didn't notice the latter. Your works consist only of accusations. *Feast of the Victors* is malicious, vile, offensive! And this foul thing is disseminated, and the people read it! When were you imprisoned? Not in 1937. In 1937, *we* went through a great deal, but nothing stopped us! Konstantin Alexandrovich was right in saying that you must speak out publicly and strike out against Western propaganda. Do battle against the foes of our nation! Do you realize that thermonuclear weapons exist in the world and that, despite all our peaceful efforts, the United States may employ them? How then can we, Soviet writers, not be soldiers?

SOLZHENITSYN: I have repeatedly declared that it is dishonest to discuss *Feast of the Victors*, and I demand that this argument be excluded from our discussion.

SURKOV: You can't stop everyone from talking.

KOZHEVNIKOV: The long lapse between the receipt of Solzhenitsyn's letter and today's discussion is, in fact, an expression of the *seriousness* with which the Secretariat approaches the letter. If we had discussed it at the time, while the impact was still hot, we would have treated it more severely and less thoughtfully. We ourselves decided to find out just what kind of anti-Soviet manuscripts these were, and we spent a good deal of time reading them. The military service of Solzhenitsyn has been confirmed by relevant documents; yet we are not now discussing the officer but, rather, the writer. Today, for the first time, I have heard Solzhenitsyn renounce the libellous depiction of Soviet reality in *Feast of the Victors*, but I still cannot get over my first impression of this play. For me, this moment of Solzhenitsyn's renunciation of *Feast of the Victors* still does not jibe with my perception of the play. Perhaps this is because in both *The First Circle* and *Cancer Ward* there is a feeling of the same vengeance for past suffering. And, if it is a question of the fate of these works, the author should remember that he is indebted to the journal that discovered him. Some time ago, I was the first to express apprehension concerning *Matryona's Home*. We spent time reading your manuscript, which you did not even venture to give to any editorial board. *Cancer Ward* evokes revulsion from the abundance of naturalism, from the surfeit of all manner of horrors. All the same, its basic orientation is not medical but social . . . And it is apparently from this that the title of the work is derived. In your second letter, you demand the publication of your novel, which still requires further work. Is such a demand worthy of a writer? All of our writers willingly listen to the opinions of the editors and do not hurry them.

SOLZHENITSYN: Despite my explanations and objections, despite the utter senselessness of discussing a work written twenty years ago, in another era, in an incomparably different situation, by a different person – a work, moreover, that was never published or read by anyone and that was stolen from a drawer – some of the speakers have concentrated their attention on this very work. This is much more senseless than, say, at the First Writers' Congress, rebuking Maxim Gorky for 'Untimely Thoughts' or Sergeyev Tsensky for the *osvagovskie* correspondence, which had been published a good fifteen years earlier.* Korneichuk has stated here that 'such a thing has never happened and will not happen in the history of Russian literature'. Precisely!

OZEROV: The letter to the Congress proved to be a politically irresponsible act. First of all, the letter reached our enemies. It contained things that were incorrect. Zamyatin was put in the same heap together with unjustly repressed writers. As regards the publication of *Cancer Ward*, we can make an agreement with *Novy Mir* that the thing may be printed only if the manuscript is corrected and the corrections are discussed. There remains some other very important work to be done. The story is uneven in quality. There are good and bad points in it. Most objectionable is the penchant for sloganeering and caricatures. I would ask that quite a number of things be deleted, things that we simply do not have time to discuss now. The philosophy of moral socialism does not belong merely to the hero. One senses that it is being defended by the author. This cannot be permitted.

SURKOV: I, too, have read *Feast of the Victors*. The mood of it is: 'be damned, the whole lot of you!' The same mood pervades *Cancer Ward* as well. Having suffered so much, you had a right to be angry as a human being, Alexander Isayevich, but, after all, you are also a writer! I have known communists

---

*Gorky's column 'Untimely Thoughts' appeared in the paper *Novaya Zhizn* (Petrograd) in 1917–18. Gorky argued that Lenin's policies might lead to a return to barbarism and oriental despotism. Sergeyev Tsenksy, the author of *The Ordeal of Sevastopol*, also initially expressed misgivings about Lenin's revolution.

who were sent to camps, but this in no measure affected their world view. No, your story approaches fundamental problems not in philosophical terms but in political terms. And then there is [the reference to] that idol in the theatre square, even though the monument to Marx had not yet been erected at that time.

If *Cancer Ward* were to be published, it would be used against us, and it would be more dangerous than Svetlana's memoirs. Yes, of course, it would be well to forestall its publication in the West, but that is difficult. For example, in recent times I have been close to Anna Andreyevna Akhmatova. I know she gave [her poem] 'Requiem' to several people to read. It was passed around for several weeks, and then suddenly it was printed in the West. Of course, our reader is now so developed and so sophisticated that no measly little book is going to alienate him from communism. All the same, the works of Solzhenitsyn are more dangerous to us than those of Pasternak: Pasternak was a man divorced from life, while Solzhenitsyn, with his animated, militant, ideological temperament, is a man of principle. We represent the first revolution in the history of mankind that has changed neither its slogans nor its banners. 'Moral socialism' is a philistine [*burzhuazny*] socialism. It is old and primitive, and [*speaking in the direction of Salynsky*] I don't understand how anyone could fail to understand this, how anyone could find anything in it.

SALYNSKY: I do not defend it in the least.

RYURIKOV: Solzhenitsyn has suffered from those who have slandered him, but he has also suffered from those who have heaped excessive praise on him and have ascribed qualities to him that he does not possess. If Solzhenitsyn is renouncing anything, then he should renounce the title of 'continuer of Russian realism'. The conduct of Marshal Rokossovsky and General Gorbatov is more honest than that of his heroes. The source of this writer's energy lies in bitterness and wrath. As a human being, one can understand this. [*To Solzhenitsyn*] You write that your things are prohibited, but not a single one of your novels has been censored. I marvel that Tvardovsky asks permission from us. I, for example, have never asked the Writers' Union for permission to print or not to print. [*He asks Solzhenitsyn to heed the recommendations of* Novy Mir *and promises page-by-page comments on* Cancer Ward *from 'anyone present'.*]

BARUZDIN: I happen to be one of those who, from the start, has not been captivated by the works of Solzhenitsyn. *Matryona's Home* was already much weaker than the first thing [*One Day*]. And *The First Circle* is much weaker, so pitifully naïve and primitive are the depictions of Stalin, Abakumov, and Poskrebyshev. But *Cancer Ward* is an anti-humanitarian work. The end of the story leads to the conclusion that 'a different road should have been taken'. Did Solzhenitsyn really believe that his letter 'in place of a speech' would be read [from the rostrum of] the Congress? How many letters did the Congress receive?

VORONKOV: About 500.

BARUZDIN: Well! And would it really have been possible to get through them in a hurry? I do not agree with Ryurikov: it is proper that the question of permission be placed before the Secretariat. Our Secretariat should more frequently play a creative role and should willingly advise editors.

ABDUMOMUNOV: It is a very good thing that Solzhenitsyn has found the courage to repudiate *Feast of the Victors*. He will also find the courage to think of ways of carrying out the proposal of Konstantin Alexandrovich [Fedin].* If we publish his *Cancer Ward*, there will be still more commotion and harm than there was from his first letter [to the Congress]. Incidentally, what's the meaning of 'sprinkled tobacco into the

---

*Konstantin Fedin, born 1892 in Saratov, is a well-known Soviet novelist. In the early twenties he was a member of the literary group 'Serapion Brothers'. His better-known works include *Cities and Years* (1924), *Brothers* (1928), *The Rape of Europe* (1933–5), *First Joys* (1945), and *The Bonfire* (1960). In 1959 he was made the First Secretary of the Soviet Writers' Union. He was considered then to be 'middle-of-the-road', but following the general political tightening he acted more and more like a die-hard. He played a decisive role in preventing *Cancer Ward* from appearing in *Novy Mir*.

eyes of the Rhesus monkey – just for the hell of it'? Why the 'just for the hell of it'? This is against our entire style of narration. In the story, there are the Rusanovs and the great martyrs from the camp – but is that all? And where is Soviet society? One shouldn't lay it on so thick and make the story so gloomy. There are many tedious passages, turns, and naturalistic scenes – all these should be eliminated.

ABASHIDZE: I was able to read only 150 pages of *Cancer Ward* and therefore can make no thoroughgoing assessment of it. Yet I didn't get the impression that the novel should not be published. But I repeat, I can't make a thorough assessment. Perhaps the most important things are farther on in the book. All of us, being honest and talented writers, have fought against embellishers even when we were forbidden to do so. But Solzhenitsyn tends to go to the other extreme: parts of his work are of a purely essayist, exposé nature. The artist is like a child, he takes a machine apart to see what is inside. But genuine art begins with putting things together. I have noticed him asking the person sitting next to him the name of each speaker. Why doesn't he know any of us? Because we have never invited him. The proposal of Konstantin Alexandrovich was correct: let Solzhenitsyn himself answer, perhaps first of all for his own sake.

BROVKA: In Belorussia, there are also many people who were imprisoned. For example, Sergei Grakhovsky was also in prison for twenty years. Yet he realized that it was not the people, not the Party, and not Soviet power that was responsible for illegal acts. The people have already seen through Svetlana's notes – that fishwife twaddle – and are laughing at them. But before us stands a generally acknowledged talent, and therein lies the danger of publication. Yes, you feel the pain of your land, even to an extraordinary degree. But you don't feel its joys. *Cancer Ward* is too gloomy and should not be printed. [*Like all preceding and subsequent speakers, he supports Fedin's proposal that Solzhenitsyn himself speak out against the Western slander concerning his letter.*]

YASHEN: The author is not tortured by injustice: he is, rather, poisoned by hatred. People are outraged that there is such a writer in the ranks of the Union of Writers. I would like to propose his expulsion from the Union. He is not the only one who suffered, but the others understand the tragedy of the time better. The hand of a master is discernible in *Cancer Ward*. The author knows the subject better than any physician or professor. As for the siege of Leningrad, he now blames 'still others' besides Hitler. Whom? We don't know. Is it Beria? Or today's outstanding leaders? He should speak out plainly. (*All the same, the speaker supports Tvardovsky's decision to work on the story with the author,* [*remarking that*] *it could then be shown to a limited number of people.*)

KERBABAYEV: I read *Cancer Ward* with a feeling of great dissatisfaction. Everyone is a former prisoner, everything is gloomy, there is not a single word of warmth. It is downright nauseating to read. Vera offers the hero her home and her embraces, but he renounces life. And then there is [the remark] 'twenty-nine weep and one laughs' – how are we to understand this? Does this refer to the Soviet Union? I agree with what my friend Korneichuk said. Why does the author see only the black? Why don't I write about the black? I always strive to write only about joyful things. It is not enough that he has repudiated *Feast of the Victors*. I would consider it courageous if he would renounce *Cancer Ward*. Then I would embrace him like a brother.

SHARIPOV: I wouldn't make any allowances in his case – I'd expel him from the Union. In his play, not only everything Soviet but even Suvorov is presented negatively. I completely agree: let him repudiate *Cancer Ward*. Our republic has reclaimed virgin and disused lands and is proceeding to score one success after another.

NOVICHENKO: The letter with its inadmissible appeal was sent to the Congress over the head of the formal addressee. I approve Tvardovsky's stern words that we should decisively condemn this kind of conduct. I disagree with the principal demands of the letter: it is impossible to let everything be printed. Wouldn't that also mean the publication of *Feast of the Victors*? Concerning *Cancer Ward*, I have complicated feelings. I am no child, my time will come to die, perhaps in an agony like that of Solzhenitsyn's heroes. But then the crucial issue will be: how is your conscience? What are your moral reserves? If the novel had been confined to these things, I would have considered it necessary to publish it. But there was the base interference in our literary life – the caricatured scene with Rusanov's daughter, which is not congruent with our literary traditions. The ideological and political sense of moral socialism is the negation of Marxism-Leninism. All these things are completely unacceptable to us, to our society, and to our people. Even if this novel were put into some kind of shape, it would not be a novel of socialist realism but only an ordinary, competent work.

MARKOV: This has been a valuable discussion. [*The speaker notes that he has just returned from Siberia, where he spoke before a mass audience five times.*] I must say that nowhere did Solzhenitsyn's name create any particular stir. In one place only was a note submitted to me. I ask your forgiveness, but this is exactly the way it was written: 'Just when is this Dolzhenitsyn [sic!] going to stop reviling Soviet literature?* We await a completely clear answer from Solzhenitsyn to the bourgeois slander; we await his statement in the press. He must defend his honour as a Soviet writer.

As for his declaration with regard to *Feast of the Victors*, he took a load off my mind. I view *Cancer Ward* in the same light as Surkov does. After all, the thing does have some worth on some kind of practical plane. But the social and political settings in it are utterly unacceptable to me. Its culprits remain nameless. What with the excellent collaboration that has been established between *Novy Mir* and Alexander Isayevich, this story can be finished, even though it requires very serious work. But, of course, it would be impossible to put it into print today. So what next? [Let me suggest some] constructive advice: That Alexander Isayevich prepare the kind of statement for the press that we talked about. This would be very good just on the eve of the holiday.* Then it

*Markov must be referring here to the fiftieth anniversary of the October Revolution. The authorities were most anxious then to prevent any unseemly publicity.

would be possible to issue some kind of communiqué from the Secretariat. All the same, I still consider him our comrade. But, Alexander Isayevich, it's your fault and no one else's that we find ourselves in this complicated situation. As to the suggestions concerning expulsion from the Union – given the conditions of comradeship that are supposed to prevail, we should not be unduly hasty.

SOLZHENITSYN: I have already spoken out against discussion of *Feast of the Victors* several times today, but I shall have to do so again. In the final analysis, I can rebuke all of you for not being adherents of the theory of development, if you seriously believe that in twenty years' time and in the face of a complete change in all circumstances, a man does not change. But I have heard an even more serious thing here: Korneichuk, Baruzdin and someone else mentioned that 'the people are reading *Feast of the Victors*', as if this play was being disseminated. I shall now speak very slowly; let my every word be taken down accurately. If *Feast of the Victors* is being widely circulated or printed, I solemnly declare that the full responsibility lies with the organization that had the only remaining copy – one not read by anyone – and used it for 'publication' of the play during my lifetime and against my will; it is this organization that is disseminating the play! For a year and a half, I have repeatedly warned that this is very dangerous. I imagine that there is no reading room there, that one is handed the play and takes it home. But at home there are sons and daughters, and desk drawers are not always locked. I had already issued a warning before, and I am issuing it again today!

Now, as to *Cancer Ward*. I am being criticized for the very title [of the story], which is said to deal not with a medical case but with some kind of symbol. I reply that this symbol is indeed harmful, if it can be perceived only by a person who had himself experienced cancer and all the stages of dying. The fact is that the subject is specifically and literally cancer, [a subject] which is avoided in literature, but which those who are stricken with it know only too well from daily experience. This includes your relatives – and, perhaps soon, someone among those present will be confined to a ward for cancer patients, and then he will understand what kind of a 'symbol' it is.

I absolutely do not understand why *Cancer Ward* is accused of being anti-humanitarian. Quite the reverse is true – life conquers death, the past is conquered by the future. By my very nature, were this not the case, I would not have undertaken to write it. But I do not believe that it is the task of literature, with respect to either society or the individual, to conceal the truth or to tone it down. Rather, I believe that it is the task of literature to tell people the real truth as they expect it. Moreover, it is not the task of the writer to defend or criticize one or another mode of distributing the social product or to defend or criticize one or another form of government organization. The task of the writer is to select more universal and eternal questions, [such as] the secrets of the human heart and conscience, the confrontation between life and death, the triumph over spiritual sorrow, the laws in the history of mankind that were born in the depths of time immemorial and that will cease to exist only when the sun ceases to shine.

I am disturbed by the fact that [some] comrades simply did not read certain passages of the story attentively and hence formed the wrong impressions. For example, 'twenty-nine weep and one laughs' was a popular camp saying addressed to the type of person who would try to go to the head of the queue. Kostoglotov comes out with this saying only so that he may be recognized, that's all. And, from this, people draw the conclusion that the phrase is supposed to apply to the entire Soviet Union. Or the case of 'the Rhesus monkey'. She appears twice [in the story], and, from the comparison, it becomes clear that this evil person who spills tobacco in people's eyes is meant to represent Stalin specifically. And why the protest over my 'just for the hell of it'? If 'just for the hell of it' does not apply, does that mean that this was normal or necessary?

Surkov surprised me. At first, I couldn't even understand why he was talking about Marx. Where does Marx come into my story? Alexei Alexandrovich, you are a poet, a man with sensitive artistic taste; yet, in this case, your imagination played a dirty trick on you. You didn't grasp the meaning of this scene. Shubin cites Bacon's ideas and employs his terminology. He says 'idols of the market', and Kostoglotov tries to imagine a marketplace and in the centre a grey idol; Shubin says 'idols of the theatre', and Kostoglotov pictures an idol inside a theatre – but that doesn't work, and so it must be an idol in a theatre square. How could you imagine that this referred to Moscow and to the monument to Marx that had not yet even been built? . . .

Comrade Surkov said that only a few weeks after [Akhmatova's] 'Requiem' had been passed from hand to hand, it was published abroad. Well, *Cancer Ward* (Part I) has been in circulation for more than a year. And this is what concerns me, and this is why I am hurrying the Secretariat.

One more piece of advice was given to me by comrade Ryurikov – to repudiate Russian realism. Placing my hand on my heart, I swear that I shall never do it.

RYURIKOV: I did not say that you should repudiate Russian realism but rather your role as it is interpreted in the West.

SOLZHENITSYN: Now, concerning the suggestion of Konstantin Alexandrovich. Well, of course I do not welcome it. Publicity is precisely what I am relentlessly trying to obtain. We have concealed things long enough – we have had enough of hiding our speeches and our transcipts under seven locks. Now, we had a [previous] discussion of *Cancer Ward*. The prose section decided to send a transcript of the discussion to interested editorial boards. Some likelihood of that! They have hidden it; they barely agreed to give me, the author, a copy. As for today's transcript, Konstantin Alexandrovich, may I hope to receive a copy?

Konstantin Alexandrovich asked: 'What interest would be served should your protests be printed?' In my estimation, this is clear: the interest of Soviet literature. Yet it's strange that Konstantin Alexandrovich says that I should resolve the situation. I am bound hand and foot and my mouth is closed – how am I to resolve the situation? It seems to me that this would be an easier matter for the mighty Union of Writers. My every line is suppressed, while the entire press is in the hands of the Union. Still, I don't understand and don't see why my letter was not read at the Congress. Konstantin Alexandrovich proposes that the fight be waged not against the causes but, rather, against the effects and against the furore in the West surrounding my letter. You wish me to print a refutation – of what, precisely? I can make no statement whatsoever concerning an unprinted letter. And, most important, my letter contains a general part and a personal part. Should I renounce the general part? Well, the fact is that I am still of the same mind as I was then, and I do not renounce a single word. After all, what is the letter about?

VOICES: About censorship.

SOLZHENITSYN: You haven't understood anything if you think it is about censorship. This letter is about the destiny of our great literature, which once conquered and captivated the world but which has now lost its standing. In the West, they say the [Russian] novel is dead, and we gesticulate and deliver speeches saying that it is not dead. But, rather than make speeches, we should publish novels – such novels as would make them blink as if from a brilliant light, and then the 'new novel' would die down and then the 'neo-avant-gardists' would disappear. I have no intention of repudiating the general part of my letter. Should I, then, declare that the eight points in the personal part of my letter are unjust and false? But they are all just. Should I say that some of the points [I protested about] have already been eliminated or corrected? But not one of them has been eliminated or corrected. What, then, can I declare? No, it is you who must clear at least a little path for such a statement: first, publish my letter, issue the Union's communiqué concerning the letter, and indicate which of the eight points are being corrected. Then I will be able to make my statement, willingly. If you wish, you can also publish my statement today concerning *Feast of the Victors*, even though I neither understand the discussion of stolen plays nor the refutation of unprinted letters. On 12 June, here at the Secretariat, I was assured that the communiqué would be printed unconditionally, and yet, today, conditions are posed. What has changed [the situation]?

My book *One Day* is banned. New slanders continue to be directed at me. You can refute them, but I cannot. The only comfort I have is that I will never get a heart attack from this slander because I've been hardened in the Stalinist camps.

FEDIN: No, this is not the proper sequence. You must make the first public statement. Since you have received so many approving comments on your talent and style, you will find the proper form, you can do it. Your idea of our acting first, then you, has no sound basis.

TVARDOVSKY: And will the letter itself be published in this process?

FEDIN: No, the letter should have been published right away. Now that foreign countries have beaten us to it, why should we publish it?

SOLZHENITSYN: Better late than never. So nothing will change regarding my eight points?

FEDIN: We'll see about that later.

SOLZHENITSYN: Well, I have already replied, and I hope that everything has been accurately transcribed.

SURKOV: You should state whether you renounce your role of leader of the political opposition in our country – the role they ascribe to you in the West.

SOLZHENITSYN: Alexei Alexandrovich, it really makes me sick to hear such a thing – and from you of all people: an artist with words and a leader of the political opposition. How does that jibe?

[*Several brief statements follow, demanding that Solzhenitsyn accept what was said by Fedin.*]

VOICES: Well, what do you say?

SOLZHENITSYN: I repeat once again that I am unable to provide such a statement, since the Soviet reader would have no idea what it is all about.

(*Problems of Communism*, July–August 1968)

Letter from Solzhenitsyn to three students

I feel that I have not told you everything, that I have not fully clarified my thoughts. Here then are a few more words.*

Justice has been the common patrimony of humanity throughout the ages. It does not cease to exist for the majority even when it is twisted in some ('exclusive') circles. Obviously it is a concept which is inherent in man, since it cannot be traced to any other source. Justice exists even if there are only a few individuals who recognize it as such. The love of justice seems to me to be a different sentiment from the love of people (or at least the two coincide only partially). And in periods of mass decadence, when the question is posed 'Why bother? What are the sacrifices for?', it is possible to answer with certainty: 'For justice'. There is nothing relative about justice, as there is nothing relative about conscience. Indeed, justice *is* conscience, not a personal conscience but the conscience of the whole of humanity. Those who clearly recognize the voice of their own conscience usually recognize also the voice of justice. I consider that in all questions, social or historical (if we are aware of them, not from hearsay or books, but are touched by them spiritually), justice will always suggest a way to act (or judge) which will not conflict with our conscience.

As our intelligence is usually not sufficient to grasp, to understand, and to foresee the course of history (and, as you say, it has been demonstrated that to 'plan' it is absurd) you will never err if you act in any social situation in accordance with justice (the old way of saying it in Russian is: to live by truth). In this way you will always be able to act and not just be a passive witness.

And please do not tell me that 'everybody understands justice in his own way'. No! They can shout, they can take you by the throat, they can tear your breast, but convictions based on conscience are as infallible as the internal rhythm of the heart

*This letter was sent by Solzhenitsyn to three students who visited him. The rest of the correspondence has not come to light.

(and one knows that in private life it is the voice of conscience which we often try to suppress).

For example, I am sure that the best among the Arabs understand that – according to justice – Israel has a right to exist and to live.

Ryazan, October 1967   (*Survey*, No. 73, Autumn 1969)

Pravda's Editor lashes out

Report of an unpublished speech by the Editor-in-chief of Pravda, M. V. Zimyanin, at the House of the Press in Leningrad, 5 October 1967

Recently there has been a great deal of slander in the Western press using several of our writers whose works have played into the hands of our enemies. The campaign by the Western press in defence of Tarsis ended only when he went to the West, where it became evident that he was not in his right mind.

At the moment, Solzhenitsyn occupies an important place in the propaganda of capitalist governments. He too is a psychologically unbalanced person, a schizophrenic. Formerly he was a prisoner and justly or unjustly was subsequently subjected to repression. Now he takes his revenge against the government through his literary work. The only topic he is able to write about is life in a concentration camp. This topic has become an obsession with him. Solzhenitsyn's works are aimed at the Soviet régime in which he finds only sores and cancerous tumours. He doesn't see anything positive in our society.

I have occasion to read unpublished works in the course of my duties and among them I read Solzhenitsyn's play *The Feast of the Victors*. The play is about repressions against those returning from the front. It is very genuine anti-Soviet literature. In the old days, people were even put into prison for works of this kind. Obviously we cannot publish his works. Solzhenitsyn's demand that we do so cannot be met. If he writes stories which correspond to the interests of our society, then his works will be published. He will not be deprived of his bread and butter. Solzhenitsyn is a teacher of physics; let him teach. He very much likes to make public speeches and often appears before various audiences to read his works. He has been given such opportunities. He considers himself a writer of genius.

(*Survey*, No. 64, July 1967)

Literary bureaucrats inquire

Letter from the Secretary of the Soviet Writers' Union to Solzhenitsyn

On 22 September [1967] the Secretariat of the Soviet Writers' Union discussed your letters. These discussions gave you the opportunity to learn about the attitude of the Soviet literary community towards you and towards your literary activities. At that time no resolution was adopted. It was expected that you would think the discussion over and would draw the appropriate conclusions. The Secretariat would like to know what decision you have reached.

K. VORONKOV

25 November 1967

Reply from Solzhenitsyn

I cannot understand the following points in your letter No. 3142 of 25 November 1967:

1. Does the Secretariat intend to protect me from a three-year-old uninterrupted campaign of slander against me in my country (it would be too kind to call it unfriendly)? (New facts: on 5 October 1967, in the House of the Press in Leningrad, the chief editor of *Pravda*, Zimyanin, repeated in the presence of a large audience the tired lie about my having been a prisoner of war, and he also used the hackneyed method employed against awkward people, that I am schizophrenic, while the lecturers of the MGK, referring to my camp sentence – an obsessive idea –

have put forward new mendacious versions about it, alleging that I was trying to knock together a defeatist or terrorist organization in the army, an oversight on the part of the Military Board of the Supreme Court which is difficult to understand.)

2. What measures were taken by the Secretariat to end the illegal prohibition on the use of my published works in the libraries, and the instructions issued by the censorship that my name must not be mentioned in reviews? (In *Questions of Literature* this has been done even in the translation of a ... Japanese article. In the University of Perm sanctions were applied against a group of students who tried to discuss my published works at a scholarly symposium.)

3. Does the Secretariat want to avert the danger of my book *Cancer Ward* being published abroad, or is it indifferent to this? Are any steps being taken to publish excerpts from this novel in the *Literaturnaya Gazeta*, and the whole novel in *Novy Mir*?

4. Does the Secretariat intend to ask the government to join the International Copyright Convention? This would provide our authors with the means to protect their works from illegal foreign editions and from disgusting commercial rivalries.*

5. During the last six months since I wrote my letter to the [Writers] Congress, has the distribution of the illegal edition of excerpts from my archives been stopped and has this edition been destroyed?

6. What measures have been taken by the Secretariat to get

---

*The Soviet Union is not a signatory to any of the international copyright conventions. As a result Soviet manuscripts are not protected by copyright abroad. This prevents the Soviet censorship from operating abroad in respect of the more unorthodox works which have passed the Soviet censor and been published in the USSR (such as *One Day*). This does not apply of course to the 'Samizdat' manuscripts which are illegal and therefore uncensored. But in both cases Soviet writings reaching Western publishers create a problem of establishing copyright for the texts published and this often results in competitive editions in which only the translations are protected by law. *Cancer Ward* was published in Europe by Mondadori and by Bodley Head, and in the USA by Dial Press and by Farra, Straus and Giroux. All of these firms claimed the copyright for their (competitive) editions. The KGB is of course fully aware of this situation and can use it either to make the publishers nervous by playing them off against each other or to discredit the authors politically. The Solzhenitsyn case seems to be an example of both.

my archives and my novel *The First Circle* returned to me, apart from having given public assurances (by the Secretary Ozerov, for instance) that they have already been returned?

7. Has the Secretariat accepted or rejected the proposal of K. Simonov to publish a collection of my writings?

8. Why have I not yet received the verbatim report of the meeting of the Secretariat on 22 September so that I may study it?

I would be very grateful for clarification on these points.

A. SOLZHENITSYN

1 December 1967

(*Survey*, No. 67, April 1968)

Alexander Tvardovsky to Konstantin Fedin

A letter to the Secretary of the Soviet Writers' Union, Konstantin Fedin, by the editor of Novy Mir, *Alexander Tvardovsky, written after the publication of Solzhenitsyn's novel* Cancer Ward *in* Novy Mir *was suppressed.*

Dear K. A.,

I am writing to you after our discussion at the Secretariat – we have had so many! – on the questions raised by Solzhenitsyn's letter.

This is not an official report to the First Secretary of the Board of the Writers' Union – not that I have any wish in this case to distinguish between the gifted writer Fedin and his official function, but I want to write as simply and informally as though we were talking, as when we talked in the Barvikhin woods, or at your *dacha*, or elsewhere.

To start with the most important: who and what are we really talking about when we touch on the still unresolved 'Solzhenitsyn question' which gives rise to endless prattle – prattle which does nothing but harm to the Secretariat – in literary circles as well as outside them?

Most people will agree that Solzhenitsyn stands out particularly sharply against our literary background, and attracts the warmest sympathy in some quarters and an unusually ruthless hostility in others. Without at the moment going into which is the predominating opinion, I simply want to make this point as proof at least of how unusual a figure he is.

One unusual thing about his career as a writer is that he made his debut as a mature man and a completely mature, independent artist. Writing about the manuscript of *One Day*, K. I. Chukovsky – an experienced old man who, as they say, knows what is what – headed his report 'A Literary Miracle'.

S. Ya. Marshak, whose judgements carried so much weight in the literary world, published an article in *Pravda* about this truthful book, so full of confidence in life. K. M. Simonov, writing in *Izvestia*, welcomed the appearance of this new and remarkable talent on the literary scene.

I will not enumerate the established writers at home and abroad who welcomed this first novel with enthusiasm – I will mention only two names: yours and Sholokhov's.

Your high opinion of the manuscript, submitted by an unknown writer to *Novy Mir*, played its part in shaping his destiny: when the question of its publication came up, I stressed it in writing to the then Secretary of the CPSU's Central Committee (as we know, *One Day* was published with the knowledge and approval of the Central Committee).

M. A. Sholokhov also spoke with warm approval of the novel at the time, and asked me to give the author a hug for him.

Among the younger and more numerous generation of writers who came to literature from the trenches of the Fatherland War, I could mention Baklanov; a sentence of his struck me: 'After the appearance of Solzhenitsyn's novel we clearly cannot go on writing as we have been writing up till now.' Baklanov was not, of course, 'writing off' a whole period in Soviet literature, but he was expressing more than just his own mood.

Solzhenitsyn, incidentally, outstanding as he is, is not unique or unprecedented in our literature. We should not forget the courage of Ovechkin's *Weekdays*, which appeared in *Novy Mir* as early as 1952 and marked a turning point. Nor the freshness and sharpness of Tendryakov's approach to reality in *Unwanted Bride* and *Short Circuit*. Nor Baklanov's new and deeper treatment of the war theme in *An Inch of Soil*. Ehrenburg in his memoirs repeatedly touched, perhaps for the first time, on past events which were supposed to be unmentionable. There are other examples as well. It is not for me to draw attention to it, but it would be false modesty on my part if I were to forget that some chapters of *Distances* and *Tyorkin in the Other World* (never published in their original version) were known long before Solzhenitsyn. But I am dealing now with the immense impression created by Solzhenitsyn's first novel.

True, there were writers who ascribed its huge success merely to its sensational subject – camps – and a leading member of the Writers' Union said: 'In three to four months this wretched story will be forgotten.' But this did not happen. The 'wretched story' was very soon to bring its author an ever-growing popularity at home and abroad and, whether we like it or not, he has become known as one of the most important writers of today: I have grounds for saying this and it will not be denied by those of our colleagues who have travelled more widely and followed the foreign press more closely than I have. Whereas Dyakonov's story, for instance, although it deals with the same subject as Solzhenitsyn's, is indeed forgotten – for all the notice taken of it now by either critics or the public, it might never have been written.

The fact stares us in the face that Solzhenitsyn's story is not just an individual work, remarkably talented but with no significance beyond itself. This is one of those apparently lightweight, unpretentious books which change the climate of literature and have very far-reaching consequences. There have been such cases in our classical literature – I need not remind you. And we should recognize that Solzhenitsyn's example is already having a beneficial influence on our current literature – a fact which should cause us nothing but joy.

I maintain that recent fiction, as important for its ideas and its art as Zalygin's *On the Irtysh* and *Solyonaya Pyad*, and Aitmatov's *Goodbye Gyulsary*, owes much to Solzhenitsyn's prose. They are in no way imitative but they apply, to a different subject and in their own way, that same principle of truthfulness, of facing facts instead of shying away from them – and thus achieve an infinitely higher artistic level than the sort of ephemeral writing which smooths reality over and waters it down to conform with current policy.

I have had occasion to say it before and I repeat it now: the most objective analysis of these works would only bear out my own observations as the publisher of all three writers.

When I speak of the writers' contrasting attitudes to Solzhenitsyn, I have no wish to ascribe the hostility or even malice of some of them to envy, although this is inevitable in any artistic milieu whenever one of its members achieves a great and unexpected success. The point is that, unlike Baklanov, some writers prefer to go on writing in the old way – they are used to it and it is easier. But even these writers must see that readers will no longer read them in the same old way – even those readers who may, in talking about him, be on the side of Solzhenitsyn's hostile critics. To put it in a nutshell, he has greatly complicated our life.

Please do not think that I regard Solzhenitsyn as a perfect and faultless artist who is above criticism. But we can talk about this some other time.

What matters and is very urgent now is to understand that he is not at the centre of attention just as himself – however valuable he is in himself – but because owing to complicated circumstances he stands at the crossroads of two opposite trends in our literature – one backward-looking, the other forward-looking and in keeping with the irreversible movement of history.

This is the position, and the clearest illustration of it is the dragging on for many months of the 'Solzhenitsyn affair', as the subject of the many closed and open meetings of the Secretariat has come to be known.

It has to be faced that the handling of this affair does credit neither to the Board nor to any of those on whom, as one of Chekhov's characters puts it, 'everything will depend'. One trouble – and it underlines the barrenness and frivolity of the whole proceedings – is that attention, disapproval and indignation have been wholly centred on the form of Solzhenitsyn's 'letter' to the delegates to the Writers' Congress, on his way of addressing them. The form is wrong, I agree. But however bad it is, we should not discount the content. For the content is there, the points are clearly and neatly made – and to the best of my memory, no attempt has been made to prove a single one of them false, invented, self-interested, damaging to the cause of Soviet literature, etc. Why? For the simple reason that they are basically undeniable – I, for my part, would put my signature to them with both hands. And you know that I am no exception in this, although I have not so far written or signed any 'document' concerning the 'letter', because I believe that all the questions arising from it should be settled in the normal way by discussion within the Board.

You also know the opinions I have expressed – again and again – here, at the meetings of the Board (they are in the Minutes) and in your presence at the Central Committee – on such subjects as censorship, and that I have spoken of the treatment of Solzhenitsyn perhaps more strongly than Solzhenitsyn himself.

Surely it is clear that to make any decision about the 'letter', taking into account only its form and treating the content as non-existent or negligible, is impossible. Do you not agree, K.A.?

Another trouble has arisen from the forlorn attempt to solve by 'secret' methods a question which has already had wide social and political repercussions, overshadowed the debates – most of them meaningless – at the Writers' Congress, received international publicity and is still a highly controversial subject in literary circles as well as outside them. To resolve what is already referred to as '*the* problem' by the existing methods of the Writers' Union, and in general by trying to charm it out of existence in the privacy of the literary Establishment, is impossible. The only results are recriminations in private and silence in public, so that people cannot help wondering what the leadership of the Writers' Union can be thinking of and what it is capable of saying before a large audience or in the press in order finally to conclude the 'affair'.

It seems that while Solzhenitsyn is ready at any moment to state his grievances against the Writers' Union in public or in the newspapers, the Union, which rejects his demands, can do nothing of the sort – evidently because it cannot count on the sympathy and approval of either readers or writers. Is not that how it is, K.A.? I am afraid it is.

Your own recent attitude to the case is particularly disappointing. You say: let Solzhenitsyn first make a radio or press statement rebuking the West for the anti-Soviet sensation raised over his 'letter'. Otherwise his novel *Cancer Ward* and his short stories (which, incidentally, have been printed and reprinted abroad, and not only in many bourgeois countries but in all the socialist ones as well) will not be published and we will not protect him – member of the Writers' Union though he is – against the slanders widely circulated about his past. In other words, not only shall we do nothing about any of the things he complains of in his letter, but we shall condemn Solzhenitsyn himself to political ostracism – even though not a single point of substance in the letter which is his *cri de coeur* has been denied by anyone. That this suggestion should come from you, K.A., an eminent Russian writer, a friend of Gorky and heir to his tradition of literary leadership, is to me strange and incomprehensible. You cannot, after all, join Sholokhov in his plain stated proposal to 'prevent Solzhenitsyn from touching a pen'. This would be all the more depressing after the well-known utterances by which the author of *Quiet Flows the Don* has so much demeaned himself in the eyes of his readers and admirers. It is sad enough that Fedin and Sholokhov – instead of setting the example of a worthy attitude, free from petty administrative considerations, towards a fellow artist – should on this occasion tend to share that of certain of our colleagues on the Board, whose own attitude is understandable and not surprising.

To start with, your insistent demand that Solzhenitsyn should 'express his attitude to the West', 'give a rebuff', etc., as an absolute condition of surviving as a writer and a citizen, comes strangely from you, because it points in *that* direction, it belongs to practices long since rejected and condemned: 'Confess!', 'Dissociate yourself from!', 'Sign!'. Such 'confessions' and 'rebuffs' as those recently printed in *Literaturnaya Gazeta* over the signature of G. Serebryakova, A. Voznesnensky and others do us enormous harm, because they create the image of writers who are morally undiscriminating, lacking in personal dignity and entirely at the mercy of 'directives' or 'demands' – which, incidentally, are one and the same thing. Do you really think that such confessions serve the interests of the Writers' Union, that they strengthen its authority? I cannot believe it.

While continuing to insist that Solzhenitsyn should 'brand the West', 'dissociate himself from it', etc., we forget his unequivocal statement at the open meeting of the Secretariat:

'Abroad' is being used as though 'abroad' were a highly respected court of appeal. I have never been abroad, I do not know what it is like and have not the time left to find out. I cannot understand how one can be so sensitive to opinion abroad and so insensitive to public opinion in our own country. All my life I have trodden my country's soil, all I hear is her pain, all I write about is that.

Nor can we discount the fact that modern Western trends are no temptation to Solzhenitsyn the artist and that he cannot possibly be accused of trying in any way to earn the good opinion of the West.

But to proceed, I was asked to 'use my influence with Solzhenitsyn', to persuade him to speak out against 'Western' reactions to his 'letter'. To start with, my influence with him is not so great. He is in no sense a 'beginner', a 'young writer' – incidentally, he is fifty this year – and he knows what he is about. Secondly, we should remember that 'Western comments' in this case are of various kinds. The 'rebuke' meant for ill-wishers and enemies of Soviet literature cannot be addressed to our friends abroad, those for instance who have written about Solzhenitsyn's 'letter' in the communist press. What can we insist on Solzhenitsyn doing in the circumstances? That he should 'brand' these commentators like the others?

Recently, however, in keeping with the principle of 'secrecy' adopted in regard to '*the* problem', it has no longer been a question of Solzhenitsyn writing to the newspapers, but of his 'expressing his attitude' to the 'West' in a letter to the Secretariat – a letter of which the West itself will never hear but which will be added to the file in order to satisfy even the most hostile members of the Secretariat, open the way to the publication of his novel and his book of short stories, and protect him against slander.

To think that the solution of this whole complex problem should depend on this one, never-to-be-published 'document'. That we should come to this – that a 'document' of a couple of pages is more important to us, writers, than a completed 600-page novel which, according to most of those who know Solzhenitsyn's manuscripts, would be the pride and ornament of our literature today, that a 'document' is more important than the destiny of a writer whose remarkable talent is not denied even by his bitterest opponents!

Thinking of *Cancer Ward*, I am reminded of a passage in an old but wise book: if a book inspires you, if it fills you with courage and noble aspirations, then judge it by these feelings: it is an excellent book and must have been written by a master.

Indeed it is. I can only add that Solzhenitsyn's sincere conviction that he has cured himself of cancer gives his book the tone of a truly inspiring affirmation of life, even though its subject-matter is so unartistic, dealing as it does with a threat to mankind perhaps second only to nuclear war. Those who like 'reading between the lines' and 'interpreting symbols' have for some reason overlooked the courageous and optimistic symbolism of the end, where the hero leaves the 'cancer ward' on a wonderful spring day and his release into life coincides with changes for the better which were already taking place before the Twentieth Congress.

'My peace of mind is dearer to me than the fate of my books', wrote Solzhenitsyn in his last letter to me. And I believe, K.A. that the publication of this novel would be even more in our interests than in those of the author. The point is not only that it is a crime to keep such an important work from his already wide and devoted public, or that the novel is already circulating, perhaps in thousands of copies, among the more determined of his readers. I know from reliable sources that it will soon be published (if it has not appeared already) in France and Italy. We cannot overlook this – the last thing we want is another Pasternak affair – but there are other reasons, nearer home, as well. The novel, the first eight chapters of which were to appear in the January issue of *Novy Mir* and are in galleys, heads a queue of other important and valuable works which are being held up (although their publication has not been forbidden by anyone): *100 Days* by K. Simonov, A. Bek's *A New Appointment*, E. Drabkina's work on the last years of Lenin, *Winter Journey*, and others I could name.

The publication of *Cancer Ward* would not only be a literary event in itself; it would also remove this bottle-neck – as when a car at the head of a traffic jam moves on. It would certainly benefit Soviet literature in its present, frankly speaking, critical and depressing state, and it would dispel the atmosphere of 'hushing-up', bewilderment, uncertainty, passive waiting.

Everything now depends on you, K.A.: on you alone, because the Board would of course back you up if you were to say, with however many reservations necessary, what was in fact said when *Cancer Ward* was discussed by the Board: that its publication should be left 'to the discretion of *Novy Mir*'. In other words, I beg you to return to the proposal which you have since rejected: that of the communiqué which at your suggestion I drafted and you, at the time, edited and *ipso facto* approved. The draft is in the 'Solzhenitsyn file', I will not quote it in full – this letter is long enough, though I do not seem to have said a tenth of what I could and should.

These were concrete proposals at the time, and I still think that their adoption would do good and serve our interests in every way:

1. Immediately print an extract from *Cancer Ward* in *Literaturnaya Gazeta* with a note saying that it is being 'published in full by *Novy Mir*';

2. Direct *Sovetsky Pisatel* to prepare a collection of Solzhenitsyn's works with a preface giving the facts about his past;

3. Print the preface in *Literaturnaya Gazeta* or *Literaturnaya Rossiya* with an explanatory note.

Your responsibility in this case, Konstantin Alexandrovich, which bodes so ill for the future of our literature, is very great and I do not suppose that you assume it lightly. I cannot see you cheerfully writing the concluding pages of your *Bonfire* while being directly involved in sweeping under the carpet the work of a man who is, after all, your fellow artist, a writer watched with sympathy by great masses of readers and whose importance in our literature today it would be hard to overestimate.

Based on his published works, Solzhenitsyn's popularity grows at an astonishing rate as his unpublished manuscripts come to be fairly widely known. As you know, he cannot be blamed for this. It is difficult to know the size of the manuscript editions of *Cancer Ward* and of *The First Circle* which is not even finished.

It should be borne in mind that in some cases the manuscript of an unpublished book arouses sharper interest than it would if the work were published, and that there is no guarantee against additions being made to the author's text.

Dear K.A., I am not at all so naïvely self-confident as to imagine that my arguments will bring tears to your eyes, change your attitude to the 'Solzhenitsyn case' and bring you to a different decision from the one you have taken. But I have no doubt that you will be brought to this by circumstances, willy-nilly.

'But what can I do?' you once asked me when I said that the demands we were making on Solzhenitsyn were unjust and impossible for him to satisfy. It was at a meeting where we sat side by side – I do not remember what I answered but I do remember your words; you sounded puzzled and displeased with yourself and with all of us.

There is only one thing to do: act according to you own mind and conscience. I can hardly suppose that you are subject to pressure or compulsion from outside. The times are over, thank God, when the 'finger pointed' and specific problems in art and science were decided without reference to what people who knew them inside out, thought or said. Whatever we are like, good or bad, we and no one else have to decide on literary problems. We need not wait for 'direct instructions' – they will not come, which is a good thing we could hardly dream of in times past, and we must take advantage of it, putting aside our fears but not our responsibilities.

It is always hard to tell which is more dangerous: to make a decision which may turn out to be wrong or to decide nothing for fear of a mistake. In military matters, even a wrong decision is thought better than inactivity through indecision. In our case, quite honestly, at the worst it would be better to make a mistake by permitting than to try to avoid a mistake (as though one could!) by forbidding. As things are now, I believe that the real danger for you is to give the sanction of your name either to a shameful decision or to a no less shameful indecision.

Besides, strictly between ourselves, you know as well as I do that there is not a single case in the history of world literature of the persecution of a gifted artist, even by another gifted artist, proving a success.

I have known you as a writer ever since, as a boy, I read your *Transvaal* (by the way, I do not remember your apologizing when, some time in the late twenties, the book was attacked as 'defending the kulaks').

I have known you personally for a good thirty years. I often heard from Marshak and others who knew you in your Leningrad days that 'Fedin is a man of honour, always ready to stand up for a just cause and to help a comrade'.

I had proof of this myself when things were very bad for me in 1954 and you spoke up for me 'at the very top' – your words were quoted to me by people who were present at that memorable meeting.

Yet now I am forced to speak harsh words to you, and perhaps to hurt your feelings, as I have already done at our recent meetings in connection with this 'case'. But you must know that a dog who barks is not a dog who bites. I am plain-spoken and perhaps do not always watch my tongue, often to my own disadvantage.

But I am incapable of striking a calculated blow from undercover. I do not go in for the tricks and intrigues which are known among us as 'diplomacy', and 'tactics'.

If I spoke harshly last time we met, in the presence of Markov and Vorontsov (I had the impression, incidentally, that both would gladly support you if you took up the proposals I repeat in this letter), it was because I could not understand your outburst against Solzhenitsyn.

How can we talk like that about a man and a writer who has paid for every page and every line as we, who judge him, have not? He has been through the greatest trials of the human spirit – war, prison and mortal illness. And now, after his successful debut as a writer, he faces trials perhaps no less hard: pressures which, to put it mildly, have nothing to do with literature: outright slander, the banning of any mention of his name in print, etc. What are we honestly to think of the use, for the purpose of indicting him, of a manuscript play written in the hell of the concentration camp more than twenty years ago by the nameless prisoner Shch. 232 – not by A. Solzhenitsyn, member of the Writers' Union; a play found among his papers, confiscated by 'special' authority and reproduced and circulated as allegedly his latest work!

Yes, I disapprove of the form of his letter, but I cannot as a human being attack him, knowing the degree of despair which brought him to take this step.

Two days ago I was sitting at my desk, reading this letter, when I was interrupted by a call from GOSLITIZDAT: 'In volume five of your collected works you have an article on Marshak in which you mention Solzhenitsyn's name. Our instructions are', etc.

Needless to say, I refused to take out the passage, even if it meant that the volume would not be published. But what on earth is going on!

As I have said, I have not much hope of my letter having any practical result.

I may have put something in it in the wrong way and perhaps not all of it is equally uncontroversial. But it was my duty to my conscience to write it.

I do not count on an answer – I know you are busy. However, this is not the point: it is in the 'case of A. Solzhenitsyn' that an answer, that is to say a decision, is months overdue.

We must put an end to that case, Konstantin Alexandrovich.
With my deepest respects and very best wishes,

Yours,

TVARDOVSKY

7–15 January 1968

(*Survey*, No. 69, October 1968)

Veniamin Kaverin to Konstantin Fedin

We have know each other for forty-eight years, Konstantin. We were friends in our youth and we have the right to judge each other; this is more than a right, it is a duty. Your former friends have often wondered what were the reasons for your conduct during those never to be forgotten events of our literary life, which have steeled some people and transformed others into servile officials, far removed from genuine art.

Who does not remember, for instance, the tragic and obtuse story of Pasternak's novel, which has done such harm to our country? Your role in this affair was such that you were compelled to give the impression that you did not know about the death of a poet who had been your friend, and who had lived next door to you for twenty-three years. Perhaps you could not see from your window the crowd of a thousand people who accompanied him when he was being carried past your house!

How did it happen that you not only did not support, but trampled upon, the *Literary Moscow* almanac which was so vital to our literature? After all, even on the eve of the meeting of 1,500 writers in the House of Film Actors, you were still supporting this publication. At the same time that you had in your pocket the written text of a speech of betrayal, you were praising our work, not finding in it even a shadow of political impropriety.

This is by no means all, but I am not going to make a balance sheet of your social activities in this letter. These are perfectly well known in literary circles. It was not for nothing that your name was received in complete silence on the occasion of Paustovsky's seventy-fifth birthday. I would not be surprised if now, when at your insistence Solzhenitsyn's novel *Cancer Ward*, already set up in print in *Novy Mir*, has been prohibited, your first appearance before an audience of writers were met by cat-calls and stamping.

Of course, your position in literature should to a certain extent have prepared us for this striking occurrence. One would have to go very far into the past in order to find the first step which marked the beginning of your spiritual deformation, of the irreversible change. For years and years this change was taking place deep inside you, but it did not clash in any striking way with your position, which could, at times, be, if not justified, then at least explained by historical causes. But what has pushed you NOW to take this step, as a result of which our literature will suffer heavily again? Do you not understand that the very fact of the publication of *Cancer Ward* would have eased the tension in our literature, would have undermined the unjustified lack of faith in it, and would have opened the road to other books which would have enriched our literature? The outstanding novel of Alexander Bek remains in manuscript; it was permitted at first, then prohibited, although it has been unreservedly acclaimed by the best writers in our country. It is the same with the war diaries of Konstantin Simonov. It would be difficult to find even one serious writer who does not have in his drawer a manuscript which he has conceived and produced, and which has been prohibited for inexplicable reasons, quite beyond the limits of good sense. Behind the façade of the alleged well-being, which is the theme of the declarations inspired by our leadership, grows a strong original literature, the spiritual wealth of our country, which at the moment is so necessary to her. Do you not see that great historical experience requires its [literary] embodiment, and that you are joining those who for reasons of self-interest are trying to stop this inevitable process?

But let us return to the novel of Solzhenitsyn. There is now no single editorial board, no single publishing house, where people do not say that Markov and Voronkov were FOR the publication of the novel and that the print has been broken up only because you have emphatically taken a position AGAINST it. This means that the novel will go on circulating from hand to hand in thousands of typed copies, and will be sold, they say, at high prices. This means that it will be published abroad. We will give away his work to the public of Italy, France, Britain, West Germany, i.e. the very thing against which Solzhenitsyn himself often and emphatically protested will happen.

It is possible that there are some people in the leadership of the Writers' Union who think that they will punish the writer by handing him over to foreign literature. They will punish him by bringing him world fame, which our opponents will use for political purposes. Or perhaps they hope that Solzhenitsyn 'will reform' and will begin to write differently? It is ridiculous to think thus about an artist who represents a rare example of a man who constantly brings home to us that our literary tradition is that of Chekhov and Tolstoy.

But this step also means something else. You are taking a responsibility upon yourself, not apparently realizing all its huge significance. A writer who puts a noose around the neck of another writer will be a figure who will remain in the history of literature quite independently of what he himself has written, but purely as a result of what the other has written. You are becoming, while perhaps not even suspecting it, a target of ill-will, of indignation, and of dissatisfaction in literary circles.

This can only be changed if you find enough strength and courage in yourself to go back on your decision.

You understand no doubt how difficult it was for me to write this letter to you. But I have no right to keep silent.

VENIAMIN KAVERIN

25 January 1968

(Survey, No. 68, July 1968)

Solzhenitsyn to Writers' Union members

To the Members of the Union of Writers of the USSR

Almost a year has passed since I sent my unanswered questions to the Writers' Congress. Since that time, I have written to the Secretariat of the Union of Writers and have been there three times in person. Nothing has changed to this very day: my archives have not been returned, my books are not being published, and my name is interdicted. I have urgently informed the Secretariat of the danger of my works being taken abroad, since they have been extensively circulated from hand to hand for a long time. Not only did the Secretariat not assist in the publication of *Cancer Ward*, which had already been set up in type at *Novy Mir*, but it has stubbornly acted against such publication and even hindered the Moscow prose section from *discussing* the second part of the story.

A year has passed and the inevitable has happened: recently, chapters from *Cancer Ward* were published in the [London] *Times Literary Supplement*. Nor are further printings precluded – perhaps of inaccurate and incompletely edited versions. What has happened compels me to acquaint our literary community with the contents of the attached letters and statements, so that the position and responsibility of the Secretariat of the Union of Writers of the USSR will be clear.

The enclosed transcript of the Secretariat's meeting of 22 September 1967, written by me personally, is of course incomplete, but it is absolutely accurate and will provide sufficient information pending the publication of the entire transcript.

SOLZHENITSYN

16 April 1968

Enclosures:

1. My letter to all (forty-two) secretaries of the Writers' Union dated 12 September 1967.

2. Transcript of the session of the Secretariat, 22 September 1967.

3. Letter from K. Voronkov, 25 February 1967.

4. My letter to the Secretariat, 1 December 1967.

(*Problems of Communism*, July–August 1968)

MANUSCRIPTS ABROAD

Towards the end of 1965 Sinyavsky and Daniel were arrested and their trial in February 1966 was a further step away from Khrushchev's practice of blowing hot and cold on the writers, of alternating between literary thaws and freezes. Now, under Brezhnev and Kosygin there was a more steady operation of censorship. It is not surprising that 'Samizdat' was gaining ground and that it was followed by 'Tamizdat' (publishing abroad of Soviet writings which could not be published openly at home).

But the government which had sentenced Sinyavsky and Daniel for this 'crime', although it was not at all illegal to send manuscripts abroad*, now took steps to close the juridical loophole which the trial had revealed. The Criminal Code was amended, making it easier to prosecute those who composed or circulated materials 'harmful to the Soviet state and social system'. Nonetheless, Solzhenitsyn's manuscripts began to filter to the West and were published there with enormous success. Solzhenitsyn himself never apparently authorized their publication, but they had been circulating in manuscript form in 'Samizdat', and many of them had also been in the possession of the KGB since being confiscated from Solzhenitsyn's friend. Hence, they would and indeed did find their way to the West from both of these sources quite independently of their author's preferences. Solzhenitsyn, fearing that a case was being fabricated against him to prevent the appearance of his works in the Soviet Union, emphatically denied having authorized their publication.

On 18 April 1968, Solzhenitsyn sent a letter to the Writers' Union saying that the editor of Novy Mir, *Alexander Tvardovsky, received a telegram from the Russian-language émigré journal* Grani, *published in Frankfurt, informing him that the Soviet*

---

*cf. *On Trial*, edited by Leopold Labedz and Max Hayward, Collins and Harvill Press, 1967, p. 308.

secret police 'have sent to the West still another copy of Cancer Ward with the aim of obstructing its publication in Novy Mir'. The editors of Grani, being in possession of a copy of Cancer Ward, decided therefore to print this work immediately. In a letter to the Writers' Union, Solzhenitsyn wrote: 'This episode makes one think about the strange and obscure ways through which the manuscripts of Soviet writers can reach the West.'

The aim of the KGB manoeuvres was to play on the inevitable competition between Western publishers, to confuse the issues, and to give the public the impression of squalid wrangles which might reflect on the author and his writings. Victor Louis, the London Evening News Moscow correspondent, whose assignments and accomplishments have frequently been described in the Western press in fact brought one copy to the West.

There have been other examples of such obscure activities which, if not directed against Solzhenitsyn, at least disregarded his wishes and endangered his position. His often-repeated denial that he ever authorized anybody to publish his manuscripts in the West stands in striking contrast to the statements of certain representatives and intermediaries, such as the Bratislava journalist Pavel Licko, who claimed such an authorization, following his visit to Solzhenitsyn in March 1967. In this difficult situation Solzhenitsyn had little chance to defend himself against people who not only disregarded his publicly-announced desires, but some of whom might, wittingly or unwittingly, have been party to the KGB's efforts to prepare the ground for eventual action against Solzhenitsyn.

Solzhenitsyn to writers and newspapers

18 April 1968

To: The Secretariat of the Union of Writers of the USSR
The journal Novy Mir
Literaturnaya Gazeta
Members of the Union of Writers

At the editorial offices of *Novy Mir*, I was shown the [following] telegram:

IMO177. Frankfurt-am-Main. Ch 2 9 16.20. Tvardovsky. *Novy Mir*. This is to inform you that the Committee of State Security, acting through Victor Louis, has sent one more copy of *Cancer Ward* to the West, in order thus to block its publication in *Novy Mir*. Accordingly we have decided to publish this work immediately – *The editors of the journal* Grani

I should like to protest against both the publication [of the work] in *Grani* and the actions of V. Louis, but the turbid and provocative nature of the telegram requires, first of all, the clarification of the following:

1. Whether the telegram was actually sent by the editors of the journal *Grani* or whether it was sent by a fictitious person (this can be established through the international telegraph system; the Moscow telegraph office can wire Frankfurt-am-Main).

2. Who is Victor Louis, what kind of person is he, of what country is he a citizen? Did he really take a copy of *Cancer Ward* out of the Soviet Union, to whom did he give it, and where else are they threatening to publish it? Furthermore, what does the Committee of State Security have to do with this?

If the Secretariat of the Writers' Union is interested in establishing the truth and stopping the threatened publication of *Cancer Ward* in Russian abroad, I believe that it will help to get prompt answers to these questions.

This episode compels us to reflect on the terrible and dark

avenues by which the manuscripts of Soviet writers can reach the West. It constitutes an extreme reminder to us that literature must not be brought to a state in which literary works become a profitable commodity for any scoundrel who happens to have a travel visa. The works of our authors must be printed in their own country and must not become the plunder of foreign publishing houses.

SOLZHENITSYN

(*Problems of Communism*, July–August 1968)

Author denies authorization

1. Solzhenitsyn to L'Unità

(4 June 1968)

I have learned from a news story published in *Le Monde* of 13 April that fragments from my novel *Cancer Ward* are being printed in various Western countries and that the publishers Mondadori (Italy) and The Bodley Head (England) are in litigation for the copyright of this novel. I declare that no foreign publisher has received a manuscript of this novel from me, nor any authorization to publish it. Therefore I do not recognize as legal any publication of this novel, present or future, done without my authorization, and I do not grant that anyone else can hold the copyright. All distortions of the text, which are inevitable considering the number of copies involved and their uncontrolled distribution, are harmful to me; all arbitrary film and theatrical adaptations of the book are disapproved and prohibited by me. I already know from experience that *One Day in the Life of Ivan Denisovich* was spoiled by haste, in all the translations. The same fate evidently awaits *Cancer Ward*. But besides money, there is literature.

In the same letter published three weeks later in Literaturnaya Gazeta *the reference to the unauthorized editions being harmful to Solzhenitsyn was omitted.*

2. *Solzhenitsyn to* Literaturnaga Gazeta

(26 June 1968)

I have learned from a news story published in *Le Monde* on 13 April that parts of my novel *Cancer Ward* are being printed in various Western countries, and that the publishers – Mondadori (Italy) and The Bodley Head (England) – are already fighting over the copyright to this novel since the USSR does not participate in the Universal Copyright Convention – despite the fact that the author is still living!

I would like to state that no foreign publisher has received from me either the manuscript of this novel or permission to publish it. Thus, I do not recognize as legal any publication of this novel without my authorization, in the present or the future, and I do not grant the copyright to anyone. I will prosecute any distortion of the text (which is inevitable in view of the uncontrolled duplication and distribution of the manuscript) as well as any unauthorized adaptation of the work for the cinema or theatre.

I already know from my own experience that all the translations of *One Day in the Life of Ivan Denisovich* were spoiled by haste. Evidently the same fate awaits *Cancer Ward* as well. But besides money, there is literature.

A. SOLZHENITSYN

Announcement by editorial board of *Grani**

Frankfurt-am-Main, 30 April 1968

The editors of the Russian literary journal *Grani*, issued by the Frankfurt publishing-house 'Possev', have for a considerable time already had at their disposal a copy of the manuscript of *Cancer Ward* by A. Solzhenitsyn. The journal has so far refrained from publishing this manuscript, since it seemed that there was still hope of publication of *Cancer Ward* in the Moscow [journal]

* *Grani* [*Facets*] – an émigré Russian literary journal published quarterly in Frankfurt-am-Main, West Germany.

Novy Mir. However, after the speech made by L. Brezhnev at the end of March at [a meeting of] Moscow party activists, it has become clear that the régime does not intend to permit publication of this work in the Soviet Union. At the same time it has become known to the editors of the journal *Grani* that the Soviet state security service (KGB) has embarked upon an act of sabotage and delivered to the West yet another copy of the manuscript of *Cancer Ward* – in exactly the same way as it acted with a copy of a partially amended manuscript of Svetlana Alliluyeva's memoirs.

On 8 April, the editors of *Grani* sent the editorial board of the journal *Novy Mir* the following telegram:

A. Tvardovsky, *Novy Mir*, Moscow, Maly Putnikovsky per. 1/2. Inform you Committee of State Security via Victor Louis has sent West one more copy *Cancer Ward* to block its publication in *Novy Mir* stop We have therefore decided publish this work immediately

Editors, Grani

The most important chapters of *Cancer Ward* will appear in the May issue No. 67 of *Grani*.

Furthermore, the editors of *Grani* know that several well-known West European publishing-houses are in possession of authenitic copies of A. Solzhenitsyn's manuscript, and thus it must be assumed that *Cancer Ward* will appear in foreign language editions also.

'Samizdat' paper on KGB machinations

In April [1968] Solzhenitsyn sent *Novy Mir*, *Literaturnaya Gazeta*, and members of the Writers' Union a further letter in connection with a telegram sent by the editors of *Grani* to *Novi Mir*. The telegram states that the State Security Committee [KGB] sent to the West through Victor Louis a copy of *Cancer Ward* in order to block its publication in the Soviet Union. One of the questions which Solzhenitsyn asks is – who is Victor Louis? The following can be said about him: he is the London

Evening Star's* Own Correspondent and a Soviet citizen. At the end of the 1940s and the beginning of the 1950s Louis was in a political corrective-labour camp and was already well known there as a *provocateur*. In recent years he is said to have been involved in handing over to the West a number of writings not published in the Soviet Union – and in so doing he was acting as a *provocateur*, as when he sold to the West German periodical *Stern* a doctored version of the memoirs of Svetlana Alliluyeva.

(*Chronicle of Current Events*, No. 2, 30 June 1968)

Solzhenitsyn: 'Is he nice?'

It was with some surprise that we received a letter from Mr Victor Louis in Moscow, accompanying a manuscript on Solzhenitsyn, submitted for publication in Survey. *We decided to publish it as a document of our times in the conviction that whatever the intention behind it, the writings of Solzhenitsyn are the best answer to his critics and that his books have already acquired their place in the history of twentieth-century literature.*

The text of the letter is as follows:

Dear Mr Labedz,

Here is the story of my recent visit to Mr Solzhenitsyn. It was too heavy for my own paper, the Evening News, *and I have sent copies to a number of other magazines.*

Perhaps it should be shortened, omitting the second paragraph and the beginning of the third. I don't want to sound anti-Solzhenitsyn. I admire him as a writer but was disappointed to discover that I disliked him as a person.

If you cannot use the story, I should be grateful if you could return it to me.

Yours faithfully,
Victor Louis

What could the point of this charade be?
Mr Victor Louis was the first to report to the West the ousting of Khrushchev and, more recently (in November 1968), he was, as he

*The *Chronicle* is mistaken: Louis in fact writes for the *Evening News*.

said over a drink in Phnompenh, the 'first Soviet citizen in nineteen years' to have visited Generalissimo Chiang Kai-shek's bastion on Formosa, obviously in order to re-establish contacts with the Kuomintang Chinese (Washington Post, 17 February 1969). It was he who reported that Gerald Brooke was to be re-tried (Evening News, 22 April 1969). In between these achievements, unusual even for a Soviet journalist, Mr Louis published various interesting articles in the Western press such as, for instance, 'Svetlana – by her children' (Evening News, 20 July 1967), which attempted to throw an unsympathetic light on Svetlana Alliluyeva in the same way as the article printed here does on Solzhenitsyn.

Solzhenitsyn by Victor Louis

Alexander Solzhenitsyn is probably the most controversial writer Russia has ever known. He said that he would not give any interviews, either to Russian or to foreign journalists, but I took advantage of the fact that my name had been brought into this story and went to talk to him. I found him at his home in the country.

As usual with Russian writers there has been a tendency to compare him with Tolstoy and Dostoyevsky. When I mentioned this to him he modestly replied that such comparisons could only be made after his death. A little less modest however is the way he signs his letters simply with one name – Solzhenitsyn – without preceding it with 'A.I.' or 'Alexander'. This has also been the habit of many great men in the past, and this master of words, with his understanding of nuances, is obviously not doing it by accident. Of course, it is hard for any human being to resist when people around them persuade them that they are geniuses. Perhaps he is.

So far, however, Solzhenitsyn is not a Tolstoy, but he appears to be becoming one gradually, although only in mini form. 'I am a country man, a villager. I live and breathe real air', he exclaims. He looks very well on it, and has started growing a beard but it is nothing compared with Tolstoy's. His estate compares poorly too. He has bought a small wooden dacha, about eighty km.

(forty-eight miles) south-west of Moscow and has made it his summer retreat where he lives with his wife and a few selected friends.

There are two downstairs rooms and his study is in the upstairs room which has a small balcony. The roof is covered with corrugated asbestos, painted pink. There is a built-on garage for his green Moskvich car, trestles for sawing firewood, a wide bench which he made himself and a small wooden toilet. The porch is all covered with Russian vine.

A small stream runs beside the house and a beautiful view opens on to forest and field with, near by, an abandoned church like those he has described so sympathetically in his short stories.

In this country his manuscripts are as tempting as forbidden fruit anywhere. They are copied out again and again in geometrical progression. People who would normally never bother to read a 'medical' novel read night and day when they are lent a manuscript for forty-eight hours, hurrying to finish it in time and pass it on to somebody else. Solzhenitsyn knows this very well.

He knows a lot more too. Like any Soviet citizen who has spent time in a labour camp, he is his own lawyer and knows the value of having an alibi. If he writes letters, he knows that they will eventually find their way into the Western newspapers, but he addresses them to members of the Writers' Union so that someone out of the hundreds of writer-members will send the letter to its destination. From a legal point of view no one can accuse Solzhenitsyn of anything. If, like Tolstoy, he disagrees with the régime, he will not say so openly. He uses his hard-learned knowledge of the law so that no one can blame him. It is hard to accuse him of sending his novels abroad but he is not at all surprised that they get there. 'This is quite natural', he says. 'As long as "Samizdat" ("publish-it-yourself") exists in Russia and as long as the manuscript has commercial value in the West, the leakage will go on without interruption.' He continued on this subject. 'I know of surprising leakages of manuscripts. Yevgenia Ginsburg's, for instance. Somebody sold her manuscript and I am absolutely sure that she never sent it.'

His next step was to protest about the publication of his

manuscripts abroad. This he did with admirable indignation, proclaiming that he would prosecute the publishers. I do not know whether he did it in the sincere belief that as soon as his protest reached the publisher who had bought one of these smuggled manuscripts, he would immediately call a halt to the printing, or whether he did it in naïveté or as a calculated protest; he must know that Pasternak also protested in vain and on the other hand it is the natural desire of any writer to be published.

Anyway Solzhenitsyn could not be accused like Sinyavsky or Daniel of sending his manuscript abroad, at least no one can prove that he did so. He made his public protest and at the same time suggested quite logically that 'works of our authors should be published in their motherland'.

When the Russian émigré *Grani* publishing house, which has already printed his selected works, and claimed a copyright for some of them, learned about Solzhenitsyn's 'protest against publication', they understandably continued their plans to publish and in addition sent a 'provocative cable' saying that Victor Louis had sent another copy of *Cancer Ward* to the West and so they had decided to print it immediately. Solzhenitsyn himself called this cable provocative, and agrees that there would have been no sense in sending another copy. And after all, if I am to be blamed for sending one copy, who was it who sent the others? Why are they not sharing the blame?

When I went to see Solzhenitsyn, he refused to admit that he had accused me of anything, because he had no evidence. 'My letter to the Writers' Union only contained questions based on the cable from *Grani*', he explained. 'I haven't got anything against you personally. Why don't you ask *Grani* about it?'

Solzhenitsyn can probably boast more admirers, friends and enemies than any other writer in the Soviet Union. After my own name was involved in the story of the supposed smuggling of his manuscript, I spoke to a number of people about him. Many are surprised that *Cancer Ward* has not been published. After all, no book which could be labelled anti-Soviet would be accepted by *Novy Mir* and prepared for publication. Some people suggested the fairly logical explanation that Solzhenitsyn became enormously popular after his first and only sizeable novel, *One Day in the Life of Ivan Denisovich*, appeared. The main attraction of this novel was that it told of things which are not easily found in print. There is hardly a single family in Russia which has not lost a relative or a close friend in the war or had one taken off to jail in Stalin's time. Solzhenitsyn's book started an avalanche of hundreds of other manuscripts written by those who had suffered and wished to tell their stories to the public. But most of them were not masterpieces, just sad accounts of facts so well known by word of mouth. The horrors of Beria's concentration camps are, of course, no credit to the state, and everyone would prefer to forget the unforgettable. 'After all', one writer pointed out to me, 'in Western Germany nobody encourages novels about the horrors of Nazi concentration camps, nor in the States about murdering national leaders.' These things too are a national shame and people would like to close up the dark pages of history. So why in the Soviet Union, where printing is in state hands, should this type of literature be stimulated, printed, distributed? Why should magazines put salt on open wounds? But the time Solzhenitsyn spent in camp and in exile shocked him so deeply that he became one-track-minded and can hardly keep off this subject in his work. Probably this is one of the reasons why for the time being his works do not appear in Russian magazines.

Other people have had different comments to make. Some said that because he is a gifted writer, they hope he will give them something of definite literary value, something without a double political meaning. Another writer said that he had the impression that Solzhenitsyn is trying to say that the Russian peasants have been happy only twice after the revolution, first in the time of NEP (Lenin's New Economic Policy, introduced in the 1920s) and then under the German occupation. This is an example of an extreme attitude towards the writer.

The émigré publishing house in Frankfurt does good business, reselling manuscripts to Western publishers, as they did with Yevgenia Ginsburg's book. But apart from the profit they collect, they put the writers in rather an embarrassing position. In Solzhenitsyn's case they advertised his works with such sentences as 'The construction of communist society does not worry Solzhenitsyn. He tells of the life of ordinary Soviet people and his stories, even though published in *Novy Mir* magazine, are as different from Soviet propaganda clichés as Pasternak's *Doctor Zhivago*'. Or again, 'Communists could not be brought up on his stories. Soviet power and the Party are not named in his stories, but they are present there as evil foes of life and humanity'.

Solzhenitsyn, who is a member of the Writers' Union, is put in an awkward position by this sort of publicity, and the émigrés must appreciate this. However, Solzhenitsyn has never himself sent a protest about this sort of thing. When such things are shown to him, he simply refuses to look so as to avoid giving a personal reaction. From a legal point of view, if he refuses to read or listen to statements of that kind, no one can accuse him, either of agreeing with them or of refusing to react to them. He disagrees with the Writers' Union on many counts, but he doesn't want to return his membership card because it gives him considerable advantages and to belong to the Writers' Union is the dream of many writers.

The Writers' Union would not like to expel him because he is a popular author apart from the fact that he was accepted under unusual circumstances, after no more than one of his novels had been published.

Solzhenitsyn is indignant with *Literaturnaya Gazeta* after the paper attacked him last summer. 'Why from 21 April until 26 June did not they publish my protest and my ban to publish *Cancer Ward* in the West?' he frowns. 'The paper took three months preparing a lampoon to answer my letter about the ban. So I announced that I would make no more public statements. I would not write anything at all. I have finished writing. Publicly. That's all. I have learned my lesson.'

The writer believes that if his letter had been published in *Literaturnaya Gazeta* immediately he sent it, the West would not have violated his ban, but the existence of his letter was well known to the publishers concerned, and no one paid any attention to it. 'I am a man who is quite without rights', he complains, 'who cannot answer the two or three hundred calumnies about me.' He goes on, 'I am gagged. I am bound hand and foot and I have been suffering for three years.' Russians love a martyr and Solzhenitsyn relishes the role. 'I am such an unhappy man that I wrote in my letter to the Writers' Congress absolutely openly that I am ready to accept death and indeed I am ready to accept it, even now. Let the first bayonet come and pierce me. I am ready to meet death at any moment. I am already in the earth up to my neck.'

But nobody approaches with a bayonet, and Solzhenitsyn, understanding the vulnerability of his situation, says more realistically, 'Someone of course would like to imprison me'. It seems that no one is planning to imprison him at the present moment, but the chances of *Cancer Ward* or *The First Circle* being freely printed here are almost nil.

Now Solzhenitsyn spends most of his time writing and only ventures out shopping from time to time. 'I am fulfilling my ambition as a writer', he says philosophically, 'and I am not interested in private life.'

(*Survey*, No. 70/71, Winter/Spring 1969)

Communiqué from French Union of Writers

The Union of Writers, founded in Paris in May 1968, which seeks to define the writer's place in a socialist society, has published the following communiqué:

'We have learnt that a West European specialized organization is at the present time offering to publishing-houses the manuscript of a theatrical work by Solzhenitsyn.* However, the work in question is one whose publication the author has always forbidden, and which, circulated against his will, served as grounds for political charges later brought against the author.

It is important that circles interested in the future publication of this work, whether publishers or readers, should be aware that its appearance in the West, on whatever pretext and in present-day circumstances, would be promptly used as an

*The Feast of the Victors.

argument for bringing charges against Alexander Solzhenitsyn, would conflict with both his intentions and with the author's entitlement to copyright, and finally, could only be a new weapon in the hands of those people who are seeking to discredit a Soviet intellectual in the eyes of public opinion in his own country, and perhaps force him to leave it'.

(*Le Monde*, 31 December 1969)

Solzhenitsyn and a Western literary agent

A statement by Dr Fritz Heeb

Having repeatedly and unsuccessfully asked the Soviet Writers' Union to protect his author's rights outside the USSR, and having now been expelled from the Union, Alexander Solzhenitsyn, Russia's greatest living writer, has engaged a Swiss lawyer, Dr Fritz Heeb, to act as his agent. In a letter circulated to a number of publishers last month, Dr Heeb stated that he had been authorized by Mr Solzhenitsyn to act as his attorney. The statement, issued in German and English, and dated Zürich 5 March 1970, reads:

As the authorized attorney of Alexander Solzhenitsyn, I am empowered to state the following:

1. My client has repeatedly tried to have his work published in his own country, so that it could be read by his fellow-countrymen. To this end, but without success, he has repeatedly turned to the Soviet Writers' Union for its support.

2. Alexander Solzhenitsyn has publicly protested against the publication abroad of his works without his authorization. Since neither the Union of Soviet Writers nor Mezhdunarodnaya Kniga (International Book), the organization concerned with publications abroad, have taken any measures to protect his author's rights; and since he has now, as a result of his expulsion from the Union of Writers, lost all prospect of such assistance, he has entrusted his Swiss attorney with the protection of his rights outside the Soviet Union.

3. Alexander Solzhenitsyn has empowered his attorney to: (a) forbid in future, as illegal, any publication without authorization, to take steps against the misuse of his name, if necessary applying to the

courts and proceeding against the authors of any compromising statements; (b) to examine, with the help of competent experts, the quality of translations of the works of Alexander Solzhenitsyn, whether they are newly published or new editions of already published works, and to bring about the necessary improvements; (c) to forbid film, radio and television adaptations.

4. In view of the maliciously circulated false statements, according to which royalties owed to my client have been given to subversive anti-Soviet organizations, I am empowered to state that royalties due to Alexander Solzhenitsyn are being kept intact. After his death, they will be disposed of according to his wishes.

5. All publishers are hereby informed that any publication of my client's work can, in future, take place legally only with contractual authorization by the author, or his legal representative.*

How Mr Solzhenitsyn succeeded in making this arrangement remains something of a mystery, since one would imagine that every move and act would be subject to unceasing scrutiny by disapproving Soviet authorities. Nevertheless, Dr Heeb's credentials have not been questioned. *The Times'* Zürich correspondent wrote on Tuesday: 'There is no reason to doubt the validity of Dr Heeb's statement that he is Mr Solzhenitsyn's "agent" in the west, though a doubter would have no way of checking finally except in the end speaking to the writer himself.' Mr Max Reinhardt of The Bodley Head, who published *Cancer Ward*, says that he is satisfied that Dr Heeb, whom he has met, has been given power of attorney by Mr Solzhenitsyn, and that he is ready to hand into Dr Heeb's hands the accumulated royalties – now amounting to some thousands of pounds – which The Bodley Head are holding for Mr Solzhenitsyn.

(*The Bookseller*, 18 April 1970)

*cf. p. 174.

EXPULSION

During 1969 Solzhenitsyn again failed in his efforts to get into print. Even his short letter thanking those who sent greetings on his fiftieth birthday did not appear in Literaturnaya Gazeta. *After a period of intermittent attacks on him in the Soviet Press, he was expelled in November 1969 from the Soviet Writers' Union, a decision which raised a storm both at home and abroad.*

New attack on Solzhenitsyn
(from *Literaturnaya Gazeta*)

26 June 1968

The Great October Revolution, which opened a new chapter in the history of mankind, also laid the foundation for a new art. Soviet literature, inspired by the ideas of Marxism-Leninism, has truthfully reflected the life of the people and the moral image of the new man, the active builder of communism. In the works produced by Soviet writers, one can trace the whole glorious and difficult path our country has traversed during half a century. Major works of prose, poetry, and drama have been devoted to each stage in our history – the October Revolution and Civil War, the early five-year plans and the socialist transformation of the countryside, the heroic struggle against the fascist invasion, and communist construction in the postwar years.

The strength of Soviet writers lies in wholehearted dedication to the ideas of communism and boundless loyalty to the cause of the Party. This is why the tie between Soviet literature and Communist Party politics evokes such fierce attacks by hostile propaganda. Our foes cannot understand the futility of their efforts to drive a wedge between the Party and Soviet writers.

The ideological centres of the Western world experienced a bitter disappointment last year: The Fourth USSR Writers' Congress, which reviewed major problems of the development of our literature, demonstrated the writers' firm solidarity with the Communist Party of the Soviet Union and its Leninist Central Committee. Representatives of thirty-three world literatures attended the Congress. In answer to the turbid wave of slander abroad, many statements were made that objectively appraised the work of the Congress and noted its businesslike, constructive nature, corresponding to the entire atmosphere of Soviet life.

Some six hundred writers from fifty-five countries visited our land during the [fiftieth] anniversary year, 1967. Upon returning to their own countries, they truthfully described to broad circles of readers how the Soviet people live and work and what a great role the creative work of writers plays in the life of our society.

The world significance of Soviet literature finds expression in the constant expansion of the international ties of the USSR Writers' Union. Regular meetings among heads of the writers' organizations of the socialist countries, close ties among literary periodicals, international gatherings of writers, poets, and translators – all foster creative contact among men of letters and arts throughout the world.

Western propaganda does everything in its power to distort the statements made by Soviet writers at meetings and discussions with their foreign colleagues. The enemies' provocational activities are dealt a fitting rebuff. Our writers display political maturity, lofty humanism, and communist conviction at international forums. Their speeches have won universal recognition for creative spirit, consistent defence of the fundamental principles of the art of socialist realism, and readiness to wage uncompromising struggle against the enemies of peace, democracy, and socialism.

This struggle requires class mobilization, ideological arming, and the ability to recognize the forms and methods to which bourgeois propaganda resorts. It is extremely tempting to our enemies, of course, to try to pit the Soviet people against the Party, to sow dissension among the intelligentsia, to divide it into 'right' and 'left', 'progressives' and 'dogmatists', to oppose some writers to others. They employ any means to present the wish for the reality.

Everything goes into the score. Some ne'er-do-well speculator is lured by nylon rags or is drawn into currency manipulations – and a legend is created of the moral instability of Soviet young people. Some circus acrobat fails to return to his motherland from a foreign tour, and the bells peal forth: he is allegedly seeking 'political asylum' because Marxism deprived him of freedom of acrobatic creativity. Someone sends a letter of inordinate praise to a foreign radio station in enthusiasm for its concert programmes – a perfect excuse to howl about the poverty of musical culture in the Soviet Union. But this is mostly for arithmetical score-keeping purposes and for expanding the 'assortment' of cases in the record of incidents chalked up. See, they say, how dissent against socialist surroundings spreads to every aspect of these surroundings.

Western propaganda gloats most over any incidents that can be connected in one way or another with the names of writers, artists, and composers. Naturally! After all, they enjoy such popularity among the people. This is not just one more mark in the score; it is a jackpot. Here you can expound at length the idea that a 'real' Soviet writer is not obliged to use his art to serve the people who are building communism and believe in it, since, if you please, true art stands outside and even above politics. In saying this, the gentlemen of the Western world experience no embarrassment at ignoring one awkward detail: the fact that they proclaim as ideal models for a writer those who would attack Soviet policy – that is, those who by no means stand outside politics.

Such models are not so easy to find in our country! Well then, one has to engage in cheap tricks, and, like the alchemists of old, raise homunculi – artificial dwarfs – in a flask and proclaim any mediocrity a talent. So the graphomaniac and schizophrenic V. Tarsis was promptly made a writer when he scribbled vast outpourings of untalented but openly anti-Soviet writings spiced with fierce anger and hatred for our social system. After 'escaping' from socialism to capitalism or, more precisely, after being kicked out of the Soviet land, whose bread he had eaten and which he slandered, Tarsis thundered in radio broadcasts and sensational news sheets that he would appear before the world as a new Dostoyevsky.

Although political publisher-merchants abroad managed to make something out of Tarsis's manuscripts, the interest in him was short-lived, and the businessmen did not get the profits they had expected. Tarsis himself lost the hopes of Judas millions. But the 'trainers' of this kind of 'talent' are unwilling to forgo methods that have been compromised. And so they raised another homunculus in the flask: They championed Svetlana Alliluyeva and her 'memoirs'. The outcome was the same – readers turned away disgustedly from her petty book.

Now, new supertalented 'intellectuals' have been 'discovered': Ginzburg, Galanskov, and their ilk. Never mind that none of them ever published a single line in the Soviet press or has the slightest connection with the Writers' Union. All the same, the underground lampooners who had swallowed the bait of the NTS and who linked their destinies to this bandit organization were immediately registered in the books, scores, and records kept by Western propaganda: see how many Soviet writers are actively fighting Soviet policy!

Our entire people and our entire creative intelligentsia regard renegades with scorn. Only individual writers who had failed to examine closely the spiritual make-up of these renegades gave bourgeois propaganda an excuse to list them among the 'supporters' of Ginzburg, Galanskov, and their crew and appeared before public opinion in their own country as politically immature and irresponsible persons.

Unfortunately, letters defending such anti-Sovieteers as Ginzburg and Galanskov bore the signatures of several long-respected writers. And this was just what hostile propaganda desperately needed. It hastened to circulate along with the fabrications of inveterate slanderers and adventurers, documents signed by such 'tender hearts'.

The Secretariat of the board of the USSR Writers' Union and

the secretariat of the Moscow writers' organization severely condemned the political irresponsibility of the writers who signed letters in defence of the anti-Sovieteers. Though very few did so, nevertheless, the writers' organization cannot tolerate such acts, for they represent a fundamental departure from the norms of public life customary among Soviet men of letters.

Writers who cherish their good name and the honour of their homeland, writers deeply convinced that their work cannot be divorced from the interests of the people and the Party and from the ideas of socialist society – when such writers become involuntary targets of hostile propaganda, they deal fitting rebuffs to their unbidden foreign champions. A whole series of examples can be cited. A few years ago, for instance, our ideological foes failed in an attempt to turn an Anatoly Kuznetsov novel against Soviet rule. This novel, *Continuation of a Legend*, recounted the story of a young man who, on finishing school, went to work at a construction project and developed spiritually on the job. Employees of a French publishing house took paste, scissors, and a dishonest editorial pen, changed the title, printed a spider's web of barbed wire on the cover, and tried to give readers the impression that the action of the book took place not at a construction project but in a concentration camp. Kuznetsov issued a press statement publicly slapping the swindlers' cheeks and instituted legal proceedings against them. The upshot of the trial was that even a bourgeois court was obliged to punish the falsifiers.*

In recent times, there have been more frequent instances of gross falsification of statements by Soviet writers. There has also been an increase in the frequency with which Soviet writers' manuscripts, not yet ready for publication, have been obtained in fraudulent ways and published for the purpose of presenting the authors in the role of political oppositionists. Naturally, all this arouses resolute protests from Soviet writers. This was how

*When Anatoly Kuznetsov defected to England in August 1969, he immediately wrote a letter to the French Minister of Justice asking that the sentence pronounced by the French court should be reviewed, as it was based on his false testimony obtained from him under duress.

V. Tendryakov responded on one occasion. *Literaturnaya Gazeta* published a letter from V. Katayev that categorically rejected the attempts of foreign propagandists to ascribe to him unfriendly statements about Soviet literature. G. Serebryakova protested in print against the unlawful publication in the West of a work stolen from her in unfinished form.

Today *Literaturnaya Gazeta* publishes a statement by A. Solzhenitsyn.

It must be said, however, that A. Solzhenitsyn was told many months ago, at a session of the Secretariat of the board of the USSR Writers' Union, that his name had been taken into the arsenal of reactionary Western propaganda and had been widely used for provocational anti-Soviet purposes. A. Solzhenitsyn remained deaf to such a warning at that time and was unwilling to express his attitude towards this unseemly publicity, whose 'hero' he had become.

A. Solzhenitsyn is a man of wide experience who had a higher education in physics and mathematics and has worked as a teacher. Solzhenitsyn spent the last years of the Patriotic War at the front as commander of an anti-aircraft battery and won awards. Shortly before the war ended, he was convicted on a charge of anti-Soviet activity and served his punishment in the camps. In 1957, he was rehabilitated.

A. Solzhenitsyn has not taken part in the public life of the Writers' Union. He preferred to take another path – the path of attacking the fundamental principles that guide Soviet literature and are set forth in the statutes of the USSR Writers' Union, which Solzhenitsyn had indeed pledged to observe on entering the Union.

Several days before the opening of the Fourth Writers' Congress, A. Solzhenitsyn sent the Congress a letter and simultaneously, in violation of generally accepted norms of behaviour, circulated it to at least 250 of the most diverse recipients, apparently reckoning that, now beyond control, it would be further reproduced and passed from hand to hand and would become a literary sensation.

Naturally, Western propagandists easily obtained this letter and promptly raised an anti-Soviet hullabaloo over it, since the letter claimed that our literature is in the grip of oppression and completely ignored all the achievements of Soviet literature that have gained worldwide recognition.

Furthermore, A. Solzhenitsyn demanded that the constitution of the Writers' Union include a special clause providing 'all the guarantees of protection that the Union affords to members who have been slandered and unjustly persecuted'. Such a clause would place the Writers' Union constitution above statewide laws ensuring equal protection to all Soviet citizens against slander and unjust persecution. Western propaganda greeted this demand of Solzhenitsyn exultantly and interpreted it as 'proof' of the complete defencelessness of Soviet writers in the face of the law.

Bourgeois propaganda found greatly to its liking A. Solzhenitsyn's claims that state security agencies had taken files and manuscripts from him. In answer to an inquiry from the Writers' Union, however, the USSR Prosecutor's Office reported that no searches had ever been conducted in A. Solzhenitsyn's apartment in Ryazan and no *manuscripts* or files had been taken from him. *Typewritten copies* of certain of Solzhenitsyn's manuscripts, *without his name*, were found in a search of [the apartment of] a certain Citizen Teush in Moscow and were seized along with other compromising materials; when a customs inspection of a foreign tourist brought to light slanderous manuscript fabrications about Soviet life, the course of the investigation instituted by the appropriate agencies led to Teush.

Among the manuscripts taken from Citizen Teush was, for example, the play *Feast of the Victors*, in which A. Solzhenitsyn presents the Soviet Army that had freed the world from the fascist plague as a horde of blockheads, rapists, marauders, and vandals, interested only in their own skins. He also comments quite sympathetically on the Vlasovites.* The play blasphem-

---

*The Vlasovites were members of the Russian Liberation Army organized by General Vlasov in Germany from among the Soviet prisoners-of-war. It fought on the Nazi side in 1944-5. It eventually turned against its Nazi sponsors in the last days of the war and liberated Prague. General Vlasov who withdrew to the American zone of occupation in Germany, was handed over to the Russians and hanged in Moscow.

ously ridicules the immortal exploits of Zoya Kosmodemianskaya and Alexander Matrosov. The author's sympathies are with a Captain Nerzhin, a 'hero' who helps a woman traitor to the homeland make her way secretly across the front line to the Vlasovites.

In his letter to the Fourth Writers' Congress, A. Solzhenitsyn declared indignantly: 'This play is now being described as my most recent work'. And, at a session of the Secretariat of the board of the USSR Writers' Union on 22 September 1967, which was devoted to a consideration of his letter, he objected to any mention of *Feast of the Victors* on the ground that he had composed this play in his mind in the camp and had set it down on paper only after rehabilitation. In fact, *Feast of the Victors* is not A. Solzhenitsyn's 'most recent work'. But how can we pretend that such a play does not exist if A. Solzhenitsyn, having entrusted the safekeeping of his works to a supplier of anti-Sovietism to the foreign world, thereby lost all control over them and over the play in particular? How can he object to mention of *Feast of the Victors* without protesting publicly against the central fact that his name itself, all of his literary works in general, and the letter to the Fourth Writers' Congress are being exploited by Western propaganda in the ideological struggle against the Soviet Union?

Nevertheless, at the Secretariat meeting, in which well-known Soviet writers took part, the discussion of A. Solzhenitsyn's letter and all his 'complaints' was conducted in a businesslike tone, with sincere concern for the writer's creative destiny.

The participants in the discussion naturally expected A. Solzhenitsyn to heed their advice and express his attitude towards hostile Western propaganda's political provocations connected with his name. But Solzhenitsyn's entire behaviour at the Secretariat meeting bore an emphatically demagogic stamp. Citing 'lack of time', Solzhenitsyn refused to acquaint himself with the statements of the foreign anti-Soviet press that had bestowed praise on his letter. Instead he insisted, in the tone of an ultimatum, on immediate publication of his new novel *Cancer Ward* which, as the Secretariat noted, was in need of substantial ideological revision. He then tried to strike a kind of bargain with the Secretariat regarding the 'concessions' he was prepared to make if the Secretariat would meet his demands.

On 25 November 1967, the Secretariat of the board of the Writers' Union sent A. Solzhenitsyn a letter asking him to state whether he intended, after all, to express his attitude towards the unceasing anti-Soviet publicity surrounding his name. An answer followed, again reproduced in many copies, from which it appeared that Solzhenitsyn intended to continue using 'public opinion' in the West as an instrument of pressure on the Writers' Union.

And A. Solzhenitsyn adhered to his stand at subsequent personal talks with him in the Secretariat.

In April 1968, A. Solzhenitsyn circulated two more communications, again in many copies, expressing feigned alarm over the forthcoming publication of *Cancer Ward* by extremely reactionary Western publishing houses and hypocritically placed moral responsibility for this on the Secretariat of the board of the USSR Writers' Union. This time, incidentally, the recipients of Solzhenitsyn's letter also received a supplement to it – a transcript of the Secretariat meeting, which he had prepared himself and prepared tendentiously and extremely unobjectively, hoping to create an impression of the nature and tone of the discussion that would be favourable to him. This transcript, naturally, was promptly included in the register of anti-Soviet materials circulated by bourgeois propaganda.

Radio centres hostile to us, in building up a provocational ballyhoo over *Cancer Ward*, 'armed themselves with a further document', which they called 'An Open Letter from V. Kaverin'. In giving a perverted interpretation of many events in our literary life in recent years, V. Kaverin distorted the attitude of some Secretariat members towards publication of *Cancer Ward* in the same spirit as characterized the transcript by A. Solzhenitsyn distributed in the West.

There is no need to analyse this letter in detail. Suffice it to say that, although V. Kaverin heard it recited almost every day by foreign 'voices', he did not deem it necessary to speak out against this hostile chorus.

A. Solzhenitsyn wrote his letter this April, when, according to the words of the author himself, the publication of excerpts from *Cancer Ward* in various Western publications had *already begun*. It was clear – to Solzhenitsyn above all – that publication of the letter could not change anything, especially since, in essence, it expressed concern only lest, God forbid, the publishers distort the text of the novel in their haste. But A. Solzhenitsyn failed to protest against the exploitation of his name and his works for anti-Soviet purposes.

One hoped that A. Solzhenitsyn would finally recognize the need to speak out in sharp protest against the actions of foreign publishers, would disavow his unbidden 'guardians', and would declare, for all to hear, his unwillingness to have anything to do with the enemy *provocateurs* of our country. But Solzhenitsyn did not do so.

Nor did he do so after a number of foreign publishing houses, continuing to inflame anti-Soviet passions, recently announced that they were preparing to publish another of A. Solzhenitsyn's works, *The First Circle*, containing malicious slander on our social system. It has become clear once and for all that the role assigned to A. Solzhenitsyn by our ideological foes is entirely satisfactory to him and that he is prepared to voice protests only of the kind printed here today.

The writer A. Solzhenitsyn could devote his literary abilities completely to his homeland and not to its ill-wishers. He could, but he does not want to. Such is the bitter truth. Whether A. Solzhenitsyn wishes to find a way out of this *cul-de-sac* depends primarily on himself.

History has charged Soviet writers with the great and noble responsibility of heralding the advanced ideas of our age, the ideas of communism, and of fighting for the social and spiritual values achieved by the socialist system. This is a responsibility to history, to society, and to their own talents, which flourish only in serving great goals, in serving the people. This is the responsibility of a person who feels he is not a detached observer in today's world, or a grumbling nihilist, but a fighter for communist ideals.

The decisions of the April plenary session of the CPSU Central Committee once again remind every worker on the ideological front that the spearhead of the enemy's main thrust is now aimed precisely against the spiritual values of socialism.

When we cast our mind's eye over all that our literature has accomplished in the years of Soviet rule and think of the new tasks confronting this literature, we perceive clearly that much has been accomplished – much that has been needed by and useful to the people and that the people have received gratefully and appreciated highly. A new, highly ideological and highly artistic literature of socialist realism has been established whose creative potentialities are inexhaustible. We do not delude ourselves that there have been no grievous failures along our literature's complicated, difficult path. But the writers of the land of the Soviets have always remained with the people and the Party, have undergone every trial together with them, and will march with them into new battles for the triumph of communist ideas, for peaceful labour on the entire planet, for genuine freedom for all mankind.

(*Problems of Communism*, July–August 1968)

'Samizdat' defends Solzhenitsyn

Letter from Lydia Chukovskaya*
(excerpts)

The Writer's Responsibility and the Irresponsibility of *Literaturnaya Gazeta*

... I picked up the article ... several times, and put it down again, unable to master its difficult content. It talks of a struggle of ideas, but it was precisely the ideas that I couldn't grasp. It

*Lydia Chukovskaya (adopted daughter of the late Kornei Chukovsky, the distinguished Russian novelist) is herself a writer and editor. She is very active in the Soviet 'civic resistance'. She contributed to the collection *Literaturnaya Moskva* (No. 2, 1956). Her book about Stalin's great purge, *The Deserted House*, did not appear in the Soviet Union but was published abroad in translation. She wrote several important letters of protest against the persecution of writers in the Soviet Union and against the 'rehabilitation of Stalin' (*Survey*, October 1968, p. 107). The present letter is a reply to an article in *Literaturnaya Gazeta* which appears on p. 187.

is not a struggle, but a gliding along well-oiled rails, not ideas but strings of words . . . But I read on to the end; halfway through, it began to talk about Solzhenitsyn. All those empty words were, it seems, leading up to a discussion of his life and work.

The author took it upon himself to give a biography of Solzhenitsyn. But he did so without due regard for accuracy . . . The name of Solzhenitsyn is too precious in our literature for the slightest untruth to be allowed to remain unrefuted. All the more, since in this instance the reader is utterly defenceless: there is no source where he can obtain Solzhenitsyn's books, or information about his life . . . Solzhenitsyn was indeed rehabilitated. What moral or legal right has *Literaturnaya Gazeta* publicly to gossip about a crime he never committed? . . . In 1963, in the preface to *One Day in the Life of Ivan Denisovich* it was stated that 'he was arrested on a trumped-up political denunciation'. Only five years have passed, and poor *Literaturnaya Gazeta* has got lost in the fog and once again does not know where the truth lies . . . Solzhenitsyn realized the truth about Stalin at an early age, before other writers; when he grew older and became a writer, he began exposing Stalinism, and not only in his diaries and letters. That is the reason for his victimization in the past and for the sad details of his literary biography at the present time . . .

In the same article about the ideological struggle and the writer's responsibility, *Literaturnaya Gazeta*, in an utterly irresponsible fashion, and without troubling to adduce any proof, refers to the novel *The First Circle* as 'slanderous'.

Could it be because, amongst other torturers and placed in the same category, there is a portrait of Stalin?

'But surely', the reader will ask, 'it is not forbidden to expose Stalin?'

I have never read any such directive or heard any such order, but by all appearances it does exist. Take the fact that for several years now, editors, with very rare exceptions, have been striking out of every article references to the death of our fellow-countrymen in Stalin's camps and prisons. 'We have been told', as one editor kindly informed me, 'that if it is continually being pointed out, the reader may get the impression that there were too many of THEM.'

THEM – that is, convicts. People who died.

Well, after explanations like that one, how could *The First Circle* be published, the novel by Solzhenitsyn whose main action takes place in a Moscow prison where the technical, engineering and literary intelligentsia from countless Siberian prisons and camps has been gathered together? The reader might indeed get the impression that there were many of THEM, too many! ... In 1964 the journal *Novy Mir* signed a contract with the author [to publish] *The First Circle*. Now, in 1968, *Literaturnaya Gazeta* informs us that the novel is 'a malicious slander on our social system'. What has changed? The novel? No. The system? Again, no. Our past? That is unchangeable. It is the weather that has changed. A new, soundless command has been given: cloak the past in a mist. The reader who did not catch the sound of the command will not understand why neither *Cancer Ward* nor *The First Circle* have been published to this day. Why the author's archive was confiscated two years ago and has still not been returned to him. Why libraries have stopped issuing *One Day* ('There are too many of THEM in it!'). Why year after year, on special instructions, malicious lies are circulated concerning Solzhenitsyn: that he cooperated with the Germans! he was a prisoner-of-war! a criminal, a thief! a schizophrenic!

You see, they have to invent a way of dealing with a writer who still carries on exposing Stalinism AFTER the command has been given to forget about it ...

When I read this extraordinary letter [by Solzhenitsyn] for the first time, it seemed to me that Russian literature itself had looked back at the path trodden by it, pondered over and weighed everything it had had to suffer, counted up its losses and its casualties, prayed to the memory of the persecuted – those who went to their destruction outside the prisons, weighed up the loss suffered by the spiritual wealth of our country through the hounding of writers, and, with the voice of Solzhenitsyn, uttered the words: enough! this must not go on! we will live differently!

Solzhenitsyn did all he could to make the voice of literature heard at the Congress. But despite the fact that dozens of delegates supported him and appealed to the Congress Presidium demanding a discussion of the letter, it was neither read out nor discussed . . .

The only part [of Solzhenitsyn's letter] that *Literaturnaya Gazeta* takes the risk of mentioning, and which it attempts to answer, is the suggestion that a clause on the obligation of the Union to defend unjustly persecuted [members] should be inserted into the Constitution of the Writers' Union.

What – defend? Its members? The Union?

Let us just imagine this suggestion put into practice, and we will be convinced of its fantastic nature.

For example: the signal has been given to hound Pasternak. Comrade Semichastny, a great connoisseur of literature, makes a speech and declares in public, from a platform, that the great poet is a swine. Yes, a swine, just that – I don't remember if it was champing or grunting.

But then – wait for it – instead of covering itself with eternal shame by expelling Pasternak, the Writers' Union stands up for its colleague and in its own paper in a calm and dignified manner, explains to those who did not know just who Pasternak is.

Or take another example: Solzhenitsyn. Let us imagine that, instead of reporting that the archive taken from Solzhenitsyn was not taken in Ryazan but in Moscow, and not from Solzhenitsyn's flat but from the flat of one of his friends (as though this has any significance!), the Union initiates in its paper a fight to secure the return of the archive. The paper reminds the public that a writer's archive is a holy of holies, and no one may dare to lay hands on it, that enough precious archives belonging to writers have perished already in secret cellars, that to circulate, against the author's will, a manuscript stolen from his archive and which he has long since publicly repudiated is a lawless, shameless deed . . . Alas! All this is only in our imagination! In fact the paper became an accessory to the theft, by telling us, in the same article, the content of the play repudiated by its author . . .

I do not deny it – it is a great misfortune, a great humiliation for our people, for all of ourselves to be receiving our own riches from the hands of foreigners. But there is one, and only one, way to avoid this: publish the significant works of Soviet artistic literature and Soviet social thought in our own country. And broadcast them on the networks of 'Mayak' [Beacon] and 'Yunost' [Youth]. Then the reader will obtain his spiritual food, and there will be no sensation, and no longer any need to force writers to renounce [their views] and disassociate themselves . . .

Solzhenitsyn ends his letter with these words:

'I am of course confident that I will fulfil my duty as a writer in all circumstances – from the grave, even more successfully and more irrefutably than in my lifetime. No one can bar the road to truth, and to advance its cause I am prepared to accept even death.'

And *Literaturnaya Gazeta* thought it could teach responsibility to such a man! . . .

Well, isn't it just the limit?

27 June–4 July 1968

2. Letter from V. Turchin to A. Chakovsky
(excerpts)

Literaturnayà Gazeta has published an article entitled 'The ideological struggle – the writer's responsibility'. If we disregard the introductory part, which contains merely well-known generalizations, the whole article is an attempt to discredit the writer A. I. Solzhenitsyn. The content and tone of this article arouse my deep indignation. Since the article appeared without a signature, it must be interpreted as an editorial, and I am addressing you as its author.

Your aim in this article is to smear A. I. Solzhenitsyn and represent him to your readers as a dishonourable man, [and one] hostile to his people; furthermore, you seek to do this not by indicating any real facts (and I am convinced that there are no such facts), but by unfounded, entirely unsupported accusations, literary abuse, falsification and slander . . . What right have you to speak thus of a soldier who defended his fatherland from the fascists, of a citizen who suffered unjustly from Stalin's tyranny, of a writer whose every line bears witness to his sincerity and his love for human beings?

You call *Cancer Ward* an ideologically immature work, and *The First Circle* malicious slander on our social system. I have read both these works, and I find them both truthful and profound; like those of Solzhenitsyn's stories which were published in our press, they represent a great contribution to Russian literature. Solzhenitsyn astounds the Soviet reader by the courage with which he writes the truth – as he sees and understands it. Of course, you may disagree with his vision and interpretation of truth; unlike you, I recognize every man's right to do so . . . But . . . you are afraid of truth, truth as such, in any interpretation: Solzhenitsyn's, mine, or yours . . . Yes, you are afraid even of your own interpretation of truth! You have grown so accustomed to masquerading that you regard writing what you think as nothing short of indecent; it is like finding yourself naked in the company of smartly dressed gentlemen. And that is precisely the content which is usually concealed behind the mask of an 'ideologically immature work'.

Next, on the subject of slander. Of course, I am not denying your right publicly to accuse anyone you like of slander, and a little further on [in my letter] I myself take advantage of this right. But let us remember what it is that we call slander . . . You refer to *The First Circle* as malicious slander on our social system; in other words, you assert that Solzhenitsyn did not write this work for the purpose of sharing with his fellow-countrymen what he went through and what he meditated upon during his imprisonment, but that he deliberately concocted a string of fairy-tales, prompted solely by a desire to discredit our system. I declare that I do not believe you. I do not believe that you think thus. A man who has read *The First Circle* cannot think like that . . . It is impossible to believe that Solzhenitsyn is a slanderer, and it is impossible to believe that this is your opinion of him. But hence it follows that you are disseminating a falsehood in which you yourself do not believe, and this is nothing other than slander.

Your account of the letters Solzhenitsyn wrote in connection with the refusal to print *Cancer Ward* and other matters is, putting it mildly, tendentious. As for the play *Feast of the Victors* ... until such time as a writer publishes his work or circulates it in any other way, it remains a document in his personal archive, and you have no facts to indicate that Solzhenitsyn circulated this play. On the contrary, he sent round a letter stressing the personal nature of this document and objecting to its being circulated. Had it not been for the interference of state organs, no one would have known about the play. So that, if he did 'lose control' over it, as you put it, that was certainly through no fault of his ...

Solzhenitsyn wrote a letter to *Literaturnaya Gazeta* stating that he had not passed the manuscript [of *Cancer Ward*] to publishers abroad, and therefore he was declaring all foreign editions of it illegal, and would prosecute [those responsible for] any distortion of the text, and also for any screen or stage version ... You ought to have published that declaration at the time when you received it, that is, two months ago. Why did you not do so?

I can see only one explanation: Solzhenitsyn's declaration, published alone, would have met with the sympathy of public opinion in our country, and it would have been clear to everyone that the responsibility for the fact that the first publication of *Cancer Ward* was taking place abroad and not in the author's own country, and also for the possible exploitation of this fact for anti-Soviet purposes, lay not with the author but with those who had prevented publication of the story [in the Soviet Union]. This did not suit you, and you decided to publish Solzhenitsyn's declaration only after you had spent two months concocting an offensive article with the aim of smearing Solzhenitsyn by means of abuse and falsification ...

I should like to dwell separately on the few phrases in which you touch upon Solzhenitsyn's biography, since the significance of these phrases goes beyond the bounds of the article's theme. You write: 'Shortly before the end of the war, he was convicted on a charge of anti-Soviet activity and SERVED HIS PUNISHMENT in a camp. In 1957 he was rehabilitated' ... Not 'was imprisoned' but 'served his punishment'. Do you not know that the concept of 'punishment' presupposes the concept of 'crime'? ... After the words 'was convicted and served his punishment', the words 'was rehabilitated' can be interpreted simply as 'was released', either in an amnesty or on completion of his term. Behind these lines I have a vision of one of the most repulsive types in Russian history – the obtuse, self-satisfied bourgeois, whose reasoning in 1968 would be roughly as follows: 'Yes, rehabilitated; well, so what? They got him, so there must have been a reason. But they didn't get me, not me. The Master just didn't put me in, just like that! Of course, times have changed, they HAD TO REHABILITATE HIM ... But all the same, he's an anti-Soviet, that's what he is ...' Yes, that is what is behind those lines, and don't try to say you don't feel it! Like any Soviet editor, you are a real specialist in double-text and context, you finger and sniff at every phrase thirty times over before passing it for publication ...

For some time now I have had contacts with *Literaturnaya Gazeta*, and my name has even appeared on its pages. Now I am ashamed of this. I hereby declare that as long as you remain chief editor of *Literaturnaya Gazeta* I refuse to engage in any form of cooperation with it, I refuse to subscribe to it or to buy it. I believe that, for any man who shares my attitude to the article on Solzhenitsyn, that is the only possible reaction to it.

V. F. TURCHIN

28 June 1968

Solzhenitsyn expresses gratitude for congratulations

To the editorial board of *Literaturnaya Gazeta*
Copy to the journal *Novy Mir*

I know that your paper will not publish a single line of mine without attributing to it a distorted, erroneous meaning. But there is no way I can answer the many people who have sent me their greetings except through your paper:

'I thank with emotion the readers and writers who sent their greetings and best wishes on my fiftieth birthday. I promise them never to betray the truth. My sole dream is to prove myself worthy of the hopes of the Russian reading public.'

Ryazan, 12 December 1968   SOLZHENITSYN
                                        (*Russkaya Mysl*, 22 May 1969)

Meeting of Ryazan writers

Meeting of the Ryazan writers' organization, held on 4 November 1969, from 3.00 until 4.30 p.m.

Six of the seven members of the Ryazan writers' organization were present (Ernst Safonov, secretary of the Ryazan Section, was awaiting an operation); F. N. Taurin, secretary of the RSFSR Union of Writers; Alexander Sergeyevich Kozhevnikov, secretary for campaigning and propaganda of the Ryazan regional committee of the CPSU; Povarenko, publications editor, and three other comrades from regional organizations.

The present record was made during the meeting by Solzhenitsyn.

The agenda contained one (officially) announced item: a report by Taurin, secretary of the RSFSR Writers' Union, on the decision of the Secretariat of the RSFSR Writers' Union 'Measures for intensifying ideological-educational work among writers'.

The report itself didn't take up much time. F. Taurin read out the decision of the RSFSR Writers' Union Secretariat, occasioned by the defection abroad of A. Kuznetsov, pointing out new measures to be taken for the ideological education of writers. He announced that similar meetings had already been held in several regional writers' organizations and had proceeded on a high level, more especially in the Moscow writers' organization where charges had been laid against Lydia Chukovskaya, Lev Kopelev, Bulat Okudzhava and also against a member of the Ryazan organization of the WU – Solzhenitsyn.

Discussion (time limit – ten minutes per speaker)

VASILY MATUSHKIN [*member of* WU *Ryazan – after a few general remarks about the condition of the Ryazan organization*]: I cannot refrain from referring to the attitude of comrade Solzhenitsyn to literature and to our writers' organization. This is where my responsibility too comes in: I at one time recommended him for admission to the Union of Writers. Accordingly, in criticizing him today, I am criticizing myself too. When *One Day* came out, not everything in it was immediately understood; much of it was distasteful. But, after the reviews by Simonov and Tvardovsky, we felt unable to disagree. We did, after all, cherish hopes that Solzhenitsyn would become an ornament to our organization. These hopes have not been realized. Take his attitude to our writers' organization. In all these years – no participation. He did, it is true, attend re-election meetings but did not speak. On one of the most important of our statutory duties – helping young writers – he has given no help and has taken no part in discussing the productions of budding writers. He did no *work* whatsoever. Regretfully, the view emerges that he behaves disdainfully towards our writers' organization and to our modest achievements in literature. I will honestly and frankly say that all of his recent writing (true, we have no knowledge of it, we haven't read it, we haven't been invited to discuss it) runs contrary to what we others are writing. We have a motherland and nothing else is dearer to us. Solzhenitsyn's work, though, is published abroad and then it all spills over on to our country. When our motherland is besmirched through his writings and Alexander Isayevich was told how to reply and an article was even printed in *Literaturnaya Gazeta*, he failed to react – he felt he knew better.

S. BARANOV [*Chairman*]: Your ten-minute time limit is up.

MATUSHKIN: Please, may I continue?

SOLZHENITSYN: Let the comrade have as much time as he likes. [*Extension allowed*]

MATUSHKIN: The Union of Writers is an entirely voluntary

organization. There are people who get published but are not in the Union. The Union's statutes say quite clearly: the Union brings together persons who share the same views – who build up communism, give it all their creative work, follow the path of socialist realism. Accordingly, there is no room for Solzhenitsyn in a writers' organization; let him work on his own. Bitter though it is, I am bound to say: A.I., our paths differ from yours and we will have to part company.

NIKOLAI RODIN [WU *member from Kasimov, hurriedly brought to the meeting, though ill, in order to form a quorum*]: After what Vasily Semyonovich has said, there is nothing to add. If we look at the statutes of the Union and compare with them the civic activities of Alexander Isayevich, we will find great discrepancies. After Vasily Semyonovich's speech I have nothing to add. He has not complied with the statutes, he has ignored our Union. There have been times when we had no one to whom to pass the manuscript of a budding writer for review and Solzhenitsyn didn't produce a review. I have serious complaints against him.

SERGEI KH. BARANOV [WU *member, Ryazan*]: This is an extremely serious problem and it is high time for it to be raised by the administration of the Writers' Union. In the Union we should be well acquainted with each other's minds and help one another. But what will happen if we scatter all over the place – who is going to educate the younger people? Who will take charge of the literary clubs of which we have many in industry and in educational institutions? Vasily Semyonovich was right in raising the question of Alexander Isayevich. We have no knowledge of his work, of his writings. At the outset there was a great fuss made about his writings. Personally I have always discerned in *One Day* black spots all through the book. Or take *Matryona's Home* – wherever did he find such a lonely woman with spiders and a cat and nobody around to help (her)? Where could one find such a Matryona? I was still hoping that Alexander Isayevich would write things the people needed. And where does he print his writings and what are they about? We have no idea. One must revise one's personal image and mutual regard. Solzhenitsyn has broken away from the organization and we must obviously drop him.

[SOLZHENITSYN *asks to be allowed to put one general query to the comrades taking the floor – the Chairman refuses.*]

EVGENY MARKIN [*Member of* WU, *Ryazan*]: It is especially difficult for me to speak, more so than for everybody else. To be absolutely frank, we are discussing the question of Alexander Isayevich remaining in our organization. I wasn't yet a member of the Union when you admitted him. I am feeling depressed and the reason why is the unprecedented swing of the pendulum from one level to another. I was working on the staff of *Literature and Life* when unprecedented tributes were being paid to Solzhenitsyn. Since then there has been a swing in the opposite direction: never have I heard such harsh views expressed about anyone as about Solzhenitsyn. Such extreme differences of views make themselves felt later on on men's consciences when they make decisions. Let us remember how Yesenin was reviled and then they began to praise him to the skies and now we have the odd [critic] here or there who would again like to sink him. Let us recall the harsh judgements uttered after 1946. I find it harder now than anyone else to make head or tail of it all. If Solzhenitsyn is expelled now and later admitted, expelled again and again admitted – I don't want to have anything to do with it. Where will a second 'hook' then be found by those who have 'boycotted' the discussion today? Our organization has serious defects: members of the Union aren't given housing. For two years our Ryazan writers' organization was bossed by the rascally Ivan Abramov who wasn't even a member of the Union; he pinned political labels on us. I attended the Literary Institute along with Anatoly Kuznetsov; intuition doesn't deceive one; we disliked him for his bigotry. As I see it, the articles of our Union Statutes can be interpreted in two ways; it's a stick with two ends. Of course, one would like to ask Alexander Isayevich why he took no part in social life. Why, in view of the hubbub that the foreign press created about his name, did he say nothing in our press, why didn't he tell us about it? Why did Alexander Isayevich not try to explain properly and

make his position known to the public at large. I have not
read his new works. My view on the question of A.I. being in
the Writers' Union is that he was not a member of the
Ryazan writers' organization. I fully agree with the majority
of the writers' organization.

NIKOLAI LEVCHENKO [*Member of* WU, *Ryazan*]: Basically the
problem has been clarified by the comrades who spoke
earlier. I would like to put myself in the place of Alexander
Isayevich and say how I would have behaved. If all I have
produced were put on exhibition abroad, what would I have
done? I would have gone along and taken counsel with my
comrades. He has isolated himself of his own accord. I side
with the majority.

POVARENKIN: Over a number of years Alexander Isayevich
has lost touch with the Writers' Union. He didn't come along
to re-election meetings but sent telegrams: 'I side with the
majority' – is that really taking a stand on principle? Gorky
used to say that the Writers' Union was a collective body, i.e.
a social (community) organization. Alexander Isayevich
evidently joined the Union for other purposes – to have a
writer's ticket. The ideological qualities of his writings don't
help us in building a communist society. He casts slurs on our
glowing future. He himself has a black inside. Only one who
is ideologically hostile to us could depict such an uninspiring
character as Ivan Denisovich. He has put himself of his own
accord outside the writers' organization.

[SOLZHENITSYN *again asks to be allowed to put a question.
Instead, he is told he can only make his statement. After a number
of misgivings has been voiced the question is allowed.*

SOLZHENITSYN *asks the* WU *members who have reproached
him with refusing to review manuscripts or with coming along to
talk to young writers to give specific details of even one such case.*

No response from previous speakers.]

MATUSHKIN: A member of the Writers' Union should work
actively in accordance with the Statutes and not wait to be
invited.

SOLZHENITSYN: I regret that no shorthand minute is being
made of our meeting and that not even exact notes are being

taken. Yet it may be a matter of interest not merely tomorrow but even later than in a week's time. Incidentally, there were three shorthand reporters working in the Secretariat of the CPSU WU, but the Secretariat, after declaring that my notes were tendentious, was either just unable or didn't decide to submit the shorthand record of that meeting.

First of all, I want to remove a weight from comrade Matushkin's mind. Let me remind you, Vasily Semyonovich, that you never gave me any recommendation; as the then WU secretary, you brought me merely blank questionnaire forms. At that time of excessive eulogization the RSFSR Secretariat was in such a hurry to admit me that it didn't wait to collect recommendations or to have me admitted to the initial Ryazan organization but admitted me on its own and sent me a congratulatory telegram.

The charges which have been preferred against me here can be divided into two completely different groups. The first concerns the Ryazan organization of the WU; the second concerns the whole of my literary future. In the case of the first group I would say that there is not a single well-founded charge. For instance, our secretary Safonov is not present. Yet I gave him notice *on the very same day* of every public action taken by me, of every letter I wrote to the Congress or the Secretariat, and I always asked him to acquaint all the members of the Ryazan WU with those materials and also our younger writers. Didn't he show them to you? Didn't he want to? Or was the reason that he was forbidden to do so by comrade Kozhevnikov here present? Not only did I not avoid creative contacts with the Ryazan WU but I requested Safonov and insisted that my *Cancer Ward*, which had been discussed in the Moscow writers' organization, should without fail be discussed in the Ryazan organization also. I have copies of letters to that effect. Yet *Cancer Ward* too was for some reason or other completely kept secret from the members of the Ryazan WU. Similarly, I always voiced my willingness to make an appearance or speak in public but I was never allowed to do so, apparently because it was feared that something might happen. As regards my alleged 'high and mighty' attitude, that is ridiculous; none of you will recall any such occasion, any such phrase used or demeanour; on the contrary, I felt myself on extremely frank and comradely terms with all of you. The fact that I did not always put in an attendance at re-elections – that is true, but the reason is that for most of the time I don't live in Ryazan, I live near Moscow, outside the city. When *One Day* had just been printed, I was strongly urged to move to Moscow but I was afraid I would lose my concentration there and I said no. When, several years later, I asked for permission to move, I was refused. I applied to the Moscow organization and asked them to put me on their list; its secretary, V. N. Ilin, replied that it was impossible, that I should remain a member of the organization where I had my passport registration and it wasn't important where I in actual fact resided. For that reason it was difficult for me sometimes to come over for the re-elections.

As regards the accusations of a general character, I still fail to understand what kind of 'reply' people expect me to make – *what* must I 'reply' to? To the notorious article in *Literaturnaya Gazeta* where I was contrasted with Anatoly Kuznetsov and it was said that I must give a reply to the West, as if it were from him and not from me? I have nothing to say in reply to that anonymous article. It casts doubt on the legitimacy of my rehabilitation by using the sly and evasive reference to 'served his sentence' – served the sentence and everything, do you see, that he served for the affair. The article uttered a falsehood about my novels, alleging that *The First Circle* constitutes a 'malicious slander on our social system' – but who proved, demonstrated or spelled out that allegation? Nobody knows the novels and you can say anything you like about them. And there are also many minor distortions in the article; the whole sense of my letter to the Congress has been perverted. Finally, once again the *Feast of the Victors* business, so repugnant to all and sundry, is regurgitated – one might, incidentally, very well ask oneself the question: *from what source* does the editor of *Literaturnaya Gazeta* obtain his information about this work, how did he get hold of it for perusal if the *one and only* copy of it was abstracted from a writing-desk by the KGB?

Generally, what happens with my writings is that, if I myself disown some work or other or don't want it to exist, as for instance, *Feast of the Victors*, then efforts are made to talk about and 'interpret' it as widely as possible. If, however, I press for my writings to be published, as, for instance, *Cancer Ward* or *Circle*, they are hidden away and nothing said about them.

Have I got to 'reply' to the Secretariat? But I have given them a reply already to all the questions put to me and yet the Secretariat has not replied to a single one of mine. I have received no reply in substance to my letter to the Secretariat in the whole of its general and personal content. It was regarded as of little significance alongside the other business of the Congress and was swept under the carpet, and I am beginning to think that they deliberately held their hand until it had been widely circulated for two weeks – and, when it was printed in the West, they took that as a convenient excuse for not publishing it in our country.

Exactly the same procedure was adopted also in respect of *Cancer Ward*. As far back as September 1967 I insistently warned the Secretariat of the danger that the book would be appearing in the West because it was enjoying such a wide circulation here. I hastened to give them permission to print it in *Novy Mir* but the Secretariat – waited. When, in the spring of 1968, signs began to appear that at any moment now it would be printed in the West, I sent letters: to *Literaturnaya Gazeta*, *Le Monde* and to *Unità*, in which I forbade the printing of *Cancer Ward* and withdrew all rights from Western publishers. And what do you think? The letter to *Le Monde*, sent by registered post, was not allowed out. The letter to *L'Unità*, sent with the well-known communist publicist, Vittorio Strada, was taken from him by the customs – and I found myself having to make a fervent appeal to convince the customs officials that, in the interests of our literature, it was essential that the letter should appear in *Unità*. Several days after this conversation, early in July, it

did after all appear in *Unità – Literaturnaya Gazeta* still went
on waiting. *What* was it waiting for? Why did it keep my
letter secret for a period of *nine* weeks from April to 26 June? It
was waiting for *Cancer Ward* to appear in the West. And,
when it was issued in the awful Russian Mondadori edition,
then – *then* – *Litgazeta* printed my protest, in the middle of its
own verbose anonymous article in which I was accused of
not having protested *sufficiently energetically or sharply
enough* against *Cancer Ward* being printed. Yet, why did
Litgazeta hold up the protest for nine weeks? The calculation
is obvious: Let *Cancer Ward* appear in the West, then it will be
possible to damn it and not let it get to the Soviet reader. Yet,
had it been printed at the right time, my protest could have
stopped the publication of *Cancer Ward* in the West – for
instance, two American publishers, Dutton and Praeger, as
soon as mere *rumours* reached them that I was protesting
against *Cancer Ward* being printed, dropped, in May 1968,
their plan to print the book. What would have happened if
Litgazeta had printed my protest at the time?

CHAIRMAN BARANOV: Your time is up – ten minutes.

SOLZHENITSYN: How can you insist on a time limit in this
case? It's a matter of life and death.

BARANOV: But we can't allow you more – there's a time limit.

[SOLZHENITSYN *insists on his plea. Various members intervene.*]

BARANOV: How much longer do you want?

SOLZHENITSYN: I have a lot I need to say. Give me another
ten minutes at least.

MATUSHKIN: Let him have three minutes.

[*After consultations ten minutes more are granted.*]

SOLZHENITSYN [*speeding up still further his already fast delivery*]:
I made an application to the Ministry of Communications asking them to put an end to the postal theft of my correspondence – non-delivery or hold-up of letters, telegrams, packets,
especially those from abroad, as for instance, when I was
replying to congratulations on my fiftieth birthday. But what
is one to do if the Soviet WU Secretariat itself is abetting this
banditry in the mails? After all, the Secretariat didn't pass
on to me a single letter or telegram from the heap it received

addressed to me for my fiftieth birthday. It still continues to keep mum.

The whole of my correspondence is closely inspected and, as if that weren't enough, the results of this illegal postal censorship are utilized cynically and brazenly. For example, the secretary of the Frunze district committee of the Moscow CP summoned the director of the Russian Language institute of the Academy of Sciences and banned a transcript of a tape-recording of my voice in that Institute – he had heard about it you see, from a postal censorship extract supplied to him.

To come now to the accusation of so-called 'vilification of reality'. Tell me: when and where and in what theory of cognition is the *expression* of a thing regarded as more important than the thing itself? Possibly in everyday systems of philosophy, but surely not in materialistic dialectics. It works out this way: what we do is not important; what is important is what people will say about it and that they should not say anything bad – we'll keep our mouths shut about all that goes on. But that isn't a solution. The time when one has to be ashamed about the nasty things that are being done is not when they are being talked about but when they are being *committed*. The poet Nekrasov said:

> The man who lives without feeling grief and anger
> Is no lover of his native country.

And, to take the other side of the coin, the man who is always rosily enraptured is also indifferent to his native land.

There has been talk here about the pendulum. Yes, there has certainly been an enormous swing of the pendulum and not in my case alone but in the whole of our life: people want to conceal, to forget the crimes committed under Stalin, to make no reference to them. 'Is there any point in recalling the past?' was the question put to Lev Tolstoy by his biographer Biryukov, and Tolstoy replied (I quote from Biryukov's *Biography of Tolstoy*, vol. 3/4, page 48) [*read at speed*]:

> If I had a vile disease and I were cured and cleansed from it, I
> would always be happy to talk about it. I would make no mention

of it only if I still went on suffering and getting worse and I wanted to deceive myself. We are sick – all of us are sick too. The form of the sickness has changed but it is still the same disease; only it is called by a different name. . . The disease that we are suffering from is the murdering of people. . . If we would recall the past and look it straight in the face – the violence we are now committing would be revealed.

No! it will not be possible indefinitely to keep silent about Stalin's crimes or go against the truth. There were millions of people who suffered from the crimes and they demand exposure. It would be a good idea, too, to reflect: what moral effect will the silence on these crimes have on the younger generation – it will mean the *corruption* of still more millions. The growing generation of young people are no fools; they know full well millions of crimes were committed and nobody talks about them – mum's the word all round. What is there then, is there anything to hold anyone of us whomsoever back from taking a hand in the injustices around us? Cover up – keep your mouth shut too.

It only remains for me to say that I retract not one word, not one word of what I wrote to the Writers' Union. I may conclude with the same words as in that very letter [*quotes*]:

'I am, of course, confident that I shall fulfil my duty as a writer in all circumstances – from the grave even more sucessfully and more irrefutably than in my lifetime. No one can bar the road to truth and to advance its cause I am prepare to accept even death' – yes, death and not merely expulsion from the Union. 'But may it be that repeated lessons will finally teach us not to stop the writer's pen during his lifetime? At no time has this ennobled our history.'

Well then, take the vote – you've got a majority. But remember: the history of literature will still continue to take an interest in this meeting of ours today.

MATUSHKIN: I have got a question to put to Solzhenitsyn. How do you explain the fact that people in the West are so keen to print your work?

SOLZHENITSYN: And how do you explain the fact that people are so stubbornly unwilling to print me in my country?

MATUSHKIN: No, you give me a reply to my question – it was addressed to you.

SOLZHENITSYN: I have already given a reply and answered the question; I have got more questions to put and they have been put earlier: let the Secretariat answer mine.

KOZHEVNIKOV [*interrupting Matushkin*]: All right, there's no need. Comrades, I don't want to butt into your meeting or meddle with your decision; you are absolutely independent. But I would like to enter an objection [*speaking in a metallic tone of voice*] against the political overtone which Solzhenitsyn wants to impose on us. We raise one question; he raises another one. He has got all the newspapers at his disposal to reply to people abroad but he makes no use of them. He has no desire to reply to our enemies. He doesn't want to give a retort to people abroad – without quoting Nekrasov and Tolstoy but to reply to our enemies in his own words. The Congress turned down your letter as uncalled for and as ideologically incorrect. In that letter you disclaim the guiding role played by the Party – that is what we stand on, the guiding role of the Party. I think your former comrades in the Union were right in what they said – we cannot be reconciled. We must all toe the line, go forward together, in orderly ranks – all acting as one – not under some kind of lash but in accordance with our conscience.

FRANTS TAURIN: It will now be for the RSFSR Secretariat to deal with this matter. It is true to say that the main substance of the problem is not the revision of manuscripts or help to young writers. The main point is that you, comrade Solzhenitsyn, have not resisted the use made of your name in the West. That might partly be explained even by the injustices you have suffered and the wrongs heaped upon you. Sometimes, though, one must place one's country future above one's own. Every man is the creator of his own personal fate. Believe me, no one wants to bring you to your knees. This meeting is an attempt to help you to straighten out all that has been pinned upon you in the West. The impression that is given over there is that you, with all your inborn talent, play the role of an enemy of your own country. It may be that in this struggle people allow themselves to overshoot the mark, but I am conversant with the minutes of the Secretariat meeting. The secretaries, and more especially comrade Fedin, begged you to make concessions, to give a public rebuff to the clamour aroused in the West. This means the harm done is doubled: we are blackened as a country and a talented writer is snatched from us. Any decision that will be taken today will be discussed in the RSFSR Secretariat.

LEVCHENKO [*rises to read an already typed draft resolution*]:
'. . . Paragraph 2. The meeting considers that Solzhenitsyn's conduct is anti-social in character and is radically in conflict with the aims and purposes of the USSR Union of Writers.

In view of his anti-social behaviour that is in contradiction with the aims and objectives of the USSR Union of Writers and of his gross violation of the basic provisions of the Statutes of the USSR WU, the writer Solzhenitsyn is hereby expelled from the USSR Union of Writers.

We request the Secretariat to endorse this decision.'

MARKIN: I would like to know the views of our secretary, comrade Safonov. Has he been notified or not?

BARANOV: He is unwell. Our meeting is lawfully competent to adopt the resolution.

[*On a vote being taken, five voted in favour, one against.*]

Solzhenitsyn's expulsion from the Writers' Union

A meeting has been held of the Ryazan writers' organization, concerned with problems of the intensification of ideological-educative work. In their speeches, participants in the meeting stressed that in present-day conditions why the ideological struggle is growing more acute, the responsibility of every Soviet writer for his work and his conduct in society increases.

In this connection the participants in the meeting raised the question of a member of the Ryazan writers' organization, A. Solzhenitsyn. The meeting unanimously noted that the behaviour of A. Solzhenitsyn was of an anti-social nature and fundamentally conflicted with the principles and aims formulated in the Constitution of the Union of Writers of the USSR.

As we know, the name and works of A. Solzhenitsyn have in recent years been actively used by hostile bourgeois propaganda for a campaign of slander against our country. However, A. Solzhenitsyn has not only not made a public statement on his attitude to this campaign, but, despite criticism from Soviet public opinion and repeated recommendations by the USSR Writers' Union, has, through certain of his actions and statements, substantially helped to fan the flames of anti-Soviet sensationalism around his name.

Proceeding from this, the meeting of the Ryazan writers' organization resolved to expel A. Solzhenitsyn from the Writers' Union of the USSR.

The Secretariat of the Board of the Writers' Union of the RSFSR has endorsed the resolution adopted by the Ryazan writers' organization.

(*Literaturnaya Gazeta*, 12 November 1969)

Solzhenitsyn protests against expulsion*

Shamelessly trampling underfoot your own statutes, you have expelled me in my absence, as at the sound of a fire-alarm, without even sending me a summons by telegram, without even giving me the four hours I needed to come from Ryazan and be present at the meeting. You have shown openly that the RESOLUTION preceded the 'discussion'. Was it less awkward for you to invent new charges in my absence? Were you afraid of being obliged to grant me ten minutes for my answer? I am compelled to substitute this letter for those ten minutes.

Blow the dust off the clock. Your watches are behind the times. Throw open the heavy curtains which are so dear to you – you do not even suspect that the day has already dawned

*This letter from Solzhenitsyn was sent to the Secretariat of the Soviet Writer's Union.

outside. It is no longer that stifling, that sombre, irrevocable time when you expelled Akhmatova in the same servile manner. It is not even that timid, frosty period when you expelled Pasternak, whining abuse at him. Was this shame not enough for you? Do you want to make it greater? But the time is near when each of you will seek to erase his signature from today's resolution.

Blind leading the blind! You do not even notice that you are wandering in the opposite direction from the one you yourselves announced. At this time of crisis you are incapable of suggesting anything constructive, anything good for our society, which is gravely sick – only your hatred, your vigilance, your 'hold on and don't let go'.

Your clumsy articles fall apart; your vacant minds stir feebly – but you have no arguments. You have only your voting and your administration. And that is why neither Sholokhov nor any of you, of all the lot of you, dared reply to the famous letter of Lydia Chukovskaya, who is the pride of Russian publicistic writing. But the administrative pincers are ready for her: how could she allow people to read her book [*The Deserted House*] when it has not been published? Once the AUTHORITIES have made up their minds not to publish you – then stifle yourself, choke yourself, cease to exist, and don't give your stuff to anyone to read!

They are also threatening to expel Lev Kopelev*, the front-line veteran, who has already served ten years in prison although he was completely innocent. Today he is guilty: he intercedes for the persecuted, he revealed the hallowed secrets of his conversation with an influential person, he disclosed an OFFICIAL SECRET. But why do you hold conversations like these which have to be concealed from the people? Were we not promised fifty years ago that never again would there be any secret

*Lev Kopelev (born 1912), a writer and critic, is an expert in German literature. He is a former inmate of the labour camps under Stalin. Rehabilitated after 1956, he has now been again expelled from the Party and dismissed from his post in the Institute of Art History to which he was previously re-admitted. Anna Akhmatova was expelled from the Writers' Union in 1946 after a virulent attack on her by Zhdanov. Boris Pasternak was expelled from it in 1958 after a campaign against him for the publication of *Doctor Zhivago*.

diplomacy, secret talks, secret and incomprehensible appointments and transfers, that the masses would be informed of all matters and discuss them openly?

'The enemy will overhear' – that is your excuse. The eternal, omnipresent 'enemies' are a convenient justification for your functions and your very existence. As if there were no enemies when you promised immediate openness. But what would you do without 'enemies'? You could not live without 'enemies'; hatred, a hatred no better than racial hatred, has become your sterile atmosphere. But in this way a sense of our single, common humanity is lost and its doom is accelerated. Should the antarctic ice melt tomorrow, we would all become a sea of drowning humanity, and into whose heads would you then be drilling your concepts of 'class struggle'? Not to speak of the time when the few surviving bipeds will be wandering over radioactive earth, dying.

It is high time to remember that we belong first and foremost to humanity. And that man has distinguished himself from the animal world by THOUGHT and SPEECH. And these, naturally, should be FREE. If they are put in chains, we shall return to the state of animals.

OPENNESS, honest and complete OPENNESS – that is the first condition of health in all societies, including our own. And he who does not want this openness for our country cares nothing for his fatherland and thinks only of his own interest. He who does not wish this openness for his fatherland does not want to purify it of its diseases, but only to drive them inwards, there to fester.

A. SOLZHENITSYN

12 November 1969

Western reactions to Solzhenitsyn's expulsion

Telegram to Fedin from David Carver and Pierre Emmanuel, 18 November 1969*

'Appalled and shocked news expulsion from Soviet Writers' Union great and universally respected writer Solzhenitsyn. Beg you intervene personally restore him to membership thus combating much deplored prolonged persecution one of our most eminent colleagues.'

Reply from Fedin

'I regard your telegram as an unprecedented interference in the internal affairs of the Writers' Union of the USSR, the observance of whose rules lies exclusively within its competence.'

Telegram to Fedin from David Carver and Pierre Emmanuel, 26 November 1969

'Regret tone and content your telegram. Writer Alexander Solzhenitsyn's calibre would be welcome anywhere. Soviet Writers' Union should feel honoured have him as member. Expressing such opinion does not in any way interfere with internal affairs Soviet Writers' Union.'

*The International Secretary and the President of the International PEN Club.

Statement by the French 'National Writers' Committee'

The expulsion of Solzhenitsyn from the Union of Soviet Writers, first announced, then denied, and finally confirmed, with the 'concerted propaganda' technique to which we are getting accustomed, constitutes in the eyes of the whole world a monumental mistake which not only does harm to the Soviet Union but helps confirm the view of socialism as propagated by its enemies. We feel sure that the most reasonable of men, and even those in the highest positions of power, have deeply regretted a similar mistake made previously with regard to Boris Pasternak. Is it really necessary that the great writers of the Soviet Union be treated like harmful beings? This would be quite incomprehensible if one did not see evidence that, with the curious complicity of some of their colleagues, action has been taken against the writers to frighten not only them but also intellectuals in general – to dissuade them from being anything else but soldiers marching in parade-step. We believed that the era which was stained by the blood of Isaak Babel, Osip Mandelshtam, Egiche Charentz, Mikhail Koltsov, Titian Tabidze – to name briefly the great national sources of the Soviet spirit – had ended. We had thought that that which had been produced by an epoch, now happily past, would never return. How can we believe that today, in the country of triumphant socialism – a country where a Nicholas II never dreamt of doing any such thing to Chekhov when he published his book on Sakhalin – this would be the fate of the writer most representative of the great Russian tradition, Alexander Solzhenitsyn – already a victim of Stalinist repression, whose main crime today is that he survived.

Is it necessary to ask our Soviet colleagues, those who remain silent, those who are forced to speak, and those who today add their names to these acts, whether they do not see in such acts the reflection of a recent past? They ought to remember that the signature of certain of their predecessors confirming similar expulsions too often proved to be a 'rope for the hangman'. Do they not understand that the past is already difficult enough to forget. Yet despite all this, we still wish to believe that, as at the time of the fury unleashed against the greatest Russian poet then living, there will be found in the high councils of the nation, to whom we owe the Dawn of October and the defeat of Hitlerian fascism, men capable of realizing the wrong that has been done and of putting it right. This – for the common cause for which we live, fight and die.

ELSA TRIOLET	MICHEL BUTOR	ALAIN PREVOST
VERCORS	JEAN-PIERRE FAYE	CHRISTIANE
JACQUES MADAULE	GEORGES GOVY	ROCHEFORT
ARTHUR ADAMOV	GUILLEVIC	JEAN ROUSSELOT
LOUIS ARAGON	PIERRE PARAF	JEAN-PAUL SARTRE
JEAN-LOUIS BORY	VLADIMIR POZNER	

(*Les Lettres Françaises*, 18 November 1969)

A letter from Western intellectuals to Konstantin Fedin

'We reject the conception that an artist's refusal humbly to accept state censorship is in any sense criminal in a civilized society, or that publication by foreigners of his books is ground for persecuting him … We sign our names as men of peace declaring our solidarity with Alexander Solzhenitsyn's defence of those fundamental rights of the human spirit which unite civilized people everywhere.'

ARTHUR MILLER	CARLOS FUENTES
CHARLES BRACELEN FLOOD	YUKIO MISHIMA
HARRISON SALISBURY	IGOR STRAVINSKY
JOHN UPDIKE	GÜNTER GRASS
JOHN CHEEVER	FRIEDRICH DÜRRENMATT
TRUMAN CAPOTE	HEINRICH BÖLL
RICHARD WILBUR	KURT VONNEGUT
JEAN-PAUL SARTRE	MITCHELL WILSON

3 December 1969

A letter to The Times, *London, 16 December 1969*

THE SILENCING OF RUSSIAN WRITERS

Sir,

The treatment of Soviet writers in their own country has become an international scandal. We now learn with dismay of the expulsion from the Soviet Writers' Union of Alexander Solzhenitsyn, the one writer in Russia who, in the words of Arthur Miller, 'is unanimously regarded as a classic'. The two great poets who were previously so expelled were Anna Akhmatova and Boris Pasternak. One understands Solzhenitsyn's bitter exclamation: 'Was this shame not enough for you!'

The silencing of a writer of Solzhenitsyn's stature is in itself a crime against civilization. We do not know whether any other steps are contemplated in this new witch-hunt. We can only hope that there is no repetition of the Sinyavsky-Daniel trial. Judging by experience, verbal protests do not sufficiently impress the Soviet authorities. We appeal to them, however, to stop persecuting Solzhenitsyn.

Should this appeal fail we shall see no other way but to call upon the writers and artists of the world to conduct an international cultural boycott of a country which chooses to put itself beyond the pale of civilization until such time as it abandons the barbaric treatment of its writers and artists.

Yours, etc.,

A. ALVAREZ	ROBERT GOFFIN	ARTHUR MILLER
HANNAH ARENDT	GÜNTER GRASS	MARY MCCARTHY
W. H. AUDEN	GRAHAM GREENE	MEYER SCHAPIRO
A. J. AYER	PETER HÄRTLING	MURIEL SPARK
CARLO BRONNE	KLAUS	WILLIAM SANSOM
CONSTANT	HARPPRECHT	PHILIP TOYNBEE
BURNIAUX	ROLF HOCHHUTH	EDMOND
DAVID CARVER	JULIAN HUXLEY	VANDERCAMMON
GEORGES DOPAGNE	UWE JOHNSON	VICTOR VAN
PIERRE EMMANUEL	ALFRED KAZIN	VRIESLAND
DANIEL GILLES	ROSAMOND	BERNARD WALL
BRIAN GLANVILLE	LEHMANN	

Madame Furtseva in Paris*

The Solzhenitsyn affair is a Soviet domestic affair. We do not make it our business how you conduct your affairs. We do not allow anyone, any writer to interfere in our affairs. In spite of all the appeals addressed to him, Solzhenitsyn refused to respect the constitution of the Writers' Union. He was expelled from it. We cannot allow the Soviet people to be slandered and Vlasov's troops to be glorified as they have been by Solzhenitsyn . . .

Let him write good books, and we will publish them. In issuing *One Day in the Life of Ivan Denisovich*, the Soviet Union published a testimony, the like of which has never been written in any other country. Let Solzhenitsyn describe Soviet reality, with its positive and negative aspects: but we will not tolerate distortion of this reality . . .

We begged him by telephone or telegram to come and explain himself [to the meeting of the Writers' Union which expelled him]. It was he who refused to come.

(*Le Monde*, 28–9 December 1969)

'Samizdat' paper on Solzhenitsyn's expulsion

Certain details about the expulsion of Solzhenitsyn from the Union of Soviet Writers have become known. At the beginning of November the secretary of the Ryazan writers' organization E. Safonov was summoned to Moscow to see L. Sobolev (Writers' Union of the RSFSR) and 'fix' the expulsion. On his return to Ryazan he was immediately operated on for appendicitis. On the morning of 4 November four Ryazan writers were summoned separately to the department of agitation and propa-

---

*Ekaterina Furtseva (born 1910) was made Minister of Culture in 1960. She was a protégéé of Khrushchev and once tried to commit suicide when she thought she was on the verge of dismissal. She misled her French audience by saying that Solzhenitsyn refused to attend the Union meeting at which he was expelled. As Solzhenitsyn explains (cf. p. 218), he was not even asked to come.

ganda of the party regional committee, where the head of the department, Shestapolov, broke it to each of them that it would be necessary to expel Solzhenitsyn. (E. Markin was promised an apartment and after Solzhenitsyn's expulsion he was issued with the necessary document.) The fifth writer, N. Rodin, without whom there would not be a quorum, was two hundred kilometres away in the town of Kasimov, seriously ill. On instructions from Ryazan, the secretary of the Kazimov party district committee compelled him to set off for Ryazan in the district committee's car. Rodin soon turned back, saying that he might die on the way, but the secretary of the district committee forced him to go, saying: 'There are four hospitals on the way – in Gus Zhelezny, Tuma, Spas-Klepiki and Solotcha – you can call on the doctors on the way.' Shestapolov called on Safonov in hospital after his operation and demanded his agreement to the expulsion of Solzhenitsyn. Safonov refused (but a month later just the same he was forced to approve the expulsion). An hour before the beginning of the meeting of the writers' organization, the five writers who were also party members (that is, all of them except Solzhenitsyn) were called to a 'party group meeting', where the propaganda secretary of the district committee, A. Kozhevnikov, made sure that there would be no 'deviations' in the voting. The proceedings of the actual meeting at which Solzhenitsyn was expelled are well known. It ended on the evening of 4 November. The meeting of the Secretariat of the RSFSR Writers' Union to discuss the same matter was hastily arranged and conducted in Solzhenitsyn's absence on 5 November in Moscow. Solzhenitsyn was given only a verbal invitation and received no official, written summons from the RSFSR Writers' Union.

However, it was decided to conceal the very fact of the meeting of the Secretariat of the RSFSR Writers' Union for a week, so as not to create an unpleasant impression on cultural figures abroad in the days before the November celebrations. For this reason on 5 November someone was appointed to answer the telephone in the Writers' Union in Ryazan with instructions that if there were calls from Moscow from foreign correspondents (and there were calls), he should reply either that there had been no expulsion, or that nothing was known about it in Ryazan. The

RSFSR Writers' Union answered inquiries in the same way on that day. This gave rise to the 'denial'. When the celebrations were over the *Literaturnaya Gazeta* published the announcement, but concealed the date of the expulsion.

The campaign of the progressive international community in connection with the expulsion of A. Solzhenitsyn from the Writers' Union continues.

Here is a summary of the most important articles:

1. *Pierre Emmanuel,* member of the Académie Française and president of the PEN Club.

Pierre Emmanuel comments on the protest of a large group of important writers and artists in the West, which contains the threat of an international 'cultural boycott' of the Soviet Union, as 'a country which has put itself beyond the pale of the civilized world . . .'

With complete justification all people are filled with indignation at what is happening in Greece, but at the same time their attitude to the situation of the Soviet intelligentsia is rather restrained, as they consider that totalitarianism in Russia is an accidental and transitory phenomenon. This is an error which only strengthens the machinery of tyranny in the East. . . It is the very right to think freely that is denied in the Soviet Union in the name of socialism, a socialism about which no one thinks, inasmuch as thinking is forbidden. . . The censorship and the police in the USSR forbid believers to pray, philosophers to think, and writers to create. When one examines the systematic transformation into slaves and liars of a whole generation of gifted people, one cannot help thinking of a slow genocide of the soul. If this régime continues to last, by the end of this century all Eastern Europe may have turned into a spiritual wilderness.

People will object: so Solzhenitsyn has been excluded from the Union of Writers. Well, that's bad, but Sinyavsky and Daniel are dying a slow death in Siberia. I quite agree, but I should remind you that in the USSR the profession of writer is regulated: a person who is excluded from the Union of Writers is left without a profession. . . He must be ready for anything, including being committed to a lunatic asylum. . . In their attempts to humiliate the great writer, they provoke him by suggesting to him that he emigrate. But the very purpose of Solzhenitsyn's life is precisely to remain in his own country at any price, where he is asserting his right to die for the truth.

In conclusion Pierre Emmanuel writes:

> We cannot be fooled by official delegations of Soviet writers and artists who travel in the West in semi-freedom. The Brezhnev era is not the Khrushchev era, and this is reflected in the quality of its cultural ambassadors. It is useless to pretend that you are dealing with genuine intellectuals rather than with members of a certain organization. Neither the prestige of the Bolshoi Theatre, nor the excellent film about Rublyov (which incidentally has been shown here but not in the USSR), can deceive us and conceal the organized suffocation of the spirit, which, for survival, is left only with the underground.

2. *Gabriel Laub: 'The conscience of the Soviet Union'.* (Gabriel Laub is a well-known Czechoslovak writer, now an émigré.)

In Tsarist Russia there was no special Imperial State Union of Writers, like the present Soviet one. Had there been, they would have had to expel from it such famous authors as Alexander Pushkin, 'for immorality and for bringing dishonour on the state system'; Saltykov-Shchedrin, 'for malicious attacks on the Russian civil service and the customs of society'; Anton Chekhov, 'for continuous slander of Russian reality, especially in his essays about his journey to Sakhalin Island'; Lev Tolstoy, 'for the dissemination of pacifist ideas foreign to the Russian people and weakening to the defensive capacity of the fatherland'.

The Union of Soviet Writers is not a society of literary people for the defence of their own interests. It is a state institution. It is quite understandable that if such an organization expels someone, then it will be someone who refuses to carry out the rules of the game, even if this is the greatest of living Russian writers. We should be much more indignant that such an organization contains in its title the word 'writers'.

The conscience of Russia in the 1960s, this is what Alexander Solzhenitsyn is.

In 1967, in his letter to the Congress of Writers, he spoke out passionately against the restrictions on freedom of speech and against the censorship, just as before him did Alexander Radishchev in 1790 and Saltykov-Shchedrin in 1860. The only difference is that the protests of his predecessors were published. With the passage of time the Russian censorship has been perfected.

The newspapers carry the first reports that some Soviet writers are protesting against the expulsion of Solzhenitsyn ... But I have no doubt that many members of the Union of Writers welcomed his expulsion, and moreover, not only because they are accustomed to condemn as a crime any deviation from the prescribed manner of thinking, but also because Solzhenitsyn is a great writer, in whose company they feel uncomfortable ... Their spiritual forebears persecuted Pushkin and were characterized by Lermontov in his poem 'The death of a poet':

> You who stand in a blood-thirsty crowd at the throne
> Are the executioners of freedom, genius and glory.

The first to make a public statement was Sholokhov. He spoke of writers who are published in the West, and compared them to colorado beetles which must be exterminated [*Izvestia*, 28 November 1969]. The well-known remark of [the German politician Franz-] Joseph Strauss takes on – in comparison to the words of this former writer – the appearance of innocent child's play.

(*Chronicle of Current Events*, No. 12, 28 February 1970)

Letter of 'the 39' on the expulsion of Solzhenitsyn

To the Union of Soviet Writers

The expulsion of Alexander Solzhenitsyn from the Union of Soviet Writers is shameful – not for the man expelled, but for the history of our literature and above all, for our writers, who acquiesced in it either by their silence or out loud.

The allegations made against Solzhenitsyn are of a purely political nature and constitute an expression of official criticism of his ideological standpoint, which is: the consistent exposure of Stalinist arbitrariness, 'Stalinshchina'.

His artistic significance, craftsmanship and world-wide reputation are unquestionable.

But surely it is by this very talent and craftsmanship *above all* that an artist's place in the company of his colleagues should be determined! Or would Dostoyevsky too, had he lived in our time, have been asked to leave the country?

Turning to the party and government leadership of our country, we would remind you that Lenin's blunt rejection of the teachings of Tolstoy did not prevent him from acknowledging the world-wide significance of that great writer and from admiring his books. We would remind you too of Lenin's suggestion that several stories from a White émigré anti-Soviet anthology by Averchenko should be reprinted precisely because of their literary merit. All this is a good example of a political approach to artistic creation in which it is recognized that a writer's value lies in his talent; a writer's ideological standpoint can only be an object of criticism and public debate; in no case can it serve as grounds for any persecution whatsoever.

Why is it that Soviet writers do not know these truths? ... They have excommunicated Solzhenitsyn from his Union – but do they really not understand that neither in this nor in any other way can they ex-communicate him from literature?

Expelling a non-Party writer from a non-Party organization for his non-Party views! That means leaving him defenceless in the face of more calamities that will very likely overtake him, and locking yourselves, and all your craftsmanship and your creative work, securely within the wretched confines of political expediency.

In their attitude to the fate of Solzhenitsyn, his readers are not as unanimous as his fellow-writers. We regard the expulsion of Solzhenitsyn from the Union of Soviet Writers as yet another blatant manifestation of Stalinism, and as a reprisal taken against a writer who embodies the conscience and reason of our people.

L. AGEYEVA	L. PLYUSHCH	I. KOROLYOVA
Z. ASANOVA	G. PODYAPOLSKY	A. VOLPIN
T. BAYEVA	M. RYZHIK	V. SEITOMETOV
I. BELOGORODSKAYA	I. RUDAKOV	L. TERNOVSKY
V. BELIYEV	R. SAVINA	A. PRIMAK
YU. VISHNEVSKAYA	V. GUSAROV	V. TIMACHYOV
O. VOROBYOV	R. DZHEMILEV	L. UBOZHKO

p.p. V. GERSHUNI	YU. DIKOV	R. URBAN
Z. GRIGORENKO	N. YEMELKINA	N. KHALILOV
V. KRASIN	A. AMETOV	I. KHALAPOV
L. KUSHEVA	Z. ISMAILOV	I. YAKIR
V. LAPIN	E. KOSTERINA	P. YAKIR
L. LYUBOVNIKOVA	V. KOZHARINOV	B. YAROSLAVOV

19 December 1969

Open letter from Jaures Medvedev

Solzhenitsyn was expelled because his talent as a writer, his humanism, his creative depiction and analysis of reality had overstepped the boundaries of the Ryazan region and were beyond the control of the department of the Ryazan regional party committee. They had overstepped the boundaries of the Russian Republic and ceased to conform with the obscure and constantly changing instructions of the furtive censorship. Alexander Solzhenitsyn has deservedly acquired in the USSR and the whole world the reputation of a patriot and a fighter for the real truth. He has not betrayed that truth, those humanitarian ideas, he has not betrayed his conscience or his principles, and he has not betrayed his people now that, in defiance of all logic and common sense, the arbitrariness of the Stalin era has begun to reappear in disguised form and the threat of lawlessness and violence has come to hang once more over the land. And it was for this that they expelled him from the Union . . .

On the charge brought against Solzhenitsyn of having his books published in the West, the author writes of the 'piratical practice of Soviet publishing-houses in publishing foreign authors and reproducing their works, without their permission. This is why our country refuses to sign the convention on the international defence of civil [i.e. authors'?] rights, thereby putting Soviet authors too in a defenceless position'. On the charge that Solzhenitsyn's works were written 'from a different ideological standpoint', the author writes: 'The publication of *One Day in the Life of Ivan Denisovich* was approved by the

Presidium of the Central Committee of the Soviet Communist
Party. This story was acclaimed by the whole of the Soviet press
and nominated for a Lenin Prize. Why then are you now
hurling abuse even at this story? It means that *your* "ideological
standpoint" has changed, and not that of Solzhenitsyn. It means
that the instructions to GLAVLIT [the censorship] have changed,
and not the writer's creative style.'

The expulsion of Solzhenitsyn from the Soviet Writers'
Union grieves me as an indication of deeply regrettable changes
in the way of running the Union and in the standpoint of those
circles which are accustomed to consider the Union as merely a
branch of the Ideological Commission. The expulsion of
Solzhenitsyn is a unique event. It came about as the logical
result of the new line of cautious repression directed against the
intelligentsia with the aim of instilling into them the inertia of
fear, the same fear that Stalin and his obedient minions created,
who did not shrink from the destruction of millions of innocent
citizens.

(*Chronicle of Current Events*, No. 14, 30 June 1970)

Statement by A. I. Solzhenitsyn in defence of Jaures Medvedev

THIS IS HOW WE LIVE:

without any arrest warrant or any medical justification four
policemen and two doctors come to a healthy man's house. The
doctors declare that he is crazy, the police major shouts 'We are
an ORGAN OF FORCE! Get up!', they twist his arms and drive
him off to the madhouse.

This can happen tomorrow to any one of us. It has just
happened to Jaures Medvedev, a geneticist and publicist, a man
of subtle, precise and brilliant intellect and of warm heart (I
know personally of his disinterested help to unknown, ill and
dying people). It is precisely for the diversity of his fertile gifts
that he is charged with abnormality: 'a split personality'! It is
precisely his sensitivity to injustice, to stupidity, which is pre-

sented as a sick deviation: 'poor adaptation to the social environment'! Once you think in other ways than is PRESCRIBED – that means you're abnormal! As for well-adjusted people, they must all think alike. And there is no means of redress: even the appeals of our best scientists and writers bounce back like peas off a wall.

If only this were the first case! But this devious suppression of people without searching for any guilt, when the real reason is too shameful to state, is becoming a fashion. Some of the victims are widely known, many more are unknown. Servile psychiatrists, breakers of their [Hippocratic] oath, define as 'mental illness': concern about social problems, and superfluous enthusiasm, and superfluous coldness, and excessively brilliant gifts, and the lack of them.

Yet even simple common sense ought to act as a restraint. After all, Chaadayev [a thinker declared 'officially mad' by Emperor Nicholas I in 1837] did not even have a finger laid on him, but we have now been cursing his persecutors for over a century. It is time to think clearly: the incarceration of free-thinking healthy people in madhouses is SPIRITUAL MURDER, it is a variation on the GAS CHAMBER, but is even more cruel: the torture of the people being killed is more malicious and more prolonged. Like the gas chambers these crimes will NEVER be forgotten, and all those involved in them will be condemned for all time, during their life and after their death.

In lawlessness, in the committing of crimes, the point must be remembered at which a man becomes a cannibal!

It is short-sighted to think that one can live by constantly relying on force alone, constantly ignoring the objections of conscience.

15 June 1970   A. SOLZHENITSYN
                                          (*Chronicle of Current Events*,
                                             No. 14, 30 June 1970)

NOBEL PRIZE

It is not a surprise that Solzhenitsyn was awarded a Nobel Prize for Literature and that the citation mentions both his artistic and moral achievements. His manner of accepting it confirmed once again his strength of character, just as the manner in which it was denounced in the Soviet press has once again indicated the gap between the moral values which this ex-prisoner of Stalin represents and the attitude of the post-Khrushchev leadership, steadily restoring Stalin's name – if not to its former glory, at least to a position of positive acclaim. This contrast made the award an act of high drama, whose symbolic significance could not be lost on Solzhenitsyn's countrymen. The drama was heightened by the conspicuous absence of Solzhenitsyn from the prize-giving ceremony. He had decided that in the circumstances he could not carry out his original intention of going to Stockholm for fear of not being permitted to return to Russia, as he explained in a letter to the Swedish Academy. Nor had Solzhenitsyn forgotten the inmates of the concentration camps (some of whom had congratulated him on his Nobel Prize). He reminded the world in another message to the Academy about the continued existence of the camps. The ghost of Ivan Denisovich was present at the Nobel banquet in Stockholm's City Hall. Soon after the ceremony the Soviet press, which for a few weeks had refrained from continuing its attacks on the Nobel Prize award to Solzhenitsyn, resumed them with a vengeance. A week after the ceremony, Pravda, *the official organ of the Soviet Communist Party, carried the most vicious onslaught on dissident Soviet intellectuals to appear in the Soviet press for many years. They were described as 'criminal elements, all sorts of renegades, drones, scoundrels, swindlers, and even persons in whom only psychiatrists can be interested. Solzhenitsyn was the central target of the article. Yet he remained unmoved. He quietly proceeded with his literary work. In June 1971 he published in Paris (in*

Russian) the first part of his epic work, August 1914, *which was refused publication in the Soviet Union. Soon after he addressed an Open Letter to the Head of the KGB, Andropov, protesting against his continuing persecution.*

Solzhenitsyn had also his share of troubles in the West. As Per Egil Hegge, the Moscow correspondent of the Norwegian Aften-posten *at the time of the Nobel award to Solzhenitsyn, disclosed in his book,* Go-Between in Moscow, *the Swedish Ambassador, Gunnar Jarring, would not consider Solzhenitsyn's proposal that he should be given the prize at a ceremony in the Swedish embassy in Moscow, a not unprecedented possibility. But Jarring, who entertained in the embassy the other Soviet Nobel prize-winner, Mikhail Sholokhov, refused even to give Solzhenitsyn an invitation card to the embassy to discuss the matter.*

Solzhenitsyn continued also to be plagued by the treatment of his work in the West, where his latest novel, August 1914, *which was published by the Russian language YMCA Press in Paris, was promptly reproduced in unauthorized editions in other countries.*

Nobel Prize Citation for Solzhenitsyn

For the ethical force with which he has pursued the indispensable traditions of Russian literature.

8 October 1970

Solzhenitsyn's statement

I am grateful for this decision. I accept the prize. I intend to go and receive it personally on the traditional day – in so far as this will depend on me.

I am well. The journey won't hurt my health.*

8 October 1970

*Solzhenitsyn tried here to dismiss in advance a possible excuse for denying him permission to go to the Nobel Prize ceremony in Stockholm.

French communists on Solzhenitsyn

There can be no doubt that the Nobel Prize for Literature 1970 has gone to a real writer, faithful to his vocation to speak the truth as he sees it, which is an essential part of his responsibility to society. To take such a writer by the hand and force him to write differently would be to treat him like a child.

ANDRÉ WURMSER
(*Humanité*, 9 October 1970)

The choice of Alexander Solzhenitsyn justifies the existence of the Nobel prize for literature. There can be few examples to equal Solzhenitsyn's achievement – in seven years to win such unanimous respect as a writer, such world-wide authority. There can be no doubt that, in the eyes of the world, Solzhenitsyn is carrying a great people up to the summits of great literature once more . . . He is a master of Russian prose, equal to the best that this great and rich language has ever known. His word is made of the flesh and blood of his people . . . I have never met a single writer whose mother tongue is Russian, and who is capable of literary judgement, who has not confided to me that he sees in Alexander Isayevich . . . the greatest living Russian writer. The Stockholm jury has therefore set its seal on a fact already completely recognized by those who have been able to read what he has written: the universal quality of Alexander Solzhenitsyn's art . . . To try to write off the Stockholm jury's choice as an act of partisan politics scarcely corresponds to the facts.

PIERRE DAIX
(*Les Lettres Françaises*, 14 October 1970)

Sympathy from Italian communists

The publication of *Cancer Ward* and of *The First Circle* has definitely established Solzhenitsyn's fame as a writer. Nevertheless he was expelled last year from the Soviet Writers' Union and thus deprived of any possibility of publishing his works.

It must be said that Solzhenitsyn has reacted equally critically to the silence imposed on him, and to the frequent commercial exploitation of his works abroad. He has even written a letter to *L'Unità* on this subject. He subsequently took legal action in this respect. To those who have disdainfully suggested that he should go abroad, he has replied that he has no intention at all of leaving his country, but will stay there and continue to defend his rights as a citizen and as an artist.

This is the reason why his works and actions attract our attention politically. It is a question of freedom of expression and of dissent in a socialist society, of its legitimacy, and even of its value. We have already expressed our support for such rights, when Solzhenitsyn was expelled from the Writers' Union. This is not the place for a fuller examination of Solzhenitsyn's works and ideas. They can be accepted or rejected. But they are also a part of the movement of opposing tendencies – the only way for a socialist society to assert itself and develop.

GIUSEPPE BOFFA
(*L'Unità*, 9 October 1970)

The Soviet literary organizations would be consistent if they were repudiating the Nobel Prize altogether. But it is not consistent to accept with pleasure this prize when it is conferred on a Soviet writer who is officially in favour but to reject it when the same prize is conferred on another, not less important, Soviet writer who happens to be in disfavour. Why did not Sholokhov make a grand gesture of rejecting the Prize which had already been previously 'provocatively' conferred on Pasternak and instead hurried off to Stockholm to collect it?

VITTORIO STRADA
(*Rinascità*, 16 October 1970)

Solzhenitsyn's telegram to Dr Karl Ragnar Gierow

I have received your cable and I want to thank you. The decision on the Nobel Prize I regard as a tribute to Russian literature and to our arduous history.

On this traditional day, I intend to come to Stockholm to receive the prize personally.

11 October 1970

Letter from 37 Soviet intellectuals congratulating Solzhenitsyn

On learning that Alexander Solzhenitsyn has been awarded the Nobel Prize, we salute the Nobel Prize Committee for this decision.

Solzhenitsyn's enthusiasm, the philosophic depth and high artistic skill of the works of this world-acknowledged contemporary writer, the humanity of his position, which he consistently and courageously defends – all this definitely deserved such a high and honourable award.

From the bottom of our hearts we congratulate Solzhenitsyn, wish him new and creative successes, health and fortitude on his path of work.

We are proud of our literature, which, in spite of all obstacles, produces such first-class masters.

At the same time, we expect that the award of the Nobel Prize to Solzhenitsyn will become another occasion for continuing the baiting that is consistently exercised here against him and is viewed by us as a national shame.

Moreover we consider it our duty to express anew our deep gratitude to Solzhenitsyn for his Nobel work.

V. GERSHUNI, PYOTR YAKIR and others
10 October 1970

Soviet official reactions

As the public already knows, the works of this author, which were illegally sent abroad and published there; have long been used by reactionary circles in the West for anti-Soviet purposes.

Soviet writers have frequently expressed in the press their attitude to the works and conduct of A. Solzhenitsyn, which, as noted by the Secretariat of the governing body of the Union of Writers of the Russian Federal Republic, have contradicted the principles and tasks of the voluntary association of Soviet authors. Soviet authors excluded A. Solzhenitsyn from the ranks of their union. As we know, this decision was actively supported by the entire public of the country.

One can only regret that the Nobel committee has allowed itself to be drawn into an unseemly game, undertaken by no means in the interests of the development of spiritual values and literary traditions, but dictated by speculative political considerations.

(*Izvestia*, 10 October 1970)

You probably know about the award of the Nobel Prize to Solzhenitsyn. This action has purely political aims and is, in its essence, a provocation. This decision is by no means dictated by concern for Russian literature and we Soviet men of letters consider this yet another international act of an anti-Soviet character.

(*Sovetskaya Rossiya*, 14 October 1970)

The facts speak for themselves: the Nobel Prize Committee has allowed itself to be drawn into an unworthy game. It has declared that it is concerned with the 'aesthetic aim' of literature. Yet it is quite obvious that in this case the members of the committee understood 'aesthetic aim' to mean anti-Soviet trends.

(*Literaturnaya Gazeta*, 14 October 1970)

The decision of the Nobel Prize Committee for Literature to make an award to Soviet writer Alexander Solzhenitsyn was clearly dictated by speculative political considerations, not literary merit.

That sums up the opinion of the secretariat of the Union of Soviet Writers.

In the Soviet Union people were amazed at the choice, they said. Some of Solzhenitsyn's works had been illegally taken abroad and published there for anti-Soviet purposes.

Soviet writers had repeatedly expressed their attitude to his work and behaviour, which conflicted with the principles and duties of the voluntary association of Soviet writers.

As a result, it will be recalled, he was recently expelled by the Union of Soviet Writers.

The award from Stockholm which followed is not a real literary award, but a maliciously prepared sensation.

By making it, the Secretariat of the Soviet Writers' Union comments, the Prize Committee has once more devalued the award.

Solzhenitsyn, a run-of-the-mill writer, has an exaggerated view of his own importance. His tragedy was that he gave in easily to the flattery of people who have no scruples about the means they use to struggle against the Soviet system.

But he must surely realize himself that his literary gifts are not only below those of the giants of the past, but also inferior to many of his Soviet contemporaries – writers the West choose to ignore because they find the impact of the truth in their writing most unapalatable.

Of course, few of the 'experts' praising Solzhenitsyn believe their own words for a moment. If Solzhenitsyn were not available, they would have found someone else.

In that context, you cannot help recalling the case of Tarsis – a literary 'giant' according to Western experts until he had served his purpose; then he completely faded from view.

It is ironic to note the things for which the new Nobel Prize-winner is being praised abroad – for example, the Paris *Express*, which enthused over his attempts to rehabilitate Vlasov, who fought against his country in the ranks of the Nazi army.

(*Soviet Weekly*, 17 October 1970)

It is sacrilege to place side by side the name of Solzhenitsyn with the names of Russian and Soviet creators of classical works known all over the world. Solzhenitsyn's tragedy is that having once put on dark glasses, he is deprived of seeing all the variety of colours in the life of his country ... Solzhenitsyn has made out of his solitariness not a tragedy but a business. If you look at everything he has written it is easy to see that the more he writes, the more his literary concerns are replaced by political libel – anything for a *succès de scandale* ... How could the malicious works of Solzhenitsyn receive such a sensational appraisal from a certain section of the foreign press? It is not just a question of their political tendentiousness, but also a further quality of the author, a quality remote from both civic feelings and generally accepted principles of morality. Solzhenitsyn has forgone his conscience and stooped to lies every time his Soviet fellow-writers have shown their frank concern over his fate as a creative writer ... But perhaps we are making too high moral demands of the members of the Nobel Prize Committee. There was after all the case of the 'laureate' André Gide, maligned by his own countrymen and by others for collaboration with Hitler's monsters. In cases such as those of Solzhenitsyn and André Gide, does the Nobel Prize Committee choose who should be crowned with laurels or is the committee carefully selected to play the role of false witness?

(*Komsomolskaya Pravda*, 17 October 1970)

The Swedish Academy to *Literaturnaya Gazeta**

With reference to the article published in your journal on 14 October, we should like to inform you and your readers of the following: The Nobel prizes for physics, chemistry, medicine, literature and peace are all awarded for work done in the respective fields, and not for any views of achievements in other contexts. The Nobel Prize for Literature is awarded as a result of the vote of all the members of the Swedish Academy and not only of its Nobel Committee. The right to make nominations for the Nobel Prize for Literature belongs only to certain persons and literary institutions round the world, who have been specially invited to this end. Proposals of candidates from other sources are ignored, and no attention is given to discussions in the press, or statements of opinion in various parts of the world, which quite often takes place before the award of a prize . . . No newspaper or periodical, either in Sweden or abroad, is included in the list of those with the right to make nominations for Nobel prizes. The paper in Belgium, which you mention, is unknown to the Swedish Academy.

19 October 1970

Congratulations from a prison camp†

Barbed wire and automatic weapons prevent us from expressing to you personally the depth of our admiration for your courage-ous creative work, upholding the sense of human dignity and exposing the trampling down of the human soul and the destruction of human values.

(signed) YURI GALANSKOV and others

*This is a letter from Dr Karl Ragnar Gierow referred to in the footnote on p. ix.

†This message, from a group of prisoners in the Soviet labour camp at Potma in Mordovia, was smuggled to Moscow. Yuri Galanskov is the young Russian poet imprisoned since 1968 in a strict-regime labour camp for editing the 'Samizdat' journal *Phoenix*. He died in November 1972.

Lukacs on Solzhenitsyn
(Excerpts)

The fundamental task facing socialist realism today is to carry to its limits the criticism of the Stalinist era. Such is certainly the essential mission of socialist ideology as a whole . . . If socialist realism . . . is to reach again the heights attained during the twenties, it must return to its path . . . However, this path of necessity involves presenting a truthful picture of the Stalinist decades, with all their monstrous crimes. The sectarian bureaucrats oppose this, alleging that one must not rummage into the past but attach oneself to the present. They claim that the past has gone completely, leaving no trace in the present. Such assertions are not only false – one need only consider to what extent the Stalinist cultural bureaucracy remains powerful at the present time – but represent a complete aberration . . .

When socialist literature uses its own resources to return to its true character, recovering the sense of its artistic responsibility before the great problems of the day, forces now silent can come into action and weigh on the side of renewal. In this process of transformation and regeneration, which signifies a radical change with regard to socialist realism of the Stalinist era, Solzhenitsyn represents a beacon lighting the way to the future.

(*Politique Hebdo*, 15–21 October 1970)

Rostropovich's Open Letter

Open letter to the chief editors of the newspapers Pravda, Izvestia, Literaturnaya Gazeta *and* Sovetskaya Kultura

Esteemed Comrade Editor,

It is no longer a secret that A. I. Solzhenitsyn lives a great part of the time in my house near Moscow. I have seen how he was expelled from the Writers' Union – at the very time when he was working strenuously on a novel about the year 1914. Now the Nobel Prize has been awarded to him. The newspaper campaign in this connection compels me to undertake this letter to you.

In my memory this is already the third time that a Soviet writer has been given the Nobel Prize. In two cases out of three we have considered the awarding of the prize a 'dirty political game', but in one (Sholokhov) as a 'just recognition' of the outstanding world significance of our literature.

If in his time Sholokhov had declined to accept the prize from hands which had given it to Pasternak 'for Cold War considerations', I would have understood that we no longer trusted the objectivity and the honesty of the Swedish academicians. But now it happens that we selectively sometimes accept the Nobel Prize with gratitude and sometimes curse it.

And what if next time the prize is awarded to Comrade Kochetov*? Of course it will have to be accepted!

Why, a day after the award of the prize to Solzhenitsyn, did there appear in our papers a strange report by correspondent 'X', with representatives of the Secretariat of the Writers' Union, to the effect that the entire public of the country (that is evidently all scholars and all musicians, etc.) actively supported his expulsion from the Writers' Union?

Why does *Literaturnaya Gazeta* select from numerous Western newspapers only the opinion of American and Swedish newspapers, avoiding the incomparably more popular and important Communist newspapers like *L'Humanité*, *Lettres Françaises* and *L'Unità*, to say nothing of the numerous non-communist ones?

If we trust a certain critic Bonosky†, then how should we consider the opinion of such important writers as Böll, Aragon and François Mauriac?

I remember and would like to remind you of our newspapers in 1948, how much nonsense was written about those giants of our music, S. S. Prokofiev and D. D. Shostakovich, who are now honoured.

*Vsevolod Kochetov, Soviet author and hard-line editor.
†Philip Bonosky, an American communist journalist.

For example:

Comrades D. Shostakovich, S. Prokofiev, V. Shebalin, N. Myaskovsky and others – your atonal disharmonic music is organically alien to the people . . . formalistic trickery arises when there is an obvious lack of talent, but very much pretension to innovation . . . we absolutely do not accept the music of Shostakovich, Myaskovsky, Prokofiev. There is no harmony in it, no order, no wide melodiousness, no melody.

Now, when one looks at the newspapers of those years, one becomes unbearable ashamed of many things. For the fact is that for three decades the opera, *Katerina Izmailova* [of Shostakovich] was not performed, that S. Prokofiev during his life did not hear the last version of his opera, *War and Peace*, and his Symphonic Concerto for cello and orchestra, that there were official lists of forbidden works of Shostakovich, Prokofiev, Myaskovsky and Khachaturian.

Has time really not taught us to approach cautiously the crushing of talented people? And not to speak in the name of all the people? Not to oblige people to express as their opinions what they simply have not read or heard? I recall with pride that I did not go to the meeting of cultural figures in the Central House of Cultural Workers where B. Pasternak was abused and where I was expected to deliver a speech which I had been 'commissioned' to deliver, criticizing *Doctor Zhivago*, which at that time I had not read.

In 1948 there were lists of forbidden works. Now oral prohibitions are preferred, referring to the fact that 'opinions exist' that the work is not recommended. It is impossible to establish where this opinion exists and whose it is. Why for instance was Galina Vishnevskaya* forbidden to perform in her concert in Moscow, the brilliant vocal cycle of Boris Tchaikovsky with the words of I. Brodsky†? Why was the performance of the Shostakovich cycle to the words of Sasha Chyorny obstructed several times (although the text had already been published)? Why did difficulties accompany the performance of Shostakovich's 13th and 14th Symphonies?

Again, apparently, 'there was an opinion.' Who first had the

*Mr Rostropovich's wife.

†A dissident Leningrad poet, now in exile in the U S A.

'opinion' that it was necessary to expel Solzhenitsyn from the Writers' Union? I did not manage to clarify this question although I was very interested in it. Did five Ryazan writer-musketeers really dare to do it themselves without a serious 'opinion'?

Apparently the 'opinion' prevented also my fellow citizens from getting to know Tarkovsky's film *Andrey Rublyov*, which we sold abroad and which I had the pleasure of seeing among enraptured Parisians. Obviously it was 'opinion' which also prevented publication of Solzhenitsyn's *Cancer Ward*, which was already set in type for *Novy Mir*. So if this had been published here it would have been openly and widely discussed to the benefit of the author as well as the readers.

I do not speak about political or economic questions in our country. There are people who know these better than I. But explain to me, please, why in our literature and art so often people absolutely incompetent in this field have the final word? Why are they given the right to discredit our art in the eyes of our people?

I recall the past not in order to grumble but in order that in the future, let's say in twenty years, we won't have to bury today's newspapers in shame.

Every man must have the right fearlessly to think independently and express his opinion about what he knows, what he has personally thought about and experienced, and not merely to express with slightly different variations the opinion which has been inculcated in him.

We will definitely arrive at reconstruction without prompting and without being corrected.

I know that after my letter there will undoubtedly be an 'opinion' about me, but I am not afraid of it. I openly say what I think. Talent, of which we are proud, must not be submitted to the assaults of the past. I know many of the works of Solzhenitsyn. I like them. I consider he seeks the right through his suffering to write the truth as he saw it and I see no reason to hide my attitude toward him at a time when a campaign is being launched against him.

Moscow, 31 October 1970
(*The New York Times*, 16 November 1970)

Solzhenitsyn to the Swedish Academy

In a telegram to the secretary of the Academy, I have already expressed and now again express my gratitude for the honour bestowed upon me by the awarding of the Nobel Prize. Inwardly I share it with those of my predecessors in Russian literature who, because of the difficult conditions of the past decades, did not live to receive such a prize or who were little known in their lifetime to the reading world in translation or to their country-men even in the original.

In the same telegram, I expressed the intention to accept your invitation to come to Stockholm although I anticipated the humiliating procedure, usual in my country for every trip abroad, of filling out questionnaires, obtaining character references from Party organizations – even for non-members – and being given instructions about behaviour.

However, in recent weeks, the hostile attitude toward my prize, as expressed in the press of my country, and the fact that my books are still suppressed – for reading them, people are dismissed from work or expelled from school – compel me to assume that my trip to Stockholm would be used to cut me off from my native land, simply to prevent me from returning home.

On the other hand, in the materials you sent me about the procedure of handing over the prizes, I discovered that in the Nobel celebrations there are many ceremonies and festivities that are tiring and not in keeping with my character and way of life. The formal part, the Nobel Lecture, is really not a part of the ceremony. Later, in a telegram and letter, you expressed similar apprehensions about the to-do that would accompany my stay in Stockholm.

Weighing all the foregoing, and taking advantage of your kind explanation that personal presence at the ceremony is not an obligatory condition to receiving the prize, I prefer at the present time not to apply for permission for a trip to Stockholm.

I could receive the Nobel diploma and medal, if such a format would be acceptable to you, in Moscow from your representatives, at a mutually convenient time. As provided by the rules of the Nobel Foundation, I am ready to give a lecture or present a written text for the Nobel Lecture within six months from 10 December 1970.

This letter is an open one, and I do not object to its being published.

With best wishes.

A. SOLZHENITSYN
(*The New York Times*, 1 December 1970)

Message from Solzhenitsyn*

I hope that my involuntary absence will not cast a shadow over today's ceremonies. I desire even less, however, that my words should cloud the festival. Yet I cannot close my eyes to the remarkable fact that the day of the Nobel Prize presentation coincides with Human Rights Day. The world cannot avoid its sense of responsibility on account of this coincidence. Everybody present in the City Hall must see a symbolic meaning in this.

ALEXANDER SOLZHENITSYN

*Read by Dr Karl Ragnar Gierow at the Nobel Banquet in Stockholm's City Hall on 10 December 1970. Dr Gierow told reporters afterwards that the message, in Russian, had been received on the previous day. On 12 December, Nils Staahle, Chairman of the Nobel Foundation, confirmed the reports that one sentence had been omitted from the message as it was read at the banquet: 'Let us, at this richly-laden table, not forget the political prisoners who are today on hunger strike for restitution of their limited rights, which have been completely trampled underfoot.' Mr Staahle said that Solzhenitsyn had given him and Dr Gierow a free hand in dealing with the message: Solzhenitsyn did not wish to spoil the Nobel festivities. However, the deletion was made to avoid causing trouble for Solzhenitsyn.

Address at the Nobel Festival by Dr Karl Ragnar Gierow*

Our passports show where and when we were born, facts that are needed to fix our identity. According to a current theory this also applies to authorship. A literary work belongs to its time and its creator is a product of his social and political situation. There are weighty examples to the contrary, but these must be jettisoned or the theory will founder. A case to which it does apply, however, is this year's Nobel Prizewinner in Literature. It is worth emphasizing this because from all points of the compass, not least the West, people are prone for various reasons to make exceptions in his case.

Alexander Solzhenitsyn's passport – I have in mind the one that will convey him to posterity – tells us when and where he was born, details that we need in order to establish his artistic identity. Born in 1918 in Kislovodsk, he belongs to the first generation of Soviet Russian writers who grew up with the new form of government and he is indivisible from the climate and the time in which he was born. Solzhenitsyn himself has said that he cannot contemplate living anywhere but in his native land. His books can; they are already living all around the world, now perhaps more than ever before, in the future perhaps more than now. But their vitality springs not least from the

*In his official speech at the banquet addressed to the Nobel laureates, Professor Arne Tiselius said: 'We sincerely regret that Alexander Solzhenitsyn could not be with us tonight. We appreciate, however, the motives which have prompted him not to attend. The homage just rendered is, if anything, reinforced by his absence.' Usually the reply to the official address is given by the Literature Prizewinner, but in the absence of Solzhenitsyn, it was given by the Economics Prizewinner, Professor Paul A. Samuelson, who made the following reference to Solzhenitsyn: 'I wish that Alexander Solzhenitsyn had been here tonight to speak to us from the heart, as well as from the mind. I am sure we would have been the better for his words. But even though he is absent, his spirit hangs over our festivities and celebrations.' Later on, against all precedent, there was no ceremonial handing over of the Nobel Prize to Solzhenitsyn in the Swedish Embassy in Moscow because Ambassador Jarring did not want to displease Soviet authorities.

feeling that roots his being to his country and its destiny. Here too, Solzhenitsyn is of the incomparable Russian tradition. The same background offsets the gigantic predecessors who have derived from Russia's suffering the compelling strength and inextinguishable love that permeate their work. There is little room in their description for prescribed idylls of programmed prognoses. But it would be a gross misunderstanding of their quest for the truth, not to feel in this their profound decisive identification with the country whose life provided their subject matter and for whose life their works are essential. The central figure in this powerful epic is the invincible Mother Russia. She appears in various guises under diverse names. One is Matryona, the main character in one of Solzhenitsyn's stories. Her lined face recalls constant, indomitable features and re-casts the spell of devotion that she is able to offer and which she so proudly deserves.

When Solzhenitsyn's novel, *One Day in the Life of Ivan Denisovich*, first appeared eight years ago, it was recognized at once in his own country and soon all over the world that a major new writer had entered the arena. As *Pravda* wrote, 'Solzhenitsyn's narrative is reminiscent at times of Tolstoy's artistic force. An unusually talented author has been added to our literature.' It would also be difficult to outdo *Pravda*'s exposé of the power exercised by Solzhenitsyn's narrative art: 'Why is it that our heart contracts with pain as we read this remarkable story at the same time as we feel our spirits soar? The explanation lies in its profound humanity, in the quality of mankind even in the hour of degradation.'

A message about limited circumstances seldom travels far, and the words that fly around the world are those which appeal to and help us all. Such are the words of Alexander Solzhenitsyn. They speak to us of matters that we need to hear more than ever before, of the individual's indestructible dignity. Wherever that dignity is violated, whatever the reason or the means, his message is an accusation but also an assurance: those who commit such a violation are the only ones to be degraded by it. The truth of this is plain to see wherever one travels.

Even the external form which Solzhenitsyn seeks for his work bears witness to his message. This form has been termed the polyphonic or horizontal novel. It might equally be described as a story with no chief character. Which is to say that this is not individualism at the expense of the surroundings. Nor may the gallery of persons act as a collective that devours its own constituents, the individuals. Solzhenitsyn has explained what he means in polyphonism: each person becomes the chief character whenever the action concerns him. This is not just a technique, it is a creed. The narrative focuses on the only human element in existence, the human individual, with equal status among equals, one destiny among millions and a million destinies in one. This is the whole of humanism in a nutshell, for the kernel is love of mankind. This year's Nobel Prize for Literature has been awarded to the proclaimer of such a humanism.

10 December 1970

A renewed attack

Every day the thousand voices of imperialist propaganda focus, not on the great and astounding life of a great people, but on the negligible handful of corrupt self-seekers. Well, there is a certain logic in this. The inclination to fabricate falsifications and forgeries, a predilection for the dregs of society, has long since been second nature to the belligerent anti-communists.

Suffering rogues and schizophrenics of this kind, the heralds of anti-communism decided to resort to a provocation on a somewhat larger scale, and to raise a hullabaloo around the name of Solzhenitsyn, with his tacit consent. Solzhenitsyn's lampoons on the Soviet people – *The Victor's Feast*, *The First Circle*, *Cancer Ward* – which blacken the feats and achievements of our homeland and the dignity of the Soviet people, turned out to be suitable material for the current anti-Soviet campaign being blown up in the West. The writers of Ryazan, where Solzhenitsyn lived, and the Union of Writers of the USSR tried in vain to persuade him not to abuse his talents and to repudiate publicly the witches' sabbath let loose abroad around his name. Solzhenitsyn refused to listen to this advice and tried to blackmail the Writers' Union, threatening that if his anti-Soviet productions were not published they would find their way abroad. Indeed, soon afterwards not only the works but all Solzhenitsyn's pettifogging letters and statements, which it seems should be known only to him and his correspondents, became the property of the bourgeois press. There, in the West, he found patrons and admirers.

Spiritually an internal émigré, alien and hostile to the entire life of the Soviet people, Solzhenitsyn was raised by imperialist propaganda to the calling of a great Russian writer and was recently awarded the Nobel Prize. The Nobel Committee followed the lead of anti-socialist speculators who extolled Solzhenitsyn, not for his talent, but solely because he had been besmirching Soviet life. The award of the Nobel Prize to Solzhenitsyn, wrote the West German *Die Welt*, is a political demonstration.

Fakes and base insinuations by isolated renegades – such are the weapons of propaganda used by our ideological opponents. By resorting to base slander they thereby lay bare their moral and ideological poverty. The great Shakespeare wrote about the 'quicksand of deceit'. Such sand is an unreliable support in the struggle of ideas that is taking place in the world. They crumble on contact with the truth of our life. The Soviet people have built a truly great society, a society of political equality, of genuine humanism, of freedom and democracy for working people, and it is legitimately proud of its historic achievements. This is something nobody will succeed in ignoring or belittling.

(*Pravda*, 17 December 1970)

The Nobel Prize: the problem of delivery

The New York Times *editorial (14 September 1971)*

Sweden's world prestige gains no luster from revelations of the submission by its Government to Soviet cultural policy with regard to Aleksandr Solzhenitsyn's richly deserved Nobel Prize for Literature.

Mr Solzhenitsyn, it will be recalled, decided last year not to go to Stockholm to receive his prize for fear the Soviet regime would not let him return to his native land. Now it emerges that Stockholm rejected a suggestion by the author that he be awarded the prize in a ceremony at Sweden's Embassy in Moscow. Premier Olof Palme has explained rather lamely that Mr Solzhenitsyn could have gotten the prize at the embassy without a ceremony, but 'a ceremony at the embassy might have been interpreted as a political manifestation against the Soviet Union.'

It does not appear to have occurred to Premier Palme that his veto of the ceremony could also be interpreted as a political manifestation, one signifying subservience to the Soviet Government's literary-political standards and implying at least partial repudiation of the judgment of the Nobel Prize committee in honoring Mr Solzhenitsyn. No similar concern seems to have bothered the Stockholm regime in repeatedly denouncing the United States on the Vietnam war and in giving haven to American deserters. Apparently the risks of offending Washington and Moscow are weighed on different scales in Stockholm.

Two letters to the New York Times

1. (Published on 17 September 1971):

To the Editor:

I was surprised to read the editorial of Sept. 14 in The Times concerning the Nobel Prize of [Aleksandr] Solzhenitsyn. The Times has evidently been misinformed about the facts. But it also touches upon a question of general interest, i.e., the functions of embassies in international cooperation.

The Swedish Academy selects the Nobel Prize laureates in literature. The Nobel Foundation presents the prizes. These institutions are completely independent of the Swedish Government. The King performs and members of the Government take part in the ceremonial distribution in Stockholm.

The Swedish Government does not deal with the question of fairness or justice in the choice of recipients. This is true of the laureates in physics and chemistry as well as in literature.

In the event the laureate cannot participate in the ceremony in Stockholm it has happened that the Swedish Embassy at the request of the Foundation has assisted in delivering the prize.

The Swedish Embassy in Moscow was certainly willing to present the Nobel Prize to Solzhenitsyn. The Swedish Embassy was, however, not prepared to comply with the ceremonial suggested by the representative of Solzhenitsyn's publisher, who wished such forms as would have purposely represented a political manifestation against the Government in the country where the embassy was accredited. My involvement in the question was solely to confirm to the publisher that the embassy was prepared to present the prize. I have certainly not vetoed any ceremony. I simply left this question to the good judgment of Gunnar Jarring, the Swedish Ambassador to Moscow.

It would seem as if The Times editorial is of the opinion that the Swedish Embassy dealt with this matter in a way which would reflect a submission to a great power.

Sweden has acted as host to a few hundred American deserters. This is true and according to our laws. Sweden has also acted as a host to tens of thousands of political refugees from Eastern Europe. This is also according to our laws.

It is also true that the Swedish Government has criticized the war in Vietnam, and the American commitment there. The Swedish Government has also criticized the Soviet invasion of Czechoslovakia in terms stronger than most other governments. We have clearly voiced our opinions on the position of Jews in the Soviet Union.

These are political decisions. We have never used embassies as a platform for expressing our opinions in a way that would disturb their normal functions as channels between governments. There have not been any celebrations with antiwar groups in the Swedish Embassy in Washington. This is a matter of principle.

I am strongly opposed to attacks toward the diplomatic representations of a country or actions that prevent embassies from performing their ordinary works. The counterpart of this view is that embassies should take care not to get deeply involved in the internal politics of the host country.

Small countries have a keen interest to see that embassies can work as links in the cooperation between governments, especially in cases where opinions differ.

OLOF PALME
Prime Minister of Sweden
Stockholm, Sept. 15, 1971

2. (Published on 24 September 1971):

To the Editor:

Premier Olof Palme of Sweden is wrong in maintaining in his Sept. 17 letter that 'a representative of Solzhenitsyn's publishers' proposed a ceremony in the Swedish Embassy in Moscow. As my book 'Go-Between in Moscow' makes clear, and as the Swedish Embassy in Moscow notes, it was the Nobel laureate himself who, through me, at an early stage inquired whether presentation of the award at the embassy was possible. The answer to this was no.

At the same time the embassy refused to give him an invitation card to the embassy for a conversation, stating as the reason that the embassy cannot invite private Soviet citizens.

In my view, Mr Palme should answer the following question: How does he envisage the presentation of the Nobel Prize in an embassy that flatly refuses to invite the laureate?

PER EGIL HEGGE
Oslo, Norway, Sept. 17, 1971

Shortly thereafter Solzhenitsyn commented on this exchange in a letter to Per Egil Hegge:

I was aghast at the reply by Palme in the *New York Times*: is the Nobel Prize actually a stolen property that must be handed over behind closed doors and without any witnesses? Why did he in advance so confidently expect a political speech? Could it not, after all, have turned out to be a purely literary speech?

18–20 September 1971

Dr Karl Ragnar Gierow, Permanent Secretary of the Swedish Academy and Chairman of the Nobel Committee, sent to Solzhenitsyn the following reply:

Per Egil Hegge has communicated in his letter to me the contents of the fragments of your letter to him from the 18th, 19th and 20th of September. Allow me first of all to respond to your sincere words of sympathy concerning my personal misfortune. They have touched me deeply and I am profoundly grateful to you.

Nils Staahle is at present on a long foreign assignment, but I have tried to send the contents of the letter to him as well. I would prefer not to respond to the questions you have raised until we have discussed them carefully with him after his return.

I think it superfluous to repeat what a great pleasure it would be for me personally to present to you in Moscow the diploma and medal of the Nobel Prize Laureate, and to meet you as well, regardless of the form that it might take. Our chances of coming to an agreement on the spot with the authorities there concerning the question of a public ceremony are now in fact – as you yourself noted – very slim. But if they were later to become more favourable, would not that mean also that it would be more possible for you to come here and to return home subsequently? As I have already written to you, this would not be the first time that a Nobel Prize Laureate of the preceding year has received the diploma and medal during the Nobel ceremonies in the following year or even later.

On certain occasions – twice in the course of seventy years, if I am not mistaken – it has also happened that the Swedish Academy has sought out the Laureate through its representatives, which is the relevant situation now. In those cases there were no special ceremonies. The entire ceremony – if we are to call it that – consisted of the Academy's representative congratulating the Laureate and presenting him the external symbols of the Nobel Prize. This, of course, will not hinder us from doing with pleasure all that practical circumstances will allow to meet your wishes, wherever and whenever the presentation of the Prize to you might·take place.

The rumours that the Swedish Ministry of Foreign Affairs was prepared to organize a ceremony in the Swedish Embassy in Moscow were, in my opinion, unfounded or imprudent. I have never heard of anything of the kind and I personally doubt that it would have been a very good thing. An official ceremony, organized by the Swedish government, could only deepen the misconception that the Swedish Academy and the Nobel Foundation are subordinate to somebody else's authority in their activities and decisions. Our complete independence is the condition for the proper awarding of the Prize, and any suspicions to the contrary can only do harm to the Nobel Prize and cast doubt on our impartiality.

This is precisely one of the questions I should like to discuss with Nils Staahle. Immediately after his return I shall write to you in greater detail about what can and should be done.

With very best wishes,
Yours truly,
KARL RAGNAR GIEROW

P.S. At a time when this letter, endorsed by the Swedish Academy on the 14th of October, was being translated, a Swedish writers' organization publicly referred to me as a man who is persecuting you and wishes to submit you to censorship. It seems that some kind of evil spirit attacks the notion of truth in writers' organizations. This was a reference to the last sentence in your message to the Nobel Prize ceremonial meeting last year, a sentence omitted for fear that it might compromise the possibility of your eventual visit here which we so enthusiastically desired. That there was no question of censorship is obvious, if only from the fact that this very phrase, together with the full text of your message, was published by us in the annual of the Nobel Foundation, *Les Prix Nobel 1970*, published in summer 1971.

KARL RAGNAR GIEROW

Stockholm, 14 October 1971

Postscript to the Russian edition abroad of *August 1914*

This book cannot be published now in our motherland except in 'Samizdat', because of censorship for reasons which are inconceivable to the normal human mind, and were it for no other reason, because it would be necessary to write the word God in lower case. But I cannot force myself to accept such a humiliation. The Party instruction to write God in lower case is a cheap atheistic pettiness, a mean triviality. Both believers and unbelievers would agree that, if the Bureau of Regional Purchases and Supplies of Foodstuffs is written with capital letters and the KGB state security police and ZAGS register offices with capitals thoughout, one might release one capital letter for the concept signifying the highest creative force of the universe. In addition, to write God in lower case would be historically false when referring to the use of the word by people in 1914 and the then prevailing notions.

The general idea embodied in the first part of this book occurred to me in 1936 at the time when I finished secondary school. Since then I have never stopped thinking about it. I understood it as the main task of my life; while I was deflected to writing other books only by the circumstances of my life and the overwhelming intensity of my experience, I was all the same progressing towards the fulfilment of this task, I was preparing myself to write this book and was collecting materials for it. And now it may seem that when I am finally approaching my goal, it may perhaps be too late: my life may be too short and my creative powers insufficient for this work which requires twenty years. Almost all contemporary observers of the events described here who might have corrected me, added to the evidence, and revealed things which were not written at the time or preserved, are already dead. Moreover, in my own country any collections of historical material which are available to others are closed to me.

However, Russian writers older than myself have avoided the

main theme of our modern history, or only touched upon it in a superficial manner. There is even less hope that those younger than myself will take it up, and if they did it would be an even more hopeless task for them to resurrect these years which are almost unintelligible even to our generation. So I must try.

In publishing the first part of my work for the Russian reader abroad, I appeal to him to send me his criticisms and supplementary information, particularly about the historical characters about whom I had very little information: on the generals A. D. Nechvolodov, Martos, Krymov, Postovsky, Filimonov, Artamonov, V. I. Gurko, Savitsky; on the colonels Kabanov, Pervushin, Kakhovsky, Isaev, Christinich, Lieutenant-Colonel Sukhachevsky, the Cossak captain Vedernikov, and the staff captain Semechkin.

I would be grateful for any unpublished material about subsequent years in the following strictly defined places: Petrograd, Moscow, Tambov, Rostov-on-Don, Novocherkask, Kislovoesk-Pyatigorsk. Other places are not included in my framework of volumes and parts of this work, the plan of which is now quite settled in my mind.

I hope that the publishing house will take the trouble to collect for me all the materials sent.

A. SOLZHENITSYN

May 1971

A Statement by Solzhenitsyn*

I want to declare publicly that my lawyer, Dr Fritz Heeb (Zurich), is my only genuine representative outside the confines of my own country. I respect very highly his honesty and his outstanding human qualities. I could not desire a better lawyer. He is exceptionally precise in executing my instructions.

One of the most important instructions given to him is to prevent a hasty and inadequate commercial publication of my books, a practice against which I did not have earlier any defence. It also involves stopping a piratical activity of pub-

*Cf. p. 184.

lishers like Flegon, who already have in the past distorted my books with thousands of mistakes and printing errors and who have now violated my author's rights by publishing a pirate edition of *August 1914*.*

A. SOLZHENITSYN

18 September 1971

*On 16 August 1971, the American *Publishers Weekly* printed an article, 'The Battle of *August 1914*', which contained the following passage: 'On August 9 the *New York Times* carried a story that Flegon Press, "a small London publishing house that specializes in manuscripts smuggled out of the Soviet Union," had already published last month an unauthorized edition of the Russian YMCA Press edition of *August 1914* and was also planning an English-language edition of the novel, to be published in London. The Bodley Head, authorized British publishers of the novel, have asked for a court injunction prohibiting such an English-language edition.'

Solzhenitsyn's open letter to the head of the KGB, Andropov

For many years, I have borne in silence the lawlessness of your employees: the inspection of all my correspondence, the confiscation of half of it, the search of my correspondents' homes, and their official and administrative persecution, the spying around my house, the shadowing of visitors, the tapping of telephone conversations, the drilling of holes in ceilings, the placing of recording apparatuses in my city apartment and at my garden cottage, and a persistent slander campaign against me from speakers' platforms when they are offered to employees of your Ministry. But after the raid yesterday, I will no longer be silent. My country cottage at Rozhdestvo, in the Naro-Fominsk district, was unoccupied and those people who were eavesdropping were counting on my absence. As I had gone back to Moscow having been taken ill suddenly, I had asked my friend Alexander Gorlov to get a spare part for the car from my country cottage. But it turned out there was no lock on the house, and voices could be heard from inside. Gorlov stepped inside and demanded the intruders' documents. In the small structure, where three or four can barely turn around, there were about ten of them in plain clothes.

On the command of the senior officer – 'To the woods with him and silence him!' – they bound Gorlov, knocked him down, dragged him face down into the woods and beat him viciously. While this was going on, some of the others ran down a side road to their car, taking parcels, documents, objects (perhaps also some of the equipment they had brought with them). However, Gorlov fought back vigorously and yelled, summoning witnesses. Neighbours from other garden plots came running in response to his shouts and barred the intruders' way to the highway and demanded their identification documents. Then one of the intruders presented a red identification card and the neighbours let them pass.

They led Gorlov, his face mutilated and his suit torn to ribbons, to the car. 'Fine methods you have', he said to those who led him. 'We are on an operation, and on an operation we can do anything.'

The one who, according to the papers he had shown the neighbours, was called Captain Ivanov then, as he himself stated, drove Gorlov to the Naro-Fominsk police station, where the local officers greeted 'Ivanov' with deference. Then Ivanov demanded from Gorlov written explanations of what had happened. Although he had been fiercely beaten, Gorlov put in writing the purpose of his trip and all the circumstances. After that the senior intruder demanded Gorlov sign an oath of secrecy. Gorlov flatly refused. Then they set off for Moscow, and on the road, the senior intruder bombarded Gorlov with literally the following phrases: 'If Solzhenitsyn finds out what took place at the dacha, it's all over with you. Your official career [Gorlov is a candidate of technical sciences and has presented for defence his doctoral dissertation and works in the State Institute of Experimental House Planning and Technical Research] will go no further; you will not be able to defend any dissertation. This will affect your family and children, and, if necessary, we will put you in prison.'

Those who know our way of life know the full feasibility of these threats. But Gorlov did not give in to them, refused to sign the pledge, and now he is threatened with reprisal. I demand from you, citizen Minister, the public identification of all the intruders, their punishment as criminals and an explanation of this incident. Otherwise I can only believe that you sent them.

13 August 1971   A. SOLZHENITSYN

To the Chairman of the Council of Ministers of the USSR, A. N. Kosygin

I enclose a copy of my letter to the Minister of State Security. I consider him personally responsible for all the illegalities mentioned. If the government of the USSR does not approve of these actions of minister Andropov I would expect an investigation into the matter.

13 August 1971   A. SOLZHENITSYN

THE STRUGGLE CONTINUES : *AUGUST* 1914

The October 1971 *issue of* Novy Mir (*which appeared in December*) *contained two poems by Evgeny F. Markin, which symbolically glorified Solzhenitsyn. The author expressed in them his remorse for having submitted to pressure over the expulsion of Solzhenitsyn from the Russian section of the Writers' Union. He compared the Russian intelligentsia to a fickle woman who has betrayed her lover. Shortly afterwards, Evgeny Markin and another writer associated with Solzhenitsyn, Alexander Galich, were expelled from the Writers' Union.*

By a tragic irony the slip of Soviet censorship in letting through this transparent allegory and the furore caused by it almost coincided with the death (on 18 *December* 1971*) of Alexander Tvardovsky, who had earlier lost the editorship of* Novy Mir. *The defiant lament for his friend, which Solzhenitsyn released for circulation, passed privately from hand to hand in Moscow.*

Soon Solzhenitsyn himself became the target of another sustained campaign of vilification in the press, this time on account of his new novel, August 1914. *It was obviously difficult to find writers who would join in this new witchhunt, so a different technique was used : the Soviet press began to reprint foreign articles attacking* August 1914. *They were then duly followed by the letters 'from the readers' (such as the indignant members of the literary circle of the Krasnodar Electrical Measurements Instruments Plant) joining in the chorus of condemnation without ever having seen the book (just as their predecessors, the lorry drivers from Minsk or Pinsk, who wrote letters about Pasternak and Sinyavsky, had never read* Doctor Zhivago *or* The Trial Begins*).*

However, the foreign articles castigating August 1914 *were also difficult to find, so Solzhenitsyn's persecutors have helped them to appear, as can be easily seen in the three cases reproduced below. In an interview given to Western correspondents Solzhen-*

itsyn denounced these clumsy provocations and made clear their source. He was no less explicit in his Lenten Letter *in which he criticized the subservience of the Orthodox hierarchy to the anti-religious state:* 'A church dictatorially ruled by atheists is a sight not seen in two thousand years'.

In the circumstances, the projected visit of the Permanent Secretary of the Swedish Academy, Dr. Karl Ragnar Gierow, to deliver the Nobel literature diploma and gold medal to Solzhenitsyn at a private ceremony in Moscow, proved impossible. At the beginning of April he was refused a visa and the ceremony had to be cancelled. Solzhenitsyn declared that this amounted to an irreversible ban on the presentation of the insignia to him inside the Soviet Union, but added : 'According to what I have been told about the Swedish Academy rules, the insignia can be kept by the Academy indefinitely. If my life is not long enough, I bequeath them to my son in my will'. *In a telegram to Dr. Gierow he said :* 'Do not be saddened. We can postpone it for many years. It is a disgrace, but not for us. I embrace you. Solzhenitsyn'.

In August 1972 *the Nobel Foundation published the Nobel lecture which Solzhenitsyn was supposed to deliver at the ceremony in Stockholm or Moscow. He said in it :* 'Woe to that nation whose literature is disturbed by the intervention of power'. *He also said :* 'In the struggle with falsehood art always did win and it always does win'. *These two statements sum up Solzhenitsyn's artistic* credo.

In Memoriam Alexander Tvardovsky
*by Alexander Solzhenitsyn**

There are many ways of killing a poet – the method chosen for Tvardovsky was to take away his offspring, his passion, his journal.

*Solzhenitsyn released this eulogy of Tvardovsky nine days after his death. He could only make a silent gesture at the funeral of his friend and protector: he kissed the corpse and threw a handful of soil on the coffin when it was sealed and put into the grave. In his eulogy he castigated the hypocrisy of the official tributes to the dead poet: Tvardovsky's press

The sixteen years of insults meekly endured by this hero were as nothing so long as his journal survived, so long as literature was not stopped, so long as people could be printed in it, so long as people could go on reading it. But then they heaped the coals of disbandment, destruction and mortification upon him, and within six months these coals had consumed him. Within six months he took to his deathbed; and only his characteristic fortitude sustained him till now, to the last drop of his consciousness, of his suffering.

Third day. The portrait over the coffin shows the dead man still only forty, his brow unfurrowed by the sweetly bitter burdens of his journal, radiant with that childishly luminescent trust that he managed to carry with him throughout his mortal life and that returned to him even when he was already doomed.

To that best of all music they bear wreaths, they bear wreaths – 'From Soviet soldiers' . . . And with reason. I remember how the lads at the front as one man preferred to marvel at his trusty "Tyorkin" to all other wartime books. And let us remember too how army libraries were forbidden to subscribe to *Novy Mir*, and how not so long ago men were hauled before the CO for questioning for reading the light blue journal.

And now the whole gang from the Writers' Union has flopped onto the scene. The guard of honor comprises that same flabby crowd that hunted him down with unholy shrieks and cries. Yes, it's an old, old custom of ours, it was the same with Pushkin: it is precisely into the hands of his enemies that the dead poet falls. And they hastily dispose of the body, covering up with glib speeches.

They crowd round the coffin in a solid ring and think they have fenced it off. Just as they destroyed our only journal and think they have won.

But you need to be deaf and blind to the last century of Russia's history to regard this as a victory and not an irreparable blunder.

---

obituary, signed, among others, by Brezhnev, Kosygin and Podgorny, did not even mention his sixteen-year-long work as the editor of *Novy Mir*, a post from which he was removed in Februray 1970.

Madmen! When the voices of the young resound, keen-edged, how you will miss this patient critic, whose gentle admonitory voice was heeded by all. Then you will be set to tear the earth with your hands for the sake of returning Trifonovich [Tvardovsky's patronymic]. But then it will be too late.

27 December 1971   (*Index*, Vol. 1, No. 1, Spring 1972)

Guns on *August*

1. The magazine Stern *about the Solzhenitsyn family** (abridged)

At the end of last year the Hamburg magazine *Stern* carried a long article on the occasion of the publication of A. Solzhenitsyn's novel *August 1914* in the German Federal Republic.

The appearance of this book in the West (the author sent the manuscript abroad himself, together with authorization to publish and detailed instructions on the disposition of royalties) proved quite opportune for anti-Sovieteers of all breeds.

Although this book seemed to be dealing with an historical theme (it described the Germans' defeat of General Samsonov's army in August 1914), the anti-Sovieteers immediately saw the 'wealth' of possibilities that A. Solzhenitsyn was providing for them . . .

*This was the first of the reprints in Soviet papers of articles on Solzhenitsyn which first appeared in foreign press and which he described in his interview as part of a centrally organized campaign against him (see pp. 285-291). Several passages in the *Stern* article (in its 21 November 1971 issue) were omitted in the *Literaturnaya Gazeta* translation. Their style was apparently considered unsuitable for Soviet readers, being either too ambivalent or too explicit. One such omitted passage read : ' In disregard of the *Dummköpfe* in the Soviet censor-bureaucracy, Solzhenitsyn has voiced his soul-felt hatred of the powers-that-be who harass patient Mother Russia. He cleverly employed a tested method that protects him from imprisonment for anti-state activities. ' The author of the article, Dieter Steiner, denied in a letter to *Die Zeit* (1 September 1972) Solzhenitsyn's allegations, but did not answer some of his precise charges (e.g., about his relations with Victor Louis. Cf. p. 285).

A host of such rapturous 'reviews' and 'analyses' has appeared in the West. The magazine *Stern* did not remain on the sidelines. However, it did not stop at pointing out the anti-Soviet trend of *August* 1914 (and at times joining in this trend). The editors of the Hamburg magazine posed the question – raised, incidentally, in other Western publications: how autobiographical is Solzhenitsyn's book ? Or, more precisely, to what degree did the author's parentage, education and inherited views affect this work ? They succeeded in uncovering something exceedingly curious.

However, let the reader, to whose attention we offer an abridged version of the *Stern* article, judge for himself:

'They were a family of boors', says Irina, aunt of Nobel Prizewinner Solzhenitsyn, about his relatives, once very wealthy landowners. In his new novel, for the rights to which Western publishers are vying, he cleverly employed a tested method that enables him to avoid imprisonment for anti-state activities. He transferred the action to prerevolutionary times. However, the reader immediately realizes that, in describing historical events, the author has contemporary problems in mind. He describes the Battle of Tannenberg, where in August 1914, the Second Russian Army was encircled and wiped out...

All the characters who appear in Solzhenitsyn's book under their real names are no longer alive, with one exception. Her name is Irina, and the writer presents her at the very beginning of the narrative as a charming, young and very wealthy woman, whose husband, Roman, is a landowner who dresses in British style. Who is Irina ? *Stern* reporter Dieter Steiner established that the name of this woman is Irina Ivanovna Shcherbak and that she is Solzhenitsyn's aunt, the sister-in-law of his mother Taisia, who died of tuberculosis in 1944 ...

Up to now the Solzhenitsyn family history remained absolutely unknown. The records state: 'Alexander Isayevich Solzhenitsyn was born into a teacher's family in Kislovodsk, North Caucasus, on 11 December 1918'. This indicates petit-bourgeois ancestry. But Irina Shcherbak has more accurate information. Solzhenitsyn's father Isai was the son of a rich landowner. When he married in 1917, he added his wife's capital to his own. He married Taisia, the daughter of a big landholder, Zakhar Shcherbak.

Solzhenitsyn's mother grew up in a manor house that resembled a castle. Her brother Roman made a good match: his wife Irina, now languishing in poverty, inherited an estate of millions from her father. She was the wealthiest of them and, since she turned over all her money to her husband, the latter could strut like a feudal lord.

Irina sadly recalled her life before World War 1, in the years when she and her husband went on long foreign tours. They visited the Daimler works in Stuttgart and bought a cigar-shaped sports car, which Roman decided to drive in a Moscow–St. Petersburg rally. He already owned a Rolls-Royce at that time. In all Russia there were only nine such cars then. During the war the Supreme Commander-in-Chief, Grand Duke Nikolai Nikolayevich, requisitioned this luxurious car for his personal use.

Solzhenitsyn, after he returned from exile in 1956, visited his aunt Irina in Georgiyevsk and questioned her for days on end about their family history. Part of what she told him appeared in the book *August 1914* . . .

Solzhenitsyn's parents married in 1917 at the front where his father, a young officer, was fighting. In 1918 the father returned to his farmstead at Sablya. The Civil War had begun by then, and the Red Army was after the landowners. Many were shot. One day Irina received a telegram from Solzhenitsyn's mother Taisia: 'Isai is dying'.

Irina and her husband went to them immediately and found Solzhenitsyn's father mortally wounded in a hospital. The official version was that it was a hunting accident, but apparently it was suicide. A few minutes before he died, he told Irina: 'Look after my son. I am sure I will have a son'. Taisia was three months pregnant.

Alexander Solzhenitsyn was born in the home of his aunt Irina. The Reds had confiscated all the belongings of the family. Taisia could hardly make both ends meet, working as a typist in Rostov. Uncle Roman found a job as a bus driver. After he died in 1944 Irina was left without any means of livelihood . . .

It is not without bitterness that Irina Shcherbak recalls her last meeting with the famed nephew. This was in 1970. Solzhenitsyn had invited his aunt to come to Ryazan and sent money for her fare. 'When I stepped out of the train', the old woman related, 'I saw Natasha [Solzhenitsyn's wife] and Sanya [Alexander] suddenly going into the station and hiding there. In my old clothes I looked too shabby. They were ashamed of me. If I had money, I would have turned back at once, but I had only 20 kopeks left'.

Irina Shcherbak does not agree at all that Solzhenitsyn, who was expelled from the Soviet Writers' Union in 1969 and since then cannot publish a line in the Soviet Union, lives in abject poverty. 'They set up a household like that of a rich bourgeois family', she reports. (Solzhenitsyn's royalties in the West have earned him a fortune of several millions.) 'They made regular trips to Moscow – to the theater or the movies' . . .

We are, of course, far from the thought of establishing a vulgar sociological link between a man's origins, education and the surroundings of his youth, on the one hand, and his activities at a mature age, on the other.

Literaturnaya Gazeta decided to check the facts set forth in *Stern* and sent a correspondent to Stavropol Territory.

Indeed, old-timers in the village of Sablya still remember the wealthy Solzhenitsyns. The grandfather, Semyon Yeumovich Solzhenitsyn, had up to 2,000 dessiatins of land and about 20,000 head of cattle at the opening of the century. More than 50 field hands worked for him. According to those who had worked for him, Semyon Solzhenitsyn and his four sons, Isai, Vasily, Konstantin and Ilya and his daughter Maria lived on two farmsteads, from which he ran his extensive estate. In addition, he had two large manor houses in the village of Sablya.

A big landowner, a prominent figure on the board of a Rostov bank and a man of stern temper, S. Ye. Solzhenitsyn held the entire region under his thumb.

(*Literaturnaya Gazeta*, 12 January 1972)

2. *When history is stood in the corner* (abridged)

We have already informed our readers, in *Literaturnaya Gazeta* (No. 2, 1972), that the publication of A. Solzhenitsyn's novel, *August 1914* in the West (the author sent the manuscript abroad himself) served as the signal for a sensational anti-Soviet campaign. The buorgeois press continues to extol Solzhenitsyn's new book.

What stirred up this frenzied publicity ? What kind of book is *August 1914*, in actuality ? The answers are provided by the prominent Finnish writer Martti Larni*, in an article in the Swedish newspaper *Norrskensflamman*.

. . . Historical experience convinces us that history has been falsified more than once ; attempts to falsify it are encountered nowadays, too. It is easy to expose a direct lie, but a falsehood cloaked in the trappings of literature often acquires verisimilitude. Some writers have a gift for treating facts so as to make black appear white . . .

These reflections were prompted by Aleksandr Solzhenitsyn's new novel, *August 1914*.

It is customary for writers to publish their books in their own country and in their own language. Frequently, if the

*Martti Larni worked on the staff of *Elanto*, the organ of the Finnish Cooperative Movement, from 1937 and was its editor from 1943 to 1951. His novels have been translated into many languages, but he is not well known. He is described in the Finnish *Who's Who* as non-political, though his articles bear a distinctly pro-Soviet character and he frequently writes for Soviet papers. In an interview in *Uusi Suomi* (26 February 1972) Larni denied having written his article for *Norrskensflamman*, a small-circulation Swedish communist newspaper published in Luleå. He did not even know of such a paper and said that he wrote the article for *Literaturnaya Gazeta* at its request. He also stated that he was dealing in the article with Anatol Shub's review of *August 1914*, and not with the book itself which he had not read. His article also appeared in the Czechoslovak *Rude Pravo* (11 Feb. 1972), which asserted that it was written especially for it. *Literaturnaya Gazeta* omitted just one passage which appeared in *Rude Pravo*, a sentence with an anti-Semitic innuendo describing Anatol Shub's review of *August 1914* as coming ' from the front ranks of the world Zionist choir '.

work possesses literary merit and the critics view it favorably, it is translated into foreign languages and published abroad. But Solzhenitsyn is an exception to the general rule. He immediately sent the manuscript of his novel abroad, with full authorization to publish. *August* 1914 appeared last year under the imprint of a West German publisher and created something of a sensation in the West: naturally – the world had finally obtained 'an authentic picture of the Russian way of life'! Although the novel treats of events of 1914, some Western critics relate the novel to modern times; they find a basis for this in the work itself. Solzhenitsyn's novel hypnotized Anatole Shub, the notorious *Washington Post* correspondent who used to titillate the philistines by transmitting fabrications of various kinds from Moscow to the USA. Shub considers *August* 1914 an indictment of the Soviet Union and its social system.

In Solzhenitsyn's novel the enemies of the Soviet Union sought and found four aces for their political poker game: Tsarist Russia was simply an ideal state; the October Revolution was a big, tragic mistake; the consequence of the revolution was humiliation of the nation; the Russians lost the sense of patriotism. Shub and other political cardsharps hide these four aces up their sleeves at times and then, at the required moment, cast them on the table to prove the 'universal weakness' of the Soviet Union. Poor history, which Solzhenitsyn, in company with the Shubs, stands in the corner like an offending schoolboy! . . .

Solzhenitsyn, in his novel, admires the high educational level of the Germans and their military skill. From certain hints an attentive reader can conclude that the author would not have been averse to seeing the Germans win the war. Obviously, the Germans themselves wanted to win, in order to turn Russia into a colony of militarist Germany. The same desire drove the Nazi armies into the Soviet Union in 1941, when Hitler promised to topple 'the colossus with the feet of clay' in a matter of a few days.

World literature contains many instances in which a writer, in describing the events of one epoch, had in mind another epoch, most often his own. Solzhenitsyn, while placing the action of his novel in prerevolutionary times, tries to draw a parallel with our days. The attentive reader who is at all familiar with the history of Europe will catch on quickly, however. If *August 1914* is deliberately aimed against the Soviet Union (as Anatole Shub, citing the novel, affirms), one can say of the author himself that he belongs to that 'homeless intelligentsia' that does not know its country and its history and does not love its people.

(*Literaturnaya Gazeta*, 23 February 1972)

3. *Aleksander Solzhenitsyn's* August 1914, *or The truth about the book and about the myth* (abridged)
by Jerzy Romanowski*

. . . There was no need to spend hundreds of pages of paper to prove that the armies of [Russian Generals] Rennenkampf and Samsonov, invading enemy territory, were badly led. This is an elementary truism, expounded long ago by military historians and set forth popularly in memoirs and writers' works . . .

*There can be little doubt that this article proves conclusively Solzhenitsyn's assertions about the coordinated character of the campaign against him (see pp. 280–293). It appeared originally on 26 March 1972 in the small Polish magazine, *Wroclawski Tygodnik Katolikow* (Wroclaw Catholic Weekly), published by the notorious P A X organization, led by Boleslaw Piasecki, the Polish prewar fascist leader, who after the war became a tool of the communist regime in its fight against the Catholic Church. The author of the article, Jerzy Romanowski, is quite unknown in Poland and 'his' article bears all the indications of a clumsy translation from Russian, a translation which must have been produced in haste. The Russian text of the article has no traces of an alien origin, while the Polish 'original' contains Polonized Russian words and sentences, as well as expressions which are grammatically or stylistically Russian rather than Polish. Moreover, the translator, being obviously in a hurry, retained the Russian transliteration of foreign names (which are spelled phonetically in the Cyrillic alphabet, while they retain their original Latin spelling in Polish). In retranslating the proper names from the Russian text, the Polish translator has rendered them phonetically. Thus in the Polish text of the article

This is not the place for a detailed operational-strategic analysis of the East Prussian operation, for the novel, despite all the boundless pretensions of the author, is by no means a military study. My purpose is much simpler: to trace, through the example of key moments of the military operations, the extent to which Solzhenitsyn's personal interpretation corresponds to the objective course of events (as they have gone down in history). It is instructive here to turn to a disinterested party.

Among the many books about the first World War that have appeared in the West in recent years, *The Guns of August*, a popular work by the American writer Barbara Tuchman, first published in 1962 and repeatedly reissued since then, compels attention. This book, recognized in America as a best seller, is similar to Solzhenitsyn's novel in the facts it deals with: both writers set out to describe the first month of the war, although the theme of Tuchman's work is broader – she covers all the fronts.

The author of *August* 1914 constantly emphasizes that his one and only concern is the truth, but even a cursory comparison with the popular American book leads to the lamentable conclusion that the transoceanic writer is much more objective about Russia than Solzhenitsyn is . . .

Solzhenitsyn did not seek objective truth, he sought only to present events in a propagandist version similar to the position of apologists of German militarism . . .

Barbara Tuchman becomes Barbara Takman, Schlieffen becomes Szlifen, and many other proper names quoted in the article are given in their Russian phonetic spelling. The translator was obviously ignorant of these names and therefore could not give their correct Latin spelling in Polish. Ironically, a footnote in the Russian text of the article (probably added only after the text was given for translation into the ' original Polish ') has a footnote in which the name of Barbara Tuchman, properly spelled, is printed in the Latin alphabet. At the beginning of 1973, 10 years after its appearance in the West, Barbara W. Tuchman's *The Guns of August* appeared in the Soviet Union. Mrs. Tuchman was very skeptical about its being 'a very effective counter' to Solzhenitsyn's book circulating clandestinely, and said that her assessment of the events of August 1914 would not be very different from Solzhenitsyn's (*The New York Times*, 8 January 1973).

We should not be surprised that Solzhenitsyn is so popular in the West, particularly in certain literary-political circles, and that his books have become 'pointers on the scales' for these circles. *August 1914* has not escaped this fate.

As was to have been expected, this book was received in the West with open arms as a work whose value – political value, we might add – consists in hatred for the Soviet Union. (The magazine *Stern* does not conceal that this is indeed the chief merit of the book: 'In describing historical events, the author raises contemporary problems'.) Thus, over there they hail the story as an anti-Soviet work and simultaneously give Solzhenitsyn a vote of confidence.

Such is the truth about the book, about the writer, and about the myth spread around his personality and his latest book *August 1914*.

(*Literaturnaya Rossiya*, 7 April 1972)

Solzhenitsyn's interview with western correspondents*, 30 March 1972

What is he working on now?

October 1916, the second 'knot' (volume) of the same book.

Will he finish it soon?

No. In the course of work it became clear that this 'knot' was more complicated than I had supposed. It will be necessary to take into consideration the history of social and intellectual currents from the end of the nineteenth century, for they imprinted themselves on the characters. Without the preceding events, there can be no understanding of the people.

*Solzhenitsyn's interview has appeared in the Western press (*The New York Times* and *The Washington Post* of 3 April 1972) in an incomplete form. The text, reproduced here, received a wide distribution in *Samizdat*.

Is he not apprehensive that, in delving
into the detailed history of Russia, he will isolate himself
from universal, timeless subjects ?

On the contrary, I think that much that is universal, and even timeless, will become clear here.

Is it necessary to study a lot of material ?

Very much so. And in one sense this work is not what I am used to, for until recently I was involved only with the present day and wrote out of my life's experience. On the other hand, there are so many adverse external circumstances that it was far easier for an obscure student in provincial Rostov in 1937–38 to gather material about the Samsonov disaster (not yet knowing that I was also fated to go through the same places, only this time it was not we who were going to be surrounded, but we who were to surround the others). And although the hovel where my mother and I lived was demolished by a bomb in 48, and all our effects, books, papers burned up – these two notebooks by some miracle were saved, and when I returned from exile they were handed over to me. Now I have used them.

Yes, in those days they didn't put special obstacles in my way. But now . . . You Western people can't imagine my situation. I'm living in my native country, writing a novel about Russia, but it is more difficult for me to gather material for it than if I were writing about Polynesia. For this next 'knot' I need to visit certain historic premises, which are now housing various institutions, but the authorities won't give me a pass. My access to central and province archives is blocked. I have to travel around the sites of events and conduct interviews with old men, the last expiring witnesses, but for this I need the approval and aid of local authorities, which I cannot get. And without that, everybody will shut up, no one will tell anything because of suspicion, and without authorization I would be detained at each step. This has already been tested.

Can others – assistants, secretaries –
do this for him ?

They cannot. In the first place, as a non-member of the Union of Writers I do not have the right to a secretary or assistant. In the second place, such a secretary, representing my interests, would be as boxed in and restricted as I am. And in the third place, I simply have nothing with which to pay a secretary. You see, after the royalties from *Ivan Denisovich*, I had no earnings, except for money left me by the late K. I. Chukovsky, and now that is running out. I lived six years on the former and three years on the latter. I managed because I limited my expenditures to my former level, when I was a teacher. I never spend more on myself than would be necessary to pay a secretary.

Cannot money be obtained from the West ?

I have made out a will, and when the opportunity arises to execute it, all the royalties will be channeled by my attorney into social uses in my homeland. (The straight-from-the-heart, never-tell-a-lie *Literaturnaya Gazeta* wrote : 'He gave detailed instructions on how the royalties are to be disbursed', but it innocently omitted to mention that they are to be used for social purposes in my homeland.) I myself will use only the Nobel Prize money. However, they have made my receipt of that money degrading, difficult, and indefinite. The Ministry of Foreign Trade has notified me that special permission of the collegium is required for each incoming sum : will they pay it to me at all, in what form, and what percentage ?

How, then, in spite of everything, does he
manage to collect material ?

Here, again, is a peculiarity of our life that for the Western man is probably difficult to understand. So far as I can visualize, possibly wrongly, it is an established practice in the West that each act of labor must be remunerated, and it is not customary to do work gratis. But among us, with what, for example, does *Samizdat* support itself, if not by unpaid labor ? People expend their labor, their free time, sitting up nights over work for which all they can expect is persecution.

So it is with me. My work and my themes are widely known in the society at large, even beyond the limits of Moscow ; well-wishers, often people unknown to me, send me (not by mail, needless to say, for then it would not reach me) various books, even extremely rare ones, their own reminiscences, etc. Sometimes it is *à propos* and very valuable, sometimes it's inappropriate, but it always touches me and strengthens my vivid sense that I am working for Russia, and Russia is helping me. And another thing. Often I myself ask knowledgeable people, specialists, for consultations, at times quite complex, or to select materials, which demands time and labor, and not only has no one ever asked for payment, but all are delighted to help.

And after all, this is still quite dangerous. A kind of forbidden, contaminated zone has been created around me and my family. And to this day there are people in Ryazan who have been dismissed from work for visiting my home a few years ago. A corresponding member of the Academy of Sciences, T. Timofeyev, Director of a Moscow institute, having just learned that a mathematician working under him was my wife, became so fearful that he forced her dismissal with indecorous haste, although this was against all the laws and was almost immediately after she had given birth to a child. A family made a perfectly legal apartment exchange, until it became known that this family was mine. Scarcely had this been found out when several bureaucrats in the Moscow City Soviet were disciplined : how could they have allowed Solzhenitsyn, although not him personally, but his infant son, to be registered in the center of Moscow ?

By the same token, an informant will meet me, and we will consult for an hour or two – and at that point constant surveillance begins, as if it were a question of a state criminal, and identification is sought. Then they investigate still further : whom this man dares to meet.

Incidentally, it's not always that way. The state security has its own schedule and its own deep perceptions. Some days there is no outside observation, or only the simplest. On other days it seems they are all over, for example, before the arrival of Heinrich Böll. They'll park cars at each of the two entries, with three of them sitting in a car, and there is more than one shift; they drive off after my visitors, and chase pedestrians as well. If you keep in mind that they monitor telephone and ordinary conversations around the clock, analyze tape recordings and all correspondence, and in some spacious building collate all the data received and compare them (this is not the task of the lower ranks), then you have to be amazed at the number of idlers in the prime of life and at the peak of their powers who would be able to be employed in productive labor for the good of the home-land, who are instead occupied with my acquaintances and me and thinking up enemies for themselves. And someone else again is digging into my biography, someone is sending agents abroad to sow chaos in the publication of my books. Someone is composing and coordinating a general plan for throttling me. That plan has not yet been successful, and has therefore been revised several times in mid-course. But its development through the years can be traced by stages.

It was decided to throttle me in 1965, when they seized my files and were horrified by my works on the labor camp years – as if these works could avoid bearing the stamp of men damned for eternity! If these were the Stalin years, nothing could have been simpler: I would have disappeared and no one would have asked any questions. But after the Twentieth and Twenty-second Party Congresses it became more complicated.

First, it was decided to SILENCE me. Not a line would ap-pear anywhere, no one would mention me even menda-ciously, and in a few years I would be forgotten. Then I could be taken away. But by then the era of *Samizdat* had arrived, and my books spread through the country, then went abroad as well. Silencing didn't work.

At some point they started (and have not ended to this day) SLANDER FROM CLOSED PLATFORMS.

This too is almost impossible for a Western man to

imagine. There exists throughout the country an established network of party and public education and a lecture network. There is no institution or military unit, no district center or state farm, where lecturers and propagandists do not appear according to a definite schedule, and all of them, in all places, simultaneously say the same thing, on instructions from a single center. There are certain variations – depending on the audiences, whether they are in the capital, or in the provinces, in the army, or in the universities, etc. Thanks to the fact that only reliable collaborators or residents in a given area are admitted, such lectures are in fact of a closed nature, or are closed outright. Sometimes orders are given, even to the scientific staff, to surrender all notebooks and pens. Any information, any slogan can be fed into this network. In 1966 the order went out to say the following about me: first, that under Stalin I was jailed WITH REASON, that I was wrongly rehabilitated, that my works are criminal, and so forth. Meanwhile, the lecturers themselves have never in their lives read these works, because the authorities were afraid to give them to them, but they were ordered to speak in that way.

The system, or its purpose, is that they lecture only to their own collaborators. Outside, serenity and good will, no maligning at all, while unanswerable slander spills over the country: you can't travel to all the towns, they won't let you into these closed auditoriums, but there are thousands of these lecturers, and while there is no one to complain to, the slander takes possession of minds.

How does this become known?

This is a new era, a different era. Quite a lot leaks through to me both from the provinces and through Moscow. The times are such that at all these lectures, even the most closed, my well-wishers are sitting everywhere, and later they inform me through various channels: on such and such a date in some auditorium or other a lecturer named this or that said this particular lie or slander about you. The most lurid stuff I write down, it may come in handy some day, for confronting one or another of these lecturers with it. Maybe the time will come in our country when they will personally answer for this in court.

Why don't the audiences object right there,
if they see distortion ?

Oh, this is impossible here, even today. No one dares to stand up and object to a party propagandist, or tomorrow it's good-by to your job, or even good-by to your freedom. There have been cases where they have used me like litmus paper to check applicants for graduate school or preferred employment: 'Have you read Solzhenitsyn ? What is your attitude toward him ?' – and the fate of the candidate depends on the answer.

They talk a lot of nonsense at these lectures. At one time they were hashing over my family history, not knowing the least thing about its particulars, and at the lowest backstairs level. Imagine what kind of occupations there are in this country, what wages are paid for, if it is not the fishwives but the official propagandists in the network of EDUCATION who are examining on the platforms someone's marriage or the birth and baptism of a son. There was a time when they were quite eagerly rubbing their hands over my patronymic 'Isayevich'. They would say, trying to seem casual: 'Incidentally, his real surname is SolzheniTSER or SolzheniTSKER, but in our country, of course, this is of no importance'.

But one charge was taken seriously, one that would always catch the ear of the audience: TRAITOR TO THE HOMELAND. When it comes to smearing, we generally adopt not reasons, but the most primitive labels, the grossest and the simplest epithets, in order, so to speak, to arouse the 'wrath of the masses'. In the 1920's it was the 'counterrevolutionary', in the 1930's the 'enemy of the people', in the 1940's and after, the 'traitor to the homeland'. Ah, how they thumbed through my military records, how they searched – was I not even for two little days a prisoner of war, like Ivan Denisovich – that would have been a find ! But, perhaps, in a closed lecture you can convince a gullible public of any lie. And the word went out for years – YEARS – in all the auditoriums near and far, throughout the whole country: Solzhenitsyn voluntarily surrendered to the Germans as a prisoner! No, he surrendered a whole battery! After that he served as a policeman for the occupiers! No, he was a Vlassovite!* No, he served right in the Gestapo! Outwardly, all is calm, but under the skin there is this cancer of slander. *Novy Mir* once organized a readers' conference in Novosibirsk, and they sent Tvardovsky a note: 'How could you allow an officer of the Gestapo to be printed in your magazine?' Thus, public opinion the country over was fully prepared for any reprisal against me. Still, we are no longer in that era, when you could crush someone without it becoming known.

The truth had to be admitted publicly that I was an army officer, and that my wartime service was irreproachable. The fog hung in the air with no rain and started to clear away.

Then began a new campaign of accusations that I myself gave *Cancer Ward* to the West. What lies did they not tell in the closed lectures: how somewhere abroad (where – is not known) they apprehended an acquaintance of my acquaintance (no name), and his suitcase had a false bottom, and there were my works (no titles). And this drivel was seriously propagated in all the provinces, and people were horrified – what a villain I am, again, a traitor to the homeland. Later, with my exclusion from the Union of Writers, there were open hints that I should get out of the country, under the same 'treason to the homeland' pretext. Then it started all over again in connection with the Nobel Prize. From all the rostrums they wailed: THE NOBEL PRIZE IS JUDAS PAY FOR BETRAYING ONE'S HOMELAND. They repeat it even now, not embarrassed that they may be casting a shadow on Pablo Neruda, for example. They are unreservedly insulting all Nobel laureates and the Nobel Foundation itself.

*Cf. p. 193.

But, after all, you yourself sent August 1914
abroad – do you mean to say that this act
is not incriminating ?

So far, people have had the good sense not to incriminate me. But the honorable *Literaturnaya Gazeta* has been guilty of an omission, innocent, like all of its 'omissions': 'Solzhenitsyn AT ONCE sent the manuscript of his novel abroad' – oh, that's not a lie ! – only the smallest thing has been left out: AFTER HE OFFERED IT TO SEVEN SOVIET PUBLISHERS – Artistic Literature, Soviet Writer, Young Guard, and various magazines, asking, DID THEY NOT WISH TO READ IT THROUGH, or at least to leaf through my novel – AND NOT ONE MANIFESTED A DESIRE even to take it in their hands. As if they had entered into collusion. Not one answered my letter, not one asked for the manuscript.

However, the appearance of *August* suggested to my pursuers a new course. The point was that in this novel I told in detail about my maternal and paternal lineage. Although many friends and acquaintances who are alive today knew my relatives, the omniscient state security, absurd though this may seem, learned about them only from this novel. So at that point they plunged into a 'follow-up' with the aim of compromising me – by Soviet standards. In this they redoubled their efforts. First, the RACIAL line was again revived. Or rather, more precisely, the Jewish line. A special major of state security named Blagovidov rushed off to check the personal files of all the Isaaks in the archives of Moscow University for 1914 in the hope of proving that I am a Jew. This would yield a tempting opportunity to 'explain' my literary position. After all, with the appearance of my historical novel the task of those who are baiting me grows complicated: it is not enough to defame the author, it is necessary also to undermine trust in his views of Russian history – those already expressed and possible future ones.

Alas, the racial research was thwarted: I turned out to be a Russian.

Then they traded the racial line for a class line, for which they approached an old aunt, pasted together an article out of her stories, and assigned it to the *boulevard* magazine *Stern** to print.

The editor-in-chief of *Stern* now insists that it was none other than his correspondent (Steiner) who visited my auntie in September, after having gone to Livadia. But it's all a lie. In AUGUST, not September, three Soviet citizens who spoke Russian beautifully (and Steiner, it would appear, does not speak it) arrived and called on my auntie five times, being in no rush. They were quite captivated with her own life story, asked her if they might read her notes for a few hours – and did not return; they stole them. Being almost blind, she did not see what they looked like, but in manner, in psychological makeup – resembling the character of Dickens' Job Trotter – the guests were from Victor Louis'† crowd, in fact, I don't rule him out in person. *Stern's* tie with Victor Louis has long been public knowledge. For example, when Louis came to me with his alibis about not having sold *Cancer Ward* to the West, the details of our conversation and some photographs (thievishly taken with a telescopic lens from the bushes) appeared in none other than *Stern*, but not under his by-line. Even in my slight experience I have noticed that *Stern* enjoys special privileges in our country, that it has access to telephone numbers and addresses that are possible to obtain only from those who are monitoring my telephone conversations and censoring my letters. The *Stern* article had scarcely appeared when Verchenko, a secretary of the Writers' Union, said at a party meeting: 'THIS IS THAT SOURCE WHICH WE HAVE EVERY GROUND FOR BELIEVING' – the publication in *Stern* is directed from the same center as the pirate publications of Flegon and Langen-Müller, with which someone wanted to undermine my books' protection under international copyright.

There is an opinion that Langen-Müller's translation is not bad.

*See pp. 268–271.
†See pp. 176–183.

I am convinced that the translation is flattened out, that is, the linguistic multi-dimensionality is lost. I often have elliptical syntax there, that is, omissions of what would seem to be even essential words, and that's very difficult for a foreigner to render, moreover, in 4 months' time? Did they perhaps gather a collective of translators, since they did not spare any expense? But a collective does not improve a translation.

The publisher Fleissner maintains that
he received the manuscript as early as the spring,
from Samizdat.

He is also a liar. How could he have received it, when I released only one copy from my desk before June, and it went to the YMCA Press? Well, let him name the person FROM WHOM he received it. It would have to be a person very close to me or a thief of the category that comes to a home because he has it on reliable authority that the occupant is absent. Fleissner wants to hide ignobly behind our noble *Samizdat*. He indulges in a logical fallacy: *since* my previous works first appeared in *Samizdat, it means this* time it is so, too. But it is precisely not so! I freely gave out my earlier writings to be read. But I wanted to take this book all the way into print myself. Only when the book came out – only then would I begin to give the manuscript to those who wanted to read it.

So you see, from the state of the *Stern* article and from the mischievous prompting, certain familiar hands are discernible, especially there where they have decided to judge the nature of literary creation. We learn that Solzhenitsyn has employed a WILY literary device; he has transferred the action to prerevolutionary times – for that he delved into people of another era, read quite a few military and historical works, and took pains to depict not the war he went through himself but another, dissimilar one – all in order to erupt on one page of the book with just one phrase, which *Stern* insinuates is to be understood in a figurative sense, so that Solzhenitsyn should be put in prison. It is exactly the same

manner in which leaders of the Writers' Union reproached
me for occupying myself with a study of cancer, for entering
a cancer clinic, and for deliberately contracting cancer in
order to sneak in some kind of symbol. Cowardly bullies
butt in to judge the nature of *belles lettres*. It is impossible
for them to get it through their skulls that one has for a long
time had no need for subterfuges and has been saying everything he thinks about the present day openly.

How authentic is the information in the Stern *article ?*

Let's call it by its proper name – the *Literaturnaya Gazeta*
article. It is authentic in what coincides with what has already been published in my novel. The rest is ludicrous
nonsense, rubbish, and very pointed, deliberate lying. Only,
in their zeal they overshoot the mark. For example, they
assert that both my grandfathers were LANDOWNERS in the
Northern Caucasus. It is embarrassing that *Literaturnaya
Gazeta* is so ignorant of the fatherland's history. Apart from
a few Cossack generals known to everyone, there never were
any LANDOWNERS (that is, landholding nobles, the progeny
of the ancient notables who received land for military service)
at all in the Northern Caucasus. All the lands belonged to
Terek and Kuban Cossack regular troops. Many of those
lands, right up until the twentieth century, were empty and
abandoned; there was a shortage of working hands. The
peasant settlers could gain possession of only small holdings,
but Cossack troops willingly rented out as much land as
could be wanted, at fantastically low rents.

My grandfathers were not Cossacks, both of them were
muzhiks. By pure accident, the peasant origins of the Solzhenitsyns is even established by documents of 1698, when
my forbear Filipp suffered from the wrath of Peter I (cf.
Voronezhskaya kommuna, 9 March 1969, article about the
city of Bobrov). And my great-great-grandfather was exiled
for taking part in a rebellion from the Voronezh *gubernia*
to the lands of the Caucasus military settlements. There,
evidently because he was a rebel, they didn't place him
among the Cossacks, but let him live on an abandoned land.

The Solzhenitsyns were ordinary Stavropol peasants. In Stavropol before the revolution, a few oxen and horses, ten cows, and two hundred sheep were by no means considered as wealth. The whole large family worked with its hands. In the farmstead stood a simple clay hut, I remember it. But to justify the CLASS line, in order to demonstrate the truth of the Most Advanced Theory, it is necessary to invent a bank, to add zeros onto the sum of possessions, to concoct a story of 50 farm hands, to call my half-sister working on a collective farm to the administration offices for questioning, and to present the Shcherbak's *dacha* in Kislovodsk, where I was born, as the picture of a 'country manor' of the Solzhenitsyns. But any fool can see that it is not even a house in a Cossack *stanitsa*. That's the kind of 'Landowners' we were. The scum blew up this lie also to impute to my father, a *narodnik* and a *Tolstoyan*, a cowardly suicide 'out of fear of the Reds' – without having seen his much-desired firstborn and having scarcely lived with his beloved wife! The judgment of a reptile.

About his mother.

She raised me in incredibly hard circumstances. Widowed before my birth, she did not remarry – mainly for fear that a stepfather might be too harsh with me. We lived in Rostov for 19 years up until the war – and for 15 of them we couldn't obtain a room from the state, and the whole time rented various dilapidated shacks from private owners for high payments; and when we finally did get a room, it was part of a reconstructed stable. It was always cold and drafty, it was heated with coal, which was hard to get, and water had to be brought in from afar. I learned what running water in an apartment means only recently. Mama knew French and English well and on top of it learned stenography and typing, but in the institutions that paid well she was never employed because of her SOCIAL ORIGIN, even in the non-sensitive ones, like *Melstroi* (the Flour Mill Construction Administration), they subjected her to a PURGE, which means that they dismissed her with restrictions on her future rights. That

forced her to look for extra evening work, she did her house-
work late at night, and was always short of sleep. Because
of our living conditions she suffered from frequent colds,
then contracted tuberculosis and died at the age of 49. I was
at the front at the time and I did not get to see her grave
until 12 years later, after prison camp and exile.

Aunt Irina.

Mama sent me twice or three times to her place for
summer holidays. The rest is the fruit of her imagination,
which is already hazy. I never lived at her place.

What does he remember about his father ?

Only snapshots, and the accounts of my mother and
people who knew him. From the university he went as a
volunteer to the front and served in the Grenadier Artillery
Brigade. Once, when the battery was set on fire, he himself
pulled out ammunition boxes. He received three officers'
decorations during the first World War, but in my childhood they were considered dangerously incriminating, so
my mother and I, I remember, buried them in the ground,
fearing a search. Almost the whole front had already col-
lapsed but the battery in which my father served remained
on the front lines until the Peace of Brest-Litovsk itself.
He and Mama were married at the front by the brigade
chaplain. Papa returned in the spring of 1918 and soon afterwards died as a result of an accident and poor medical care.
His grave in Georgiyevsk was plowed up by a tractor during
the construction of a stadium.

About the other grandfather.

My maternal grandfather came from *Tavria* as a young
boy to herd sheep and work as a farmhand. He started with
nothing, then became a tenant farmer, and by the time he
was old he actually became quite rich. He was a man of rare
energy and industry. In his fifties he gave the country more
grain and wool than many of today's state farms, and he
worked no less hard than their directors. And he treated his

workers in such a way that after the revolution they voluntarily supported the old man for 12 years before he died.
Let a state farm director try to ask his workers to do that
after he retires.

*Are people still considered guilty nowadays
because of their [social] origin ?*

Of course, the practice is not as rampant as it was in the
twenties and thirties, but that old guilt by social origin is
still very firmly implanted in the consciousness and still
quite alive in our country, and it would take very little to
fan the fires again at any moment. In fact, quite recently
Tvardovsky's enemies were publicly condemning him for
his so-called *kulak* origins. So why not with me ? If 'treason
against the homeland' hasn't worked out through my 'cap-
ture' by the enemy, it might squeeze by on a CLASS BASIS ?
So the latest articles in *Literaturnaya Gazeta*, for all their
illiteracy and stupidity, are by no means simple, purposeless
tooth-baring.

Incidentally, you notice that *Literaturnaya Gazeta*, which
never discussed THE SUBSTANCE of my works and views,
which never dared to print a single genuine critical review
about me, even the most hostile, for that could uncover a
portion of the intolerable *truth* – in its judgments about me
seems to have lost its voice altogether, as if its own critics
and authors had disappeared. In its attacks on me it hides
itself behind reprints, behind a *boulevard* magazine, behind
foreign journalists, and even music-hall singers or jugglers.
I do not understand this business. Maybe it is because those
who, as they say in Finland, 'are reared on vinegar from
childhood' are somehow becoming model socialist realists
and even making their way into the management of the Union
of Writers and of *Literaturnaya Gazeta* itself ?

When, on a *Literaturnaya Gazeta* assignment, the Finnish
journalist Larni* undertook to write and publish [an article
about Solzhenitsyn] not at home in Finland, but in a third
country, he committed himself to stretching out a steel coil

*See pp. 272–274.

with his teeth. A death-defying act. You know how it is in
the circus: a silly-looking clown comes out, everyone laughs
at him, he climbs up somewhere near the star performers,
under the roof, on a wire, and suddenly he is dangling by
his teeth – and the whole circus falls silent and sees he is not
a clown at all, that he has gone into a death-defying act.
Larni HINTS at certain IMPLICATIONS, which I can understand: that in my novel the social democrat-defeatist,
Lenartovich, expresses in 1914 sympathy for the idea that
Russia should suffer a defeat, so that it could then be reconstructed socially. All the social democratic defeatists
wished and reasoned *exactly so*, in contrast with the so-called
SOCIAL-PATRIOTS, that is, the social democrats who stood
for the defence [of Russia] and Larni, as a communist,
probably knows this, and yet he recklessly stretches out the
steel coil with his teeth, not realizing how easily he can himself be broken. He stretches the argument to imply that the
AUTHOR himself, that is I (by no means a social democrat!),
'is not averse to seeing the Germans as victors' – and, it
seems, not in 1914 but in 1941 (why not transpose the '1'
and the '4', are your hands not free?).

If there is anything that is totally absent in my novel – it
is this spirit of defeatism. But they stretch it that way anyway. They need at all costs a newspaper bridgehead in order
to print subsequently 'angry letters from the working
people', as has already happened more than once. A shameless fraud by the press, which is not accustomed to corrections and retractions. Ah, how the PLAN is needed by them,
how their LITERARY CRITIQUE needs a testimonial from the
Gestapo . . . If they stretch things so in front of the whole
circus, what wonders could they perform in their unscru-
tinized closed lectures!

Of course, this is not the last lie, there are probably more
ahead than behind, and you cannot defend yourself against
all the lies, let them hang there. Yes, someone else may
answer for me. Interviews are not the writer's business. I
have abstained from interviews for nine years and I am not
the least bit sorry.

In general, fame is a heavy burden, it eats up lots of time. They do not yet drag me along to meetings as they do others; I am grateful that they expelled me. It was good to work when nobody knew me, nobody exerted himself to write fairy tales about me, to collect backstairs gossip, like those rascals Burg and Feifer.

What is the PLAN ?

The PLAN consists in driving me out of this life or out of the country, tossing me into a ditch or sending me to Siberia, or having me dissolve 'in an alien fog' as they frankly write. How confident they are that those who are pandering to censorship have more rights on Russian soil than others who are born there. In general, all this defamation shows the stupidity and shortsightedness of those who direct it. They do not want to know the complexity and richness of history in all its diversity. They care only about silencing all voices that are unpleasant for them to hear or spoil their peace of mind today, and they do not think about the future. So, they have now senselessly silenced *Novy Mir* and Tvardovsky – thus making themselves poorer and even more blind – but they do not want to understand their loss.

Incidentally, about two weeks ago the *New York Times* printed a letter from a certain Soviet poet, Smelyakov, in which he attacks my eulogy of Tvardovsky.

About the access to the Western press.

No, we don't see it, but sometimes Western radio stations are audible through the screeches of the jamming. If we learn anything about our own events, it is there.

This new onslaught against me is striking IN ITS FORM : it would seem that all the press is in their hands, so is there nowhere nearer for answering me than in the *New York Times ?* This is what it means to fear the truth : answer me in the Soviet press, and you would have to quote me at least a little, and that is impossible. But let's take the content : surprisingly, Smelyakov argues, as it were, without having quoted me. I write that they strangled *Novy Mir* and in that way they have killed Tvardovsky. Smelyakov dodges this :

'Tvardovsky had some grievous moments'. I write that Tvardovsky wrote more candidly about the battle-front, and more purely than anyone else. Smelyakov distorts: that means, 'Tvardovsky had a negative attitude toward the Soviet army?' Where does he get this? I wrote literally about his 'gentle, admonitory voice [which] was heeded by all', and Smelyakov turns it inside out: 'Solzhenitsyn ascribes to Tvardovsky his own illusions that someday Soviet rule will crumble and a new generation will build a new Russia'. Read my eulogy – where is there anything like that?

And that last paragraph is indeed filled with meaning, but what can you do if they refuse, or if they are unable, to read it through? The study of Russian history, which today has taken me already to the end of the last century, has shown me how precious for the country are the PEACEFUL outlets, how important it is that the authority, however autocratic and unrestrained it may be, should listen benevolently to society, that society should understand the real position of the authorities ; how important it is that the country be led NOT BY FORCE AND COERCION, but by RIGHTEOUSNESS. Obviously, the realization of this helped me to recognize in Tvardovsky's activity precisely that conciliatory line. Alas, even the softest, the most judicious voice is intolerable, and they silence it too. How reasonably, with what good will did Sakharov and Grigorenko speak out here recently – no one even LISTENED TO THEM – get lost, shut up . . .

Therein lies the shallowness, the baseness of calculation of those who are leading the campaign against me. It honestly does not enter their heads that a writer who thinks differently from the majority of his society is an enrichment to that society, not the shame and ruination of it.

Solzhenitsyn's Lenten Letter* (abridged)

Most Holy Master !

That – which presses upon the head like a gravestone and

*The letter was sent in March 1972 to Patriarch Pimen, the head of the Russian Orthodox Church. In his answer to Solzhenitsyn, Father Sergei

crushes the breast of a moribund Russian Orthodox people –
– is the subject of this letter. Everyone knows this, and it has
already been shouted aloud, but everyone has again reverted
to a doomed silence. And a small stone needed to be placed
on top of the large one to make it no longer possible to remain
silent. I was weighed down by such a small stone when I heard
your message on Christmas Eve . . .

Why is your earnest appeal directed only to Russian émigrés ? Why do you call only on those children to be brought
up in the Christian faith, why do you admonish only the distant
flock to 'discern slander and falsehood' and be strong in truth
and justice ? And we – what should we discern ? Should we or
should we not foster in our children a love for the church ? . . .

The right to propagate the faith of our fathers has been
broken, as well as the right of parents to bring up their children
within the precepts of their own world outlook. And you,
leaders of the church, have yielded to this and condone it by
accepting as reliable evidence of religious freedom the fact
that we must place our defenseless children not into neutral
hands but into those of the most primitive and unscrupulous
kind of atheistic propagandists. You find evidence of religious
freedom in the fact that adolescents torn away from Christianity (God forbid that they should be infected by it) are left
with the ravine between the agitator's manual and the criminal
code for their moral upbringing . . .

The Russian Church has its indignant opinion on every evil
in distant Asia or Africa, yet on internal ills – it has none –
ever. Why are the messages which we receive from the church
hierarchy traditionally tranquil ? Why are all church documents
so complacent, as if they were issued among the most Christian
of peoples ? One serene message follows another, in the course

Zheludkov criticized him for lack of ' realism '. Solzhenitsyn replied on
28 April 1972, stressing again the need for personal sacrifices : ' What is
lacking is an inner defense of the faith. That women can go to church after
50 years [of Soviet history] is due to the women and not to the Church. It
is precisely this inner power of resistance that has been lost and this is
what is pernicious. It has been lost primarily by the Church leaders, and
the higher they are the more irrevocably they have lost it . . . It is through
PERSONAL SACRIFICES that the world around us can be reeducated '.

of the same inclement year? Will not the need for these messages soon cease altogether? There will no longer be anyone left to whom they should be addressed; the flock will disappear, with the exception of the Patriarchal Chancellery office . . .

The entire administration of the church, the appointment of priests and bishops (including even sacrilegious churchmen who make it easier to deride and destroy the church), all of this is secretly managed by the Council for Religious Affairs. A church dictatorially ruled by atheists is a sight not seen in two thousand years. Also under their control is the church economy and the use of church resources, those coins deposited by the fingers of the devout. Five million rubles are donated to outside funds with magnanimous gestures, while beggars are chased away from the portico and there is no money to repair a leaking roof in a poor parish. Priests are powerless within their own parishes, only the conduct of church services is still entrusted to them, and even then, only if they remain within the church building. But if they wish to visit the bedside of the sick or a cemetery they must first ask for approval of the city council.

What sort of reasoning can be used to convince oneself that the consistent destruction of the spirit and body of the church by atheists is the best means for its preservation? Preservation for whom? Certainly not for Christ. Preservation by what means? Falsehood? But after falsehood – what sort of hands should perform the Eucharist?

Most Holy Master! Do not scorn entirely my unworthy outcry . . . Do not let us suppose, not make us think that for the high priests of the Russian Church earthly authority is higher than heavenly authority, earthly responsibility more frightening than responsibility before God.

Let us not deceive the people, and more importantly, let us not deceive ourselves while praying, by thinking that external fetters are stronger than our spirit. It was not any easier at the time of Christianity's birth, but it has survived and flourished and has shown us the way: that of sacrifice. He who is deprived of all material power is always victorious through sacrifice. The same martyrdom worthy of the first centuries was accepted by our priests and fellow believers in our living memory. But at that time they were thrown to the lions, today one can only lose well-being.

During these days, when the Cross is brought out to the middle of the church and you kneel before it, ask the Lord: What other purpose could there be for your serving a people which has lost the spirit of Christianity and the Christian image ?

Great Lent, Sunday of Veneration of the Cross, 1972
(*The New York Times*, 9 April 1972)

Solzhenitsyn and the Nobel prize
by Per Egil Hegge★

FIRST INQUIRIES

It was in June 1970 that I first attempted to make contact with Alexander Solzhenitsyn's circle – a tight circle, whose members have always been as much concerned for his protection as for their own, and who have therefore never been particularly anxious to have dealings with foreigners.

I knew of the wariness of this circle and assumed that there was not the slightest chance of meeting Solzhenitsyn, still less of securing an interview, unless he should receive the Nobel Prize for Literature that autumn. I accordingly asked one of his friends whether Solzhenitsyn would be prepared to grant an interview to Scandinavian journalists in the event of his winning the prize . . . I eventually received an answer, through channels which I am unable to disclose, to the effect that, in that event, he might possibly allow himself to be interviewed. And there the matter rested.

I was later to learn that my enquiry had aroused enormous interest in that small, closed circle. In the spring of 1970 the Swedish Academy had made very discreet enquiries among these same friends to discover whether the award would make

★These are extracts from the book *Go-Between in Moscow* (*Mellommann i Moskva*), J. W. Cappelens Forlag (Oslo, 1971). They are published here with the kind permission of the author.

his position more vulnerable than it already was. Thus they knew that there was some possibility. And their reply to the Swedish initiative had been unequivocal: he would be in a stronger position with the prize than without it . . .

PHONE CALL TO SOLZHENITSYN

In late September and early October I talked to one or two people who knew Solzhenitsyn and learnt that the imminent Nobel announcement had brought the excitement of his closest friends to fever pitch. At that time it had been made known that the decision would be announced on 22 October, and throughout September Swedish newspapers applied considerable pressure to the Academy, demanding that the prize should go to Solzhenitsyn. This was evidently what caused the Academy to announce on 7 October that their decision would be made public the following day.

That very evening I sought out one of Solzhenitsyn's acquaintances, making sure as usual that no one followed me there . . . I interpreted this acceleration of the Stockholm announcement as an indication that Solzhenitsyn was *not* this year's winner, that the Swedish Academy wished to escape from the pressure of public opinion, and, moreover, to spare the candidate any unnecessary suspense in his present, rather exposed situation.

We agreed that I would in any case ring a friend of his the following day to tell him who had won the prize, whether or not it was Solzhenitsyn. I expected to hear the decision a few minutes after it was made known in Stockholm and promised to ring at about five past three in the afternoon. UPI, the American telegraphic agency, has its offices in the building where I was then living, and a piece of news like this is transmitted as an urgent bulletin the moment it becomes available.

That afternoon a handful of colleagues and I were gathered round the teleprinter up in the UPI office. At a few minutes past three transmission was interrupted and the words 'Stockholm – Flash – ' were tapped out onto the paper, followed by: 'Nobel prize to Russian writer Alexander I. Solzhenitsyn'. It promised to be a lively and difficult evening.

Together with four or five colleagues I went downstairs to my apartment and called up Solzhenitsyn's friend. At first he could not grasp what I was saying, but at last this gave way to jubilation. My colleagues and I sat down to wait . . .

At about 3.45 the telephone rang. It was my acquaintance once again. He sounded extremely agitated. 'I've spoken to him and told him he's won the Nobel prize, but he won't believe it. Could you please ring him and tell him it's true. He'll believe you.'

So I was given a phone number and was told that a lady would answer the phone. I should then ask to speak to 'the neighbor', and Solzhenitsyn would come to the phone. I was also asked to speak loudly as he was living out of town and the line was bad . . .

I dialled the number. A woman answered, sounding very busy, and I asked if I might speak to 'the neighbor'. I subsequently learnt, from someone who will figure again in this story, that I was the fourth person to ring. The three previous callers were friends who had heard the news from foreign radio broadcasts. However, Solzhenitsyn himself had somehow become convinced that this year's winner was to be announced on 17 October, the day he had planned to finish his new novel, *August 1914*. Hence he refused to believe them . . .

Almost a minute went by before another person took the receiver.

'Alexander Isayevich ?' I asked.

'Yes.'

I introduced myself as a correspondent for *Svenska Dagbladet* and said : 'May I congratulate you on winning the Nobel Prize for Literature ?'

'Where did you get this information from ?' He sounded almost irritated, and I was told later that he had had so many phone calls that day that he had not been able to get very much work done on his novel.

I replied that the Swedish Academy had officially announced the news in Stockholm 45 minutes before. There was no reaction.

I then asked if he had any comment to make.

'I am not prepared to give interviews. But I should like you to convey my thanks to the Swedish Academy privately. I repeat – privately.'

'I can do that, of course, but can't I write in the paper that you are grateful for the award ?'

'No, I want you to convey my thanks to the Swedish Academy privately.'

'But Alexander Isayevich, that's not really good enough for us. You must realize that the whole world is interested in your reaction.'

There was a moment's silence. Then he said: 'All right, I'll dictate a statement to you, but only on condition that it is quoted exactly word for word. I intensely dislike being misquoted.'

'Agreed.'

He then dictated: 'I am grateful for the award. I accept the prize. I intend to come and receive it on the traditional day in so far as this depends on me. I am in good health. The state of my health is no obstacle to my making the trip.'

[*Solzhenitsyn promised to call Hegge should he have anything further to say.*]

THE DECISION NOT TO GO TO STOCKHOLM

Two weeks after the Swedish Academy had announced its decision I was back in Oslo for a thorough medical examination, as I had been troubled for quite some time by attacks of dizziness. On the way back to Moscow I talked to a number of people in Stockholm about the preparations for the Nobel ceremony. Naturally, they were chiefly interested in knowing whether Solzhenitsyn would be coming. They had a fairly good idea of the considerable difficulties he would encounter in attempting to obtain an exit and reentry visa.

Now there was no real doubt that he would be allowed to travel *out* of the country. When he was expelled from the Writers' Union, *Literary Gazette* wrote that he was more than welcome to settle abroad, where his slanderous writings were so highly valued. He did not deign even to reply to this suggestion, and in Moscow no one, not even foreigners, really believed that he would ever leave his homeland of his own accord . . . It was not until 27 November, 13 days before the Nobel ceremony, that Solzhenitsyn announced his decision not to go to Stockholm. I am convinced that he made up his mind not later than 25 October, less than three weeks after saying that he would go.

The men who persuaded him to remain at home were one of his closest friends, whom I shall not name here, and the physicist, Andrei Sakharov, who 'worked on him' one week-end out at Rostropovich's dacha. This happened either on 17–18 October, or on 24–25 October. They persuaded him that Russia needed him more than did the Swedes, and that the danger that he would not be allowed back was too great to risk. He yielded to these arguments . . .

NEGOTIATIONS WITH THE SWEDISH EMBASSY

I was strengthened in my belief that Solzhenitsyn would not go to Stockholm when, on 28 October, I was contacted by a man to whom I shall refer as Ivanov. This is the commonest of names, whereas he is the rarest of men, and I may well write more about him on another occasion. He had, and probably still has, good contacts with Solzhenitsyn's circle of friends.

Ivanov told me that Solzhenitsyn wished to visit the Swedish Embassy at the end of November, to arrange for his Swedish entry visa, or else to advise them that the trip had come to nothing, as the case might be. The novelist would have liked to come on Friday, 27 November and wanted a card inviting him to come for a talk on that day. This was to avoid the risk of being stopped by a police guard outside the building. Ivanov asked me to inform the Embassy of his request.

I explained to him that there were no policemen posted outside the offices of the Swedish Embassy and hence no written invitation would be required. He replied that it was quite conceivable that the authorities would station a policeman there as the day of the ceremony, 10 December, approached, and that was why Solzhenitsyn wanted an invitation . . .

On 2 November I had a talk with A., one of the Swedish

diplomats in Moscow. Like all confidential talks in Moscow our conversation took place as we strolled through the streets ... I informed A. of my talk with Ivanov and passed on Solzhenitsyn's request for an invitation to visit the Embassy at 12 noon on 27 November. I also told him of Solzhenitsyn's desire to explore the possibility of a presentation ceremony being held in the Swedish Embassy ...

On 5 November I had a phone-call from A. asking me to come down to the Embassy. We went for another walk, during which he told me that the Embassy could not invite Solzhenitsyn to come; that is, they could *not* give him the written invitation he had asked for. However, should he still wish to come on the date and at the time he had indicated, that would be in order. A. added that a presentation ceremony at the Embassy would not be possible, and he repeated that the Embassy's task was to maintain good relations with the local authorities. He made it clear that this decision emanated from Stockholm and asked me to inform Solzhenitsyn – or rather, Ivanov – of this.

I promised to do so and said that I would very likely be meeting Ivanov the following week. I also told him that, in my own opinion, he ought to draw the attention of the Foreign Office in Stockholm to two points: firstly, it was possible that this refusal would embitter Solzhenitsyn and that he would not come to the Embassy; secondly, the Swedish Government ought to be prepared to defend its action in case it became known ... In addition I reminded him that, five years before, Ambassador Jarring had not only congratulated that year's Nobel prizewinner, Mikhail Sholokhov, but had invited him to the Embassy, and A. could doubtless imagine how the conduct of the Swedish authorities in 1970 would appear by comparison.

A. said that he quite realized that it didn't look 'particularly heroic', but he repeated that the first duty of the Embassy was to preserve the good relations between Sweden and the Soviet Union ...

I did not know, and still do not know, the best way to go about telling a winner of the Nobel Prize that he is just a private person and cannot be invited to the Swedish Embassy because the Embassy wishes to maintain the good relations between two states. Perhaps I should have asked. I refrained from doing so, but was not looking forward to my meeting with Solzhenitsyn . . .

[*At a meeting with C., another Embassy official, Hegge was rebuked for allegedly suggesting that the Embassy was 'afraid' to make contact with Solzhenitsyn. Hegge observes that this episode might have served the previous year's prizewinner, Samuel Beckett, as the basis for a 'new and very absurd play:* Waiting for Solzhenitsyn'. *Meanwhile, the official campaign against Solzhenitsyn was increasing in intensity.*]

On 19 November I had finally managed to contact a man whom I shall here call Petrov. He too deserves to have a novel written about him when the time is ripe. He told me that the Head of the Moscow Gorkom, Grishin, who was also a candidate-member of the Politburo and hence one of the 20 top Soviet leaders, had sharply attacked Solzhenitsyn at a closed party meeting which was not reported in the press. He also told me that there had been a meeting of the party members of the Writers' Union in Moscow, at which the chairman, Arkady Vasilev, had expressed 'his personal opinion', that Solzhenitsyn ought to be offered a one-way ticket to Stockholm. Then they would be done with an awkward problem.

Quite obviously, his friends' fear that they would lose him if he went abroad was not without foundation . . .

Solzhenitsyn's Nobel lecture in literature 1970

1. Just as that puzzled savage who has picked up – a strange cast-up from the ocean ? – something unearthed from the sands ? – or an obscure object fallen down from the sky ? – intricate in curves, it gleams first dully and then with a bright thrust of light. Just as he turns it this way and that, turns it over, trying to discover what to do with it, trying to discover

some mundane function within his own grasp, never dreaming of its higher function.

So also we, holding Art in our hands, confidently consider ourselves to be its masters, boldly we direct it, we renew, reform and manifest it; we sell it for money, use it to please those in power; turn to it at one moment for amusement – right down to popular songs and nightclubs, and at another – grabbing the nearest weapon, stick or cudgel – for the passing needs of politics and for narrow-minded social ends. But art is not defiled by our efforts, neither does it thereby depart from its true nature, but on each occasion and in each application it gives to us a part of its secret inner light.

But shall we ever grasp the whole of that light? Who will dare to say that he has DEFINED Art, enumerated all its facets? Perhaps once upon a time someone understood and told us, but we could not remain satisfied with that for long; we listened, and neglected, and threw it out there and then, hurrying as always to exchange even the very best – if only for something new! And when we are told again the old truth, we shall not even remember that we once possessed it.

One artist sees himself as the creator of an independent spiritual world: he hoists onto his shoulders the task of creating this world, of peopling it and of bearing the all-embracing responsibility for it; but he crumples beneath it, for a mortal genius is not capable of bearing such a burden. Just as man in general, having declared himself the center of existence, has not succeeded in creating a balanced spiritual system. And if misfortune overtakes him, he casts the blame upon the age-long disharmony of the world, upon the complexity of today's ruptured soul, or upon the stupidity of the public.

Another artist, recognizing a higher power above, gladly works as a humble apprentice beneath God's heaven; then however, his responsibility for everything that is written or drawn, for the souls which perceive his work, is more exacting than ever. But, in return, it is not he who has created this world, not he who directs it, there is no doubt as to its foundations; the artist has merely to be more keenly aware than others of the harmony of the world, of the beauty and ugliness of the human contribution to it, and to communicate this acutely to his fellowmen. And in misfortune, and even in the depths of existence – in destitution, in prison, in sickness – his sense of stable harmony never deserts him.

But all the irrationality of art, its dazzling turns, its unpredictable discoveries, its shattering influence on human beings – they are too full of magic to be exhausted by this artist's vision of the world, by his artistic conception or by the work of his unworthy fingers.

Archaeologists have not discovered stages of human existence so early that they were without art. Right back in the early morning twilights of mankind we received it from Hands which we were too slow to discern. And we were too slow to ask: FOR WHAT PURPOSE have we been given this gift ? What are we to do with it ?

And they were mistaken, and will always be mistaken, who prophesy that art will disintegrate, that it will outlive its forms and die. It is we who shall die – art will remain. And shall we comprehend, even on the day of our destruction, all its facets and all its possibilities ?

Not everything assumes a name. Some things lead beyond words. Art inflames even a frozen, darkened soul to a high spiritual experience. Through art we are sometimes visited – dimly, briefly – by revelations such as cannot be produced by rational thinking.

Like that little looking glass from the fairy-tales: look into it and you will see – not yourself – but for one second, the Inaccessible, whither no man can ride, no man fly. And only the soul gives a groan . . .

2. One day Dostoevsky threw out the enigmatic remark: 'Beauty will save the world'. What sort of a statement is that ? For a long time I considered it mere words. How could that be possible ? When in bloodthirsty history did beauty ever save anyone from anything ? Ennobled, uplifted, yes – but whom has it saved ?

There is, however, a certain peculiarity in the essence of beauty, a peculiarity in the status of art: namely, the convincingness of a true work of art is completely irrefutable and it forces even an opposing heart to surrender. It is possible to compose an outwardly smooth and elegant political speech, a headstrong article, a social program, or a philosophical system on the basis of both a mistake and a lie. What is hidden, what distorted, will not immediately become obvious.

Then a contradictory speech, article, program, a differently constructed philosophy rallies in opposition – and all just as elegant and smooth, and once again it works. Which is why such things are both trusted and mistrusted.

In vain to reiterate what does not reach the heart.

But a work of art bears within itself its own verification: conceptions which are devised or stretched do not stand being portrayed in images, they all come crashing down, appear sickly and pale, convince no one. But those works of art which have scooped up the truth and presented it to us as a living force – they take hold of us, compel us, and nobody ever, not even in ages to come, will appear to refute them.

So perhaps that ancient trinity of Truth, Goodness and Beauty is not simply an empty, faded formula as we thought in the days of our self-confident, materialistic youth? If the tops of these three trees converge, as the scholars maintained, but the too blatant, too direct growths of Truth and Goodness are crushed, cut down, not allowed through – then perhaps the fantastic, unpredictable, unexpected growths of Beauty will push through and soar TO THAT VERY SAME PLACE, and in so doing will fulfill the work of all three?

In that case Dostoevsky's remark, 'Beauty will save the world', was not a careless phrase but a prophecy. After all HE was granted to see much, a man of fantastic illumination.

And in that case art, literature might really be able to help the world today.

It is the small insight which, over the years, I have succeeded in gaining into this matter that I shall attempt to lay before you here today.

3. In order to mount this platform from which the Nobel lecture is read, a platform offered to far from every writer and

only once in a lifetime, I have climbed not three or four make-
shift steps, but hundreds and even thousands of them; un-
yielding, precipitous, frozen steps, leading out of the darkness
and cold where it was my fate to survive, while others – perhaps
with a greater gift and stronger than I – have perished. Of
them, I myself met but a few on the Archipelago of GULag,*
shattered into its fractionary multitude of islands; and beneath the millstone of shadowing and mistrust I did not talk
to them all, of some I only heard, of others still I only guessed.
Those who fell into that abyss already bearing a literary name
are at least known, but how many were never recognized, never
once mentioned in public? And virtually no one managed to
return. A whole national literature remained there, cast into
oblivion not only without a grave, but without even underclothes, naked, with a number tagged on to its toe. Russian
literature did not cease for a moment, but from the outside it
appeared a wasteland! Where a peaceful forest could have
grown, there remained, after all the felling, two or three trees
overlooked by chance.

And as I stand here today, accompanied by the shadows of
the fallen, with bowed head allowing others who were worthy
before to pass ahead of me to this place, as I stand here, how
am I to divine and to express what THEY would have wished
to say?

This obligation has long weighed upon us, and we have
understood it. In the words of Vladimir Solov'ev:

Even in chains we ourselves must complete
That circle which the gods have mapped out for us.

Frequently, during exhausting camp marches, in a column of
prisoners, when chains of lanterns pierced the gloom of the
evening frosts, there would well up inside us the words that we
should like to cry out to the whole world, if the whole world
could hear one of us. Then it seemed so clear: what our successful ambassador would say, and how the world would immediately respond with its comment. Our horizon embraced
quite distinctly both physical things and spiritual movements,
and it saw no lopsidedness in the indivisible world. These ideas

*The Central Administration of Corrective Labour Camps.

did not come from books, neither were they imported for the sake of coherence. They were formed in conversations with people now dead, in prison cells and by forest fires, they were tested against THAT life, they grew out of THAT existence.

When at last the outer pressure grew a little weaker, my and our horizon broadened and gradually, albeit through a minute chink, we saw and knew 'the whole world'. And to our amazement the whole world was not at all as we had expected, as we had hoped; that is to say a world living by 'the wrong thing', a world leading 'in the wrong direction', a world which could exclaim at the sight of a muddy swamp, 'what a delightful little puddle!', at concrete neck stocks, 'what an exquisite necklace!'; but instead a world where some weep inconsolable tears and others dance to a lighthearted musical.

How could this happen? Why the yawning gap? Were we insensitive? Was the world insensitive? Or is it due to language differences? Why is it that people are not able to hear each other's every distinct utterance? Words cease to sound and run away like water – without taste, color, smell. Without trace.

As I have come to understand this, so through the years has changed and changed again the structure, content and tone of my potential speech. The speech I give today.

And it has little in common with its original plan, conceived on frosty camp evenings.

4. From time immemorial man has been made in such a way that his vision of the world, so long as it has not been instilled under hypnosis, his motivations and scale of values, his actions and intentions are determined by his personal and group experience of life. As the Russian saying goes, 'Do not believe your brother, believe your own crooked eye.' And that is the most sound basis for an understanding of the world around us and of human conduct in it. And during the long epochs when our world lay spread out in mystery and wilderness, before it was encroached upon by common lines of communication, before it was transformed into a single, convulsively pulsating lump – men, relying on experience, ruled without

mishap within their limited areas, within their communities, within their societies, and finally on their national territories. At that time it was possible for individual human beings to perceive and accept a general scale of values, to distinguish between what is considered normal, what incredible; what is cruel and what lies beyond the boundaries of wickedness; what is honesty, what deceit. And although the scattered peoples led extremely different lives and their social values were often strikingly at odds, just as their systems of weights and measures did not agree, still these discrepancies surprised only occasional travelers, were reported in journals under the name of wonders, and bore no danger to mankind which was not yet one.

But now during the past few decades, imperceptibly, suddenly, mankind has become one – hopefully one and dangerously one – so that the concussions and inflammations of one of its parts are almost instantaneously passed on to others, sometimes lacking in any kind of necessary immunity. Mankind has become one, but not steadfastly one as communities or even nations used to be; not united through years of mutual experience, neither through possession of a single eye, affectionately called crooked, not yet through a common native language, but, surpassing all barriers, through international broadcasting and print. An avalanche of events descends upon us – in one minute half the world hears of their splash. But the yardstick by which to measure those events and to evaluate them in accordance with the laws of unfamiliar parts of the world – this is not and cannot be conveyed via sound waves and in newspaper columns. For these yardsticks were matured and assimilated over too many years of too specific conditions in individual countries and societies; they cannot be exchanged in mid-air. In the various parts of the world men apply their own hard-earned values to events, and they judge stubbornly, confidently, only according to their own scales of values and never according to any others.

And if there are not many such different scales of values in the world, there are at least several; one for evaluating events near at hand, another for events far away; aging societies possess one, young societies another; unsuccessful people one, successful people another. The divergent scales of values scream in discordance, they dazzle and daze us, and so that it might not be painful we steer clear of all other values, as though from insanity, as though from illusion, and we confidently judge the whole world according to our own home values. Which is why we take for the greater, more painful and less bearable disaster not that which is in fact greater, more painful and less bearable, but that which lies closest to us. Everything which is further away, which does not threaten this very day to invade our threshold – with all its groans, its stifled cries, its destroyed lives, even if it involves millions of victims – this we consider on the whole to be perfectly bearable and of tolerable proportions.

In one part of the world, not so long ago, under persecutions not inferior to those of the ancient Romans, hundreds of thousands of silent Christians gave up their lives for their belief in God. In the other hemisphere a certain madman (and no doubt he is not alone) speeds across the ocean to DELIVER us from religion – with a thrust of steel into the high priest! He has calculated for each and every one of us according to his personal scale of values!

That which from a distance, according to one scale of values, appears as enviable and flourishing freedom, at close quarters, and according to other values, is felt to be infuriating constraint calling for buses to be overthrown. That which in one part of the world might represent a dream of incredible prosperity, in another has the exasperating effect of wild exploitation demanding immediate strike. There are different scales of values for natural catastrophes: a flood claiming two hundred thousand lives seems less significant than our local accident. There are different scales of values for personal insults: sometimes even an ironic smile or a dismissive gesture is humiliating, while at others cruel beatings are forgiven as an unfortunate joke. There are different scales of values for punishment and wickedness: according to one, a month's arrest, banishment to the country, or an isolation-cell where one is fed on white rolls and milk, shatters the imagination and fills the newspaper columns with rage. While according to another, prison sentences of twenty-five years, isolation-cells where the walls are covered in ice and the prisoners stripped to their underclothes, lunatic asylums for the sane, and countless unreasonable people who for some reason will keep running away, shot on the frontiers – all this is common and accepted. While the mind is especially at peace concerning that exotic part of the world about which we know virtually nothing, from which we do not even receive news of events, but only the trivial, out-of-date guesses of a few correspondents.

Yet we cannot reproach human vision for this duality, for this dumfounded incomprehension of another man's distant grief, man is just made that way. But for the whole of mankind, compressed into a single lump, such mutual incomprehension presents the threat of imminent and violent destruction. One world, one mankind cannot exist in the face of six, four or even two scales of values: we shall be torn apart by this disparity of rhythm, this disparity of vibrations.

A man with two hearts is not for this world, neither shall we be able to live side by side on one Earth.

5. But who will coordinate these value scales, and how ? Who will create for mankind one system of interpretation, valid for good and evil deeds, for the unbearable and the bearable, as they are differentiated today ? Who will make clear to mankind what is really heavy and intolerable and what only grazes the skin locally ? Who will direct the anger to that which is most terrible and not to that which is nearer ? Who might succeed in transferring such an understanding beyond the limits of his own human experience ? Who might succeed in impressing upon a bigoted, stubborn human creature the distant joy and grief of others, an understanding of dimensions and deceptions which he himself has never experienced ? Propaganda, constraint, scientific proof – all are useless. But fortunately there does exist such a means in our world ! That means is art. That means is literature.

They can perform a miracle: they can overcome man's detrimental peculiarity of learning only from personal experience so that the experience of other people passes him by in vain. From man to man, as he completes his brief spell on earth, art transfers the whole weight of an unfamiliar, lifelong experience with all its burdens, its colors, its sap of life; it recreates in the flesh an unknown experience and allows us to possess it as our own.

And even more, much more than that; both countries and whole continents repeat each other's mistakes with time lapses which can amount to centuries. Then, one would think, it would all be so obvious! But no; that which some nations have already experienced, considered and rejected, is suddenly discovered by others to be the latest word. And here again, the only substitute for an experience we ourselves have never lived through is art, literature. They possess a wonderful ability: beyond distinctions of language, custom, social structure they can convey the life experience of one whole nation to another. To an inexperienced nation they can convey a harsh national trial lasting many decades, at best sparing an entire nation from a superfluous, or mistaken, or even disastrous course, thereby curtailing the meanderings of human history.

It is this great and noble property of art that I urgently recall to you today from the Nobel tribune.

And literature conveys irrefutable condensed experience in yet another invaluable direction; namely, from generation to generation. Thus it becomes the living memory of the nation. Thus it preserves and kindles within itself the flame of her spent history, in a form which is safe from deformation and slander. In this way literature, together with language, protects the soul of the nation.

(In recent times it has been fashionable to talk of the leveling out of nations, of the disappearance of different races in the melting pot of contemporary civilization. I do not agree with this opinion, but its discussion remains another question. Here it is merely fitting to say that the disappearance of nations would have impoverished us no less than if all men had become alike, with one personality and one face. Nations are the wealth of mankind, its collective personalities; the very least of them wears its own special colors and bears within itself a special facet of divine intention.)

But woe to that nation whose literature is disturbed by the

intervention of power. Because that is not just a violation of 'freedom of the press', it is the closing down of the heart of the nation, a slashing to pieces of its memory. The nation ceases to be mindful of itself, it is deprived of its spiritual unity, and despite a supposedly common language, compatriots suddenly cease to understand one another. Silent generations grow old and die without ever having talked about themselves, either to each other or to their descendants. When such as Akhmatova and Zamyatin – interred alive throughout their lives – are condemned to create in silence until they die, never hearing the echo of their written words, then that is not only their personal tragedy, but a sorrow to the whole nation, a danger to the whole nation.

In some cases moreover – when as a result of such a silence the whole of history ceases to be understood in its entirety – it is a danger to the whole of mankind.

6. At various times and in various countries there have arisen heated, angry and subtle debates as to whether art and the artist should be free to live for themselves, or whether they should be forever mindful of their duty towards society and serve it albeit in an unprejudiced way. For me there is no dilemma, but I shall refrain from raising once again the train of arguments. One of the most brilliant addresses on this subject was actually Albert Camus' Nobel speech, and I would happily subscribe to his conclusions. Indeed Russian literature has for several decades manifested an inclination not to become too lost in contemplation of itself, not to flutter about too frivolously. I am not ashamed to continue this tradition to the best of my ability. Russian literature has long been familiar with the notions that a writer can do much within his society, and that it is his duty to do so.

Let us not violate the RIGHT of the artist to express exclusively his own experiences and introspections, disregarding everything that happens in the world beyond. Let us not DEMAND of the artist, but – reproach, beg, urge and entice him – that we may be allowed to do. After all, only in part does he himself develop his talent; the greater part of it is breathed into him at birth as a finished product, and the gift of talent imposes responsibility on his free will. Let us assume that the artist does not OWE anybody anything: nevertheless, it is painful to see how, by retiring into his self-made worlds or the spaces of his subjective whims, he CAN surrender the real world into the hands of men who are mercenary, if not worthless, if not insane.

Our twentieth century has proved to be more cruel than preceding centuries, and the first fifty years have not erased all its horrors. Our world is rent asunder by those same old cave-age emotions of greed, envy, lack of control, mutual hostility which have picked up in passing respectable pseudonyms like class struggle, racial conflict, struggle of the masses, trade-union disputes. The primeval refusal to accept a compromise has been turned into a theoretical principle and is considered the virtue of orthodoxy. It demands millions of sacrifices in ceaseless civil wars, it drums into our souls that there is no such thing as unchanging, universal concepts of goodness and justice, that they are all fluctuating and inconstant. Therefore the rule – always do what's most profitable to your party. Any professional group no sooner sees a convenient opportunity to BREAK OFF A PIECE, even if it be unearned, even if it be superfluous, than it breaks it off there and then and no matter if the whole of society comes tumbling down. As seen from the outside, the amplitude of the tossings of western society is approaching that point beyond which the system becomes metastable and must fall. Violence, less and less embarrassed by the limits imposed by centuries of lawfulness, is brazenly and victoriously striding across the whole world, unconcerned that its infertility has been demonstrated and proved many times in history. What is more, it is not simply crude power that triumphs abroad, but its exultant justification. The world is being inundated by the brazen conviction that power can do anything, justice nothing. Dostoevsky's DEVILS – apparently a provincial nightmare fantasy of the last century – are crawling across the whole world in front of our very eyes, infesting countries where they could not have been dreamed of; and by means of the hijackings, kidnappings, explosions and fires of recent years they are announcing their determination to shake and destroy civilization! And they may well succeed. The young, at an age when they have not yet any experience other than sexual, when they do not yet have years of personal suffering and personal understanding behind them, are jubilantly repeating our depraved Russian blunders of the nineteenth century, under the impression that they are discovering something new. They acclaim the latest wretched degradation on the part of the Chinese Red Guards as a joyous example. In shallow lack of understanding of the age-old essence of mankind, in the naive confidence of inexperienced hearts they cry: let us drive away THOSE cruel, greedy oppressors, governments, and the new ones (we!), having laid aside grenades and rifles, will be just and understanding. Far from it!... But of those who have lived more and understand, those who could oppose these young – many do not dare oppose, they even suck up, anything not to appear 'conservative'. Another Russian phenomenon of the nineteenth century which Dostoevsky called SLAVERY TO PROGRESSIVE QUIRKS.

The spirit of Munich has by no means retreated into the past; it was not merely a brief episode. I even venture to say that the spirit of Munich prevails in the twentieth century. The timid civilized world has found nothing with which to oppose the onslaught of a sudden revival of barefaced barbarity, other than concessions and smiles. The spirit of Munich is a sickness of the will of successful people, it is the daily condition of those who have given themselves up to the thirst after prosperity at any price, to material well-being as the chief goal of earthly existence. Such people – and there are many in today's world – elect passivity and retreat, just so that their accustomed life might drag on a bit longer, just so as not to step over the threshold of hardship today – and tomorrow, you'll see, it will all be all right. (But it will never be all right! The price of cowardice will only be evil; we shall reap courage and victory only when we dare to make sacrifices.)

And on top of this we are threatened by destruction in the fact that the physically compressed, strained world is not allowed to blend spiritually; the molecules of knowledge and sympathy are not allowed to jump over from one half to the other. This presents a rampant danger: THE SUPPRESSION OF INFORMATION between the parts of the planet. Contemporary science knows that suppression of information leads to entropy and total destruction. Suppression of information renders international signatures and agreements illusory; within a muffled zone it costs nothing to reinterpret any agreement, even simpler – to forget it, as though it had never really existed. (Orwell understood this supremely.) A muffled zone is, as it were, populated not by inhabitants of the Earth, but by an expeditionary corps from Mars; the people know nothing intelligent about the rest of the Earth and are prepared to go and trample it down in the holy conviction that they come as 'liberators'.

A quarter of a century ago, in the great hopes of mankind, the United Nations Organization was born. Alas, in an immoral world, this too grew up to be immoral. It is not a United Nations Organization but a United Governments Organization where all governments stand equal; those which are freely elected, those imposed forcibly, and those which have seized power with weapons. Relying on the mercenary partiality of the majority UNO jealously guards the freedom of some nations and neglects the freedom of others. As a result of an obedient vote it declined to undertake the investigation of private appeals – the groans, screams and beseechings of humble individual PLAIN PEOPLE – not large enough a catch for such a great organization. UNO made no effort to make the Declaration of Human Rights, its best document in twenty-five years, into an OBLIGATORY condition of membership confronting the governments. Thus it betrayed those humble people into the will of the governments which they had not chosen.

It would seem that the appearance of the contemporary world rests solely in the hands of the scientists; all mankind's technical steps are determined by them. It would seem that it is precisely on the international goodwill of scientists, and not of politicians, that the direction of the world should depend. All the more so since the example of the few shows how much could be achieved were they all to pull together. But no;

scientists have not manifested any clear attempt to become an important, independently active force of mankind. They spend entire congresses in renouncing the sufferings of others; better to stay safely within the precincts of science. That same spirit of Munich has spread above them its enfeebling wings.

What then is the place and role of the writer in this cruel, dynamic, split world on the brink of its ten destructions? After all we have nothing to do with letting off rockets, we do not even push the lowliest of handcarts, we are quite scorned by those who respect only material power. Is it not natural for us too to step back, to lose faith in the steadfastness of goodness, in the indivisibility of truth, and just to impart to the world our bitter, detached observations: how mankind has become hopelessly corrupt, how men have degenerated, and how difficult it is for the few beautiful and refined souls to live amongst them?

But we have not even recourse to this flight. Anyone who has once taken up the WORD can never again evade it; a writer is not the detached judge of his compatriots and contemporaries, he is an accomplice to all the evil committed in his native land or by his countrymen. And if the tanks of his fatherland have flooded the asphalt of a foreign capital with blood, then the brown spots have slapped against the face of the writer forever. And if one fatal night they suffocated his sleeping, trusting Friend, then the palms of the writer bear the bruises from that rope. And if his young fellow-citizens breezily declare the superiority of depravity over honest work, if they give themselves over to drugs or seize hostages, then their stink mingles with the breath of the writer.

Shall we have the temerity to declare that we are not responsible for the sores of the present-day world?

7. However, I am cheered by a vital awareness of WORLD LITERATURE as of a single huge heart, beating out the cares and troubles of our world, albeit presented and perceived differently in each of its corners.

Apart from age-old national literatures there existed, even in past ages, the conception of world literature as an anthology skirting the heights of the national literatures, and as the sum total of mutual literary influences. But there occurred a lapse in time: readers and writers became acquainted with writers of other tongues only after a time lapse, sometimes lasting centuries, so that mutual influences were also delayed and the anthology of national literary heights was revealed only in the eyes of descendants, not of contemporaries.

But today, between the writers of one country and the writers and readers of another, there is a reciprocity if not instantaneous then almost so. I experience this with myself. Those of my books which, alas, have not been printed in my own country have soon found a responsive, worldwide audience, despite hurried and often bad translations. Such distinguished western writers as Heinrich Böll have undertaken critical analysis of them. All these last years, when my work and freedom have not come crashing down, when contrary to the laws of gravity they have hung suspended as though on air, as though on NOTHING – on the invisible dumb tension of a sympathetic public membrane; then it was with grateful warmth, and quite unexpectedly for myself, that I learnt of the further support of the international brotherhood of writers. On my fiftieth birthday I was astonished to receive congratulations from well-known western writers. No pressure on me came to pass by unnoticed. During my dangerous weeks of exclusion from the Writers' Union the WALL OF DEFENSE advanced by the world's prominent writers protected me from worse persecutions; and Norwegian writers and artists hospitably prepared a roof for me, in the event of my threatened exile being put into effect. Finally even the advancement of my name for the Nobel Prize was raised not in the country where I live and write, but by François Mauriac and his colleagues. And later still entire national writers' unions have expressed their support for me.

Thus I have understood and felt that world literature is no longer an abstract anthology, nor a generalization invented by literary historians; it is rather a certain common body and a common spirit, a living heartfelt unity reflecting the growing unity of mankind. State frontiers still turn crimson, heated by electric wire and bursts of machine fire; and various ministries of internal affairs still think that literature too is an 'internal affair' falling under their jurisdiction; newspaper headlines still display: 'No right to interfere in our internal affairs!' Whereas there are no INTERNAL AFFAIRS left on our crowded Earth! And mankind's sole salvation lies in everyone making everything his business; in the people of the East being vitally concerned with what is thought in the West, the people of the West vitally concerned with what goes on in the East. And literature, as one of the most sensitive, responsive instruments possessed by the human creature, has been one of the first to adopt, assimilate, to catch hold of this feeling of a growing unity of mankind. And so I turn with confidence to the world literature of today – to hundreds of friends whom I have never met in the flesh and whom I may never see.

Friends! Let *us* try to help if we are worth anything at all! Who from time immemorial has constituted the uniting not the dividing strength in your countries, lacerated by discordant parties, movements, casts and groups? There in its essence is the position of writers: expressers of their native language – the chief binding force of the nation, of the very earth its people occupy, and at best of its national spirit.

I believe that world literature has it in its power to help mankind, in these its troubled hours, to see itself as it really is, notwithstanding the indoctrinations of prejudiced people and parties. World literature has it in its power to convey condensed experience from one land to another so that we might cease to be split and dazzled, that the different scales of values might be made to agree, and one nation learn correctly and concisely the true history of another with such strength of recognition and painful awareness as if it had itself experienced the same, and thus might it be spared from repeating the same cruel mistakes. And perhaps under such conditions we artists will be able to cultivate within ourselves a field of vision to embrace the WHOLE WORLD: in the center observing like any other human being that which lies nearby, at the edges we shall begin to draw in that which is happening in the rest of the world. And we shall correlate, and we shall observe world proportions.

And who, if not writers, are to pass judgment – not only on their unsuccessful governments (in some states this is the easiest way to earn one's bread, the occupation of any man who is not lazy) – but also on the people themselves, in their cowardly humiliation or self-satisfied weakness ? Who is to pass judgment on the lightweight sprints of youth, and on the young pirates brandishing their knives ?

We shall be told: what can literature possibly do against the ruthless onslaught of open violence ? But let us not forget that violence does not live alone and is not capable of living alone : it is necessarily interwoven with falsehood. Between them lies the most intimate, the deepest of natural bonds. Violence finds its only refuge in falsehood, falsehood its only support in violence. Any man who has once acclaimed violence as his METHOD must inexorably choose falsehood as his PRINCIPLE. At its birth violence acts openly and even with pride. But no sooner does it become strong, firmly established, than it senses the rarefaction of the air around it and it cannot continue to exist without descending into a fog of lies, clothing them in sweet talk. It does not always, not necessarily, openly throttle the throat, more often it demands from its subjects only an oath of allegiance to falsehood, only complicity in falsehood.

And the simple step of a simple courageous man is not to partake in falsehood, not to support false actions ! Let THAT enter the world, let it even reign in the world – but not with my help. But writers and artists can achieve more: they can CONQUER FALSEHOOD ! In the struggle with falsehood art always did win and it always does win! Openly, irrefutably for everyone ! Falsehood can hold out against much in this world, but not against art.

And no sooner will falsehood be dispersed than the nakedness of violence will be revealed in all its ugliness – and violence, decrepit, will fall.

That is why, my friends, I believe that we are able to help the world in its white-hot hour. Not by making the excuse of possessing no weapons, and not by giving ourselves over to a frivolous life – but by going to war !

Proverbs about truth are well-loved in Russian. They give

steady and sometimes striking expression to the not inconsiderable harsh national experience:

ONE WORD OF TRUTH SHALL OUTWEIGH THE WHOLE WORLD.

And it is here, on an imaginary fantasy, a breach of the principle of the conservation of mass and energy, that I base both my own activity and my appeal to the writers of the whole world.

(Copyright © the Nobel Foundation 1972.
Reprinted by permission)